# INDIAN WOMEN

*A Socio-Legal Perspective*

# INDIAN WOMEN

## *A Socio-Legal Perspective*

***Nandita Saikia***

**SERIALS PUBLICATIONS**
NEW DELHI

First Published - 2008

ISBN: 978-81-8387-132-7



*Published by*

**SERIALS PUBLICATIONS**

4830/24, Prahlad Street, Ansari Road
Darya Ganj, New Delhi-110002 (India)
Phone : 23245225. Fax : 91-11-23272135
E-mail: serials@satyam.net.in

*In memory of*
*Dada :*
*Thomas Waterfield*

# CONTENTS

Preface *vii*
Introduction *ix*

**Part I: Discrimination** **1**
The Societal Status of Women 4
Independent India 13

**Part II: Violence** **24**
Female Foeticide and Infanticide 28
Honour Killings 31
Domestic Violence 34
Sati 56
Witch Killings 61
Modesty and Obscenity 64
Rape 84
Prostitution and Trafficking 100

**Part III: Protection** **116**
Constitutional Provisions 118
Education 139
Legislation 144
The Role of the Media 158

**Appendix** **171**
The Code of Criminal Procedure 172
The Commission of Sati (Prevention) Act 175
The Immoral Traffic Prevention Act 184
The Indecent Representation of Women Act 203

The Indian Evidence Act 207
The Indian Penal Code 210
The Information Technology Act 220
The National Commission for Women Act 220
The Prenatal Diagnostic Techniques Act 226
The Protection of Women against Domestic Violence Act 239

**References** **259**

**Index** **261**

# INTRODUCTION

Sometime ago, I read a book which I loved: *Fire with Fire* by Naomi Wolf. In the book, the author speaks of what she calls 'power feminism' (as opposed to 'victim feminism'), tries to analyse where the feminist movement went wrong and discusses what can be done about it–there certainly is something which has gone wrong, if not anything else, as is evidenced by the fact that the words *fat, ugly, lesbian* and *feminist* have come to be synonyms for all practical purposes.

I know that when I hear the term *feminist,* and, in particular, *radical-feminist,* it rarely conjures particularly pleasant images in my mind. I usually wind up thinking of a grotesque-looking, cigarette wielding, black lipped, extremely strident, overweight woman without an ounce of charm, who, if, say trapped in an abusive marriage, would find it difficult to obtain any more sympathy than her abuser, who is, after all, tied to her for the *rest of his life.**

And to be honest, the thought of women like that–they do exist–makes me cringe. But even so, I somehow can't help but admire 'women who assert themselves'.*

There are too few women who do so. And among those who do, most are judged extremely harshly. In January 2007, for example, I came across a couple who wanted to get a divorce. Neither I nor anyone else they had spoken to at that point had any idea of what the facts of the case were but the mere fact that the wife (rather aggressively) and unequivocally declared that she wanted a divorce was enough to leave her in the wrong in everyone's eyes. I grant that she was much less pleasant than her husband to talk to but then again, he may have simply been more adept at presenting himself in a better light than she was and in thereby garnering sympathy. No one could have known for certain. And no one, not even one of the women who heard the couple, was willing to give her, if not the benefit of the doubt, a chance to justify herself.

It's often said that the implementation of women's rights–which though guaranteed by law are virtually impossible to see in existence in the daily lives of most women–is so difficult partly because women are their own worst enemies. It's a notion I've never completely understood despite all the historical evidence which shows women protesting against movements for women's rights.*

I remember once watching a film about one of the Balkan wars–I think it was called *Saviour*–in which there was a young girl who initially could not take care of her baby because she was in shock and later managed to do so only by going into some sort of emotional paralysis.*

The woman who was watching the film with me first condemned her for not taking care of the child and later on, for being too 'matter-of-fact' and showing no reaction to the carnage all around her. Both ways, she was deemed to be callous and consequently, worthless.*

I'm not entirely sure why but for some reason, her reactions left me stunned and it wasn't just because they were so harsh and judgmental. I think it was primarily because no matter what the young woman in the film did, she somehow wound up being in the wrong and although, moving away from reel life into real life, one often winds up in situations where one is damned no matter what one does, what astonished (and still continues to astonish) me is that one can be left at the wrong end of public opinion even by people who are not normally unkind and who have no intention of hurting one or being cruel.*

I see no reason for 'feminist issues' to be any different from 'women's issues'. My own belief is that feminist issues should be brought into the mainstream and discussed instead of being restricted to (often over-the-top) academic circles which are more often than not misquoted–assuming that they are even marginally comprehensible to the average person to start off with–and that is the purpose of writing this book which comprises a socio-legal perspective of Indian women, not *the* Indian Woman because I do not believe that any such woman exists.

A French textbook for Indian students I once read described Indian women as being battered, submissive and illiterate. My experience though is that although a large fraction of Indian women are in fact 'battered, submissive and illiterate', it is ridiculous to define today's Indian women using a stereotype which has little charm and even less truth in it.

I don't care for the 'men are the enemy' brand of feminism–although I've dealt with well over my fair share of men who are *far* beneath contempt, I've had too many men in my life who've been wonderful friends for me to be willing to make unqualified generalisations–*and* I am tired of the 'you are either with us or against us' attitude which some feminists dish out, especially since the truth is that there are a lot of issues I don't truly understand and therefore simply cannot take a concrete stand on. Take abortion, for instance. In theory, I'm pro-choice but I also thank God that it isn't a choice which I have ever been required to make. I have no idea what of what I'd do and I'm certainly not going to judge anyone else for whatever they may choose to do.

This book takes a look at the legal framework which is supposed to protect women's rights in India and the social structure within which that framework is supposed to function–I use the words *supposed to* because, often, the concerned laws are either not enforced or are simply unenforceable. The way in which the system functions does, however, vary widely depending on a number of different factors including, but not limited to, region, caste, class, affluence, (local) traditions and religion. There are women who are extremely liberal and there are those who have been brought up differently.

In the city of Pune, for example, a fourteen-year-old girl, Puja Nagraj Shetty, set herself on fire on October 28, 2006 because her parents saw her talking to a boy in the locality she lived in, and she was afraid of being scolded by them for doing so. She died the next day.[1] Such a sequence of events would, however, be unthinkable for millions of other Indian women.

Belonging to the urban middle class myself, I cannot claim to be able to speak of women who belong to other classes quite simply because the most I can do is try to understand the realities of their lives. Having never been in their shoes, the truth is that no matter how much I've studied, there is no way for me to know what their lives are actually like. For example, intellectually, I know how lower caste Dalit men and women in rural India are often treated by the upper castes–their men are bodies that work, their women are bodies that please[2]–but I cannot even begin to imagine how they feel since my own experiences are different. And that is why, wherever I've spoken of issues which I have no experience of, I've relied on research, statistics and media reports without even trying to delve any deeper.

Women's issues have always been spoken about in both the West and the East although it has only been recently that they have stopped being veiled in any manner. For example, in *The Speckled Band*, Arthur Canon Doyle hinted at domestic violence by having Helen Stoner explain her bruises by saying that her stepfather, Dr Roylott, was a hard man who hardly knew his own strength–the same *explanation* which battered wives still often give–and later, Doyle hinted at his sexually abusing her by having Sherlock Holmes refer to her as Miss Roylott instead of as Miss Stoner; she did not correct him.[3]

> *There is no such thing as autobiography, there is only art and lies.*
>
> – J. Winterson

Recent years have also seen the emergence of sophisticated lesbian literature. In *Art and Lies: A Piece for Three Voices and a Bawd* by Jeanette Winterson, for example, prose and poetry merge, and words are used to sculpt images (as opposed to being used to frame sentences). It certainly isn't everyone's cup of tea though: it's the kind of work which either leaves you stunned by the beauty of its language or makes you want to throw rotten tomatoes at the author who often does nothing more than simply state the mundane albeit beautifully.*[4]

In India, there has been much literature both in vernacular languages and in English about Indian women, their lives and their rights–a great deal of it is so depressing that it's difficult to read. There hasn't been too much non-fictional material at a popular level which has been made available though.

I've tried to make this book as accessible as possible although I haven't even attempted to ensure that it is particularly nuanced. For example, while it's true that the 'victims and the perpetrators of abuse within the home are both trapped in high tension zones where the conflict-ridden logics of the household (intimacy, sexual desire, identity formation, personal habits, marriage, money, the hard work of cooking, cleaning and childcare) interact with, reinforce and often contradict virtually the same list of conflict-ridden logics of the labour market (with its additional special stresses and strains of employment, unemployment and underemployment) and its neighbouring criss-crossing social relations with the wider civil society', as John Keane pointed out while speaking of child murders, to my mind, market forces, migration and other such factors are not reasons to be either discriminatory, violent or otherwise abusive in any situation. There is no justification for abuse, there are only excuses.

Also, I have concentrated on discrimination, violence and protection seen in everyday life not directly perpetrated by the State and I have not dealt with women living in abnormal circumstances such as during riots, or in areas in which the Armed Forces Special Powers Act is in force or in which terrorism is rife.

The appendix contains details of the relevant provisions of various Indian laws which have been mentioned in the text; the main text explores the societal status of women in contemporary Indian society. *The content of this book is not professional advice and should not be construed as such.* Although every effort has been made to ensure accuracy and correctness, this book is not meant to be authoritative or binding - and it certainly isn't impartial or objective -and no action should either be taken or omitted on the basis of its contents.

There have been several unpleasant scenes all over the world–to put it mildly–in the course of the feminist movement but as Martin Luther King, Jr. once said, "Freedom is never voluntarily given by the oppressor; it must be demanded by the oppressed."

After all, the American Society for the Prevention of Cruelty of Animals was founded in 1866 and the Society for the Prevention of Cruelty to Children was established in 1875. Both of them were created before any organization to help abused women was formed, and even though a lot of people today think of 'feminism' as an objectionable word, I somehow get the feeling that if our predecessors hadn't kicked or blown open doors, women today wouldn't have been able to walk through them. History has shown us that men, on the whole, have little interest in promoting women's rights particularly when such promotion *infringes* on their own *right* to control women.*

**Nandita Saikia**
SaikiaNandita@gmail.com

## NOTES

In writing this book, I have tried to ensure that the references are as complete as possible but may have inadvertently left some out. Also, I have used material which I had previously published in articles in my blogs, Panorama published by TakingITGlobal, etc. Such material has been marked with *.

1. The Times of India; 30.10.2006
2. Thakur, Sankarshan; Justice for All, Folks; Tehelka; 11.11.2006
3. Sutherland, John; Is Heathcliffe a Murderer?; Oxford University Press; 1996.
4. The book reminded me of the film Closer–although it lacks the crudity of the film–and in particular, of one line from it:

   "It's a lie. It's a bunch of sad strangers photographed beautifully, and all the glittering assholes who appreciate art say it's beautiful 'cause that's what they want to see. But the people in the photos are sad, and alone, but the pictures make the world seem beautiful. So the exhibition's reassuring, which makes it a lie, and everyone loves a big fat lie."

   Although Art and Lies travels through the centuries with ease, it is set in a London of the near future from which its three main characters, Handel, Picasso and Sappho, are fleeing. They seem to represent Music, Art and Poetry although Handel is, in the book, a former priest turned surgeon and Picasso is a female painter who is abused by her brother. Only Sappho resembles the poet of antiquity. And their stories are often interrupted by Doll Sneerpiece, an 18th Century bawd.*

# PART - I

## DISCRIMINATION

Contemporary India, it seems to me, is a country which is desperately trying to be modern while hanging on to Colonial/ Victorian Puritanism against a backdrop of the Temples of Khajuraho and the Kamasutra. The result is that, as a nation, we are confused, to say the least. Dance bars are beyond the pale for many of us but the so-called *Kala Kendras* or *Art Centres* where girls dance for money–usually in anything but traditional styles–somehow don't seem to bother us very much.

> *The experience of Draupadi in the Court of the Kauravas has become symbolic of the ill treatment of women in our country.*
> *– Former President K.R. Narayanan*
>
> *(They tried to disrobe her in public after they won her from her husbands while gambling but Lord Krishna saved her.)*

There are an increasing number of instances of fundamentalism and orthodoxy one keeps coming across in India today; it somehow feels as though we're moving towards a society which is 'post-modern in its technology, [but] seems pre-modern in its values', to borrow a phrase which Régis Debray used in the rebuttal he wrote in *The New York Times* in response to Donald Rumsfeld's 'Old Europe' gaffe.*

Sometimes, the 'issues', such as they are, seem so trivial that it hardly seems worth arguing about them but when those same non-issues curb freedom, it becomes another story. Take Valentine's Day celebrations, for example. Personally, I see little reason to make India Inc. richer than it is but to be told that the day is against Indian Culture and should therefore not be celebrated strikes me as ludicrous. The problem is that once you add political parties, who actually seem to believe that, as well as people who are willing to indulge in vandalism and assault to stop celebrations into the mix, it stops being funny and becomes just plain frightening. Many florists in the city I live in do not stock roses on the day because they're afraid of running into trouble. I would have understood protests against the celebrations if they included arson or some out of the way illegal activity but they don't–it's the protests themselves which, to my mind, are illegal.*

The argument, in this case, is that Western Influences are corrupting *Indian Culture* by encouraging and creating the existence and incidence of STDs, promiscuous behaviour, teen pregnancies and pre-marital sex.

It's an argument that makes little sense to me. For one thing, it assumes that Indian culture is superior and for another, that Indian culture is oblivious to sex without taking into account the fact that we do not actually need Valentine's Day (which is anyway almost exclusively celebrated by the liberal urban youth) to create any of these problems–if that's how you choose to look at them–or to encourage any other form of sexual behaviour, for that matter. Immaculate conception has had nothing to do with our growing population.

The perception of the average unmarried Indian woman's virtue is nonetheless entrenched in her lack of sexual knowledge, and the *corrupting influence* of the West is blamed for any problem in India that involves sex.

I suppose being tempted to blame others for one's own problems isn't restricted to Indians though–as George Mikes, writing about English foibles, observed, "[rude] remarks are considered very un-English and are the results of foreign influence. (Dating back, however, to the era of the Danish invasion.) "

In India, where we earlier used to blame the 'foreign hand' for creating virtually all our problems, we now blame the 'foreign libido' and have somehow managed to convince ourselves that if we ban miniskirts, close down pubs early and do away with Valentine's Day and the like, we will, by extension, do away with rape, murder and other forms of violence which are, of course, completely unheard of in *Indian Culture.*

Traditionally, the position of women in Indian society is ambiguous. The ancient law-giver, Manu said that women should be honoured–the gods are pleased where women are honoured–on one hand and on the other, he said that that they are unfit for independence and need to be cared for by their fathers in childhood, their husbands during marriage and their sons in widowhood.[1] The scriptures are littered with sanctions against women although there was apparently a time–the Vedic Period–when women had substantial rights in much the same way that women supposedly had a great deal of autonomy in the early Roman Empire.

The Hindu pantheon also includes a large number of Goddesses. The feminine principle was considered to be the 'spirit of the universe' in the Rig Veda–the oldest Hindu text–but over time, Goddesses have been disempowered by the institution of marriage and made subordinate to their husbands. The ferocity of the Goddess Kali, for example, was controlled by her husband, Shiva at a time when nothing and no one else could restrain it. She is usually depicted with her tongue hanging out–myth has it that this is because Shiva lay down on a battlefield in which She was dancing in such frenzy that She danced on top of him. When she realised what she had done, she hung her tongue out, ashamed of the disrespect She had shown her Lord.

There are, obviously, a number of different factors which have contributed to the status of women in contemporary Indian Society including Hindu scriptural injunctions, Islamic influences brought to India by Muslim rulers, Western ideology which the British were largely responsible for bringing into the country, globalisation and contemporary socio-legal theory.

In his address on the eve of Republic Day in 2002, former President K.R. Narayanan observed, "One of the clearest indicators of the development of a society is the position and

> *Bringing up a daughter is like watering a neighbour's plant.*
>
> *– Indian proverb*

status women enjoy in that society. Even though women's rights are recognized as human rights... their standing in our society is deplorable. The problem of women in India is symbolic of the problem of inequalities and injustices in our society in general. Even today it is amazing that we have not become an inclusive society in spite of the political triumph of our democracy."

Sonal Manṣingh, an Odissi dancer–*the* Odissi dancer in the eyes of many people–performed a piece on the contemporary Indian woman in a performance I attended in 2005 and while introducing it, she pointed out that, nowadays, we have goodness knows how many seminars, workshops, lectures etc. to discuss women's rights but at the end of the day, they make little difference to ground realities.[2*]

## THE SOCIETAL STATUS OF WOMEN

### Ancient Indian Society

#### *The Vedic Period*

c. 4000 BC to 1000 BC

"The Hindus have received their religion through revelation, the Vedas. They hold that the Vedas are without beginning or end. It may sound ludicrous to this audience how a book can be without beginning or end. But by the Vedas no books are meant. They mean the accumulated treasury of spiritual laws discovered by different persons in different times. [They] would exist even if we forgot them. The discoverers of these laws were called Rishis and we honour them as perfected beings," said Swami Vivekananda at the Parliament of Religions in 1893. He added that he was proud to say that some of the very greatest of the Rishis were women.

The Vedic Period was the period in which the four Vedas[3]–the Rig Veda, the Yajur Veda, the Atharva Veda and the Sama Veda–were written. They are believed to have been 'revealed'–Shruti–and, in many ways, they constitute the basis of Hinduism. They are considered to be perfect because of being divinely heard. However, the laws which Swami Vivekananda speaks of are not legal norms of visible human conduct; the Vedas are not an important source of Hindu law in that sense although they do recognise the importance of such law.

Quoting from the Vedas, Holland said, "Law is the king of kings, far more powerful and rigid than they; nothing can be mightier than law, by whose aid, even the weak may prevail over the strong."[4]

In ancient India, society was patriarchal, as it is today. There are some scholars who talk of a time prior to the formation of a patriarchal society when society was matriarchal but they do not have very much solid proof to support their proposition and although some Indian societies today–such as that of the tribal Khasis and Garos–are in theory matriarchal, the fact of the matter is that in practice, matriarchy doesn't seem to do away with the need for a woman to get permission from her male relatives to do such things as sell property.

Women were educated in ancient India and there are reports of women who did not marry so as to be able to actively pursue their studies.

The Vedic period boasts of female philosophers like Gargi and Maitreyee. The Brihadaranya Upanishad speaks of a philosophical argument between Gargi and the sage, Yajnavalkya expounding the nature of God while the question '*What shall I do with that by which I do not become immortal?*' asked by Yajnavalkya's wife, Maitreyee when she was wondering whether she could achieve immortality by owning all the wealth in the world 'has been repeatedly cited in Indian religious philosophy to illustrate both the nature of the human predicament and the limitations of the material world'.[5]

However, references to female philosophers decreased as time wore on and the Manusmriti which is considered to have been written around 200 BC specifically says that 'women have no business with the text of the Veda'.[6]

It is believed that women could inherit property during this period and that widow remarriage was common. However, towards the end of the period, the caste system crystallised and the Purushashukta Hymn was added to the Rig Veda.

This hymn laid down the hierarchy among the four main castes. The Brahmin priests were at the top; they were supposedly made from the head of God. The Kshatriya warriors, who were said to have been made from His shoulders and chest, came next. After them were the Vaishya merchants from the thighs of God; they had little social status in spite of often being extremely wealthy. And finally, the Shudras (who are still considered to be the lowest caste) were said to have been created from God's feet. Thus, the Purushashukta Hymn helped to strengthen the caste system and destroy social mobility by making the membership of castes strictly hereditary.

*The Age of the Smritis*
c. 800 BC to 300 AD

The most important religious/legal texts of classical India were written in the age which followed the Vedic Period. These books include the Shastras or legal texts such as the Manu Smriti c. 200 BC, the Yajnavalkya Smriti c. 300 AD, and the Narada Smriti c. 400 AD, as well as treatises on administration such as Arthashastra by Kautilya, and Nibandhe or commentaries on individual legal texts which were written between 700 and 1700 AD.[7]

Smriti-meaning what is remembered (as opposed to what has been heard/revealed in the Vedas)-is considered to be secondary and changeable in nature. It is neither as old as Shruti and nor is it entirely religious; it speaks of secular matters as well and includes folklore. It is authoritative only as far as it conforms to Shruti.[*]

Also, custom or Sadachar was, in Ancient India, as in the rest of the world, an important source of law. There were different types of customs which were recognised: Kulachar or family customs, Lokachar or local customs and Deshachar or national customs. Although a great deal of Hindu law has been codified today, customs are still accepted as a source of law to a limited extent provided they are not illegal, immoral or opposed to public policy.

For example, one of the conditions necessary for a Hindu Marriage to be valid under the Hindu Marriage Act is that the intending spouses are not within the degrees of a prohibited relationship as defined in the Act.[8] However, this does not apply if a custom or usage governing them permits their marriage.[9]

Moving back though, it was during the age of the Smritis that a society firmly based on the caste system was established. And the caste system itself no longer affected merely a person's occupation; its effects spilled into every other sphere of life, and there was no mobility worth mentioning within it at all.

Marriage became almost entirely within one's own caste although marriages of men with women belonging to castes lower than theirs were accepted by society and their children were considered legitimate. Such a marriage was called an Anulobha Vivaha. However, the reverse was not true: a woman could not legitimately marry a man of caste lower than hers. Such a marriage was called a Pratilobha Vivaha and children born of it were considered illegitimate.

The legal texts also said that although intending spouses had to belong to the same caste, a man and a woman of the same caste belonging to the same Gotra could not marry. It was believed that Brahmins, Kshatriyas and Vaishyas were the descendents of seven ascetic Rishis, and that the descendants of each of the Rishis formed a separate Gotra. A man and a woman could get married only if they did not share the same Gotra for up to seven generations on the paternal side (Sapinda) and five on the maternal side of their families.

And if that wasn't enough, there were also eight different kinds of marriage[10] which were mentioned in the texts:

1. **Brahma:** The father gave his daughter (wearing jewellery) as a gift to a Brahmin whom he had invited.
2. **Daiva:** The father gave his daughter (wearing jewellery) as a gift to a priest who had duly officiated at a sacrifice while the sacrifice was in progress.
3. **Arsha:** The father gave away his daughter after receiving a cow and a bull or two pairs of cows from the bridegroom.
4. **Prajapatya:** A contract was signed with the intended husband and the bride's father said, "You two shall now practice your householders' duties together."

5. **Asura:** The bridegroom received a maiden after giving as much money as he could afford to the kinsmen of the bride and to the bride herself.
6. **Gandharva:** The voluntary union of a woman and her lover.
7. **Rakshasa:** The forcible abduction of a maiden from her home by the man who intended to marry her.
8. **Paishacha:** A man stealthily seduced a sleeping, intoxicated or mentally disabled girl and later married her.

The first four types were the approved forms of marriage although the others existed as well. Manu said that even if a man had married in due form, he could legally abandon his wife if she was blemished, diseased or deflowered, and had been fraudulently given to him.[11]

Today's 'love marriage' is similar to the Gandharva form of marriage which was spoken of in ancient times (and is still often looked down on). Kalidas wrote about it in his play *Shakuntala* in which a curse by the sage, Durvasas, caused Shakuntala's husband, the king, Dushyant, to forget her and therefore refuse to recognise her as being his wife. And since their marriage had been in the Gandharva form, she could not produce any witnesses to support her story.[12]

> *Patriarchy's foundation has rested for millennia on the unwritten but rigorously enforced rule that women and children keep the secrets of men and suffer abuse in silent shame.*
>
> – *Naomi Wolf*

Women also became less able to fend for themselves during this period because their lives changed in the educational arena: they were no longer either encouraged or–in many cases – permitted to study. In fact, the scriptures specifically said that women are unfit to hear the Vedas[13] although, even then, there were occasional instances of people speaking out against the control of women by men; for example, sometime between 100 and 200 AD, Tiru-Valluvar questioned the use of 'that purity which is brought about by physical restrictions and isolation to which women are subjected'.[14]

And to make matters worse, patriarchy was, by this time, so deeply entrenched in society that the Smritis not only declared that women had no property of their own but also that they were property themselves–the wealth which they earned was deemed to have been earned 'for him to whom they belonged'.[15]

## Medieval India

The Medieval Period in India was primarily dominated by Muslim rulers in most of the country. Their rule began in the 13th Century.

North Indian society in both the Delhi Sultanate and the Mughal Empire was heterogeneous. The positions of the various castes in Hindu society in the North changed slightly because the Brahmins lost their traditional positions as advisors to Hindu kings. In the South, however, the existence of the Muslim Bahamani Kingdom made the Hindu rulers of the Vijayanagar Kingdom very rigid and orthodox in their application and interpretation of Hindu laws and customs. They tried to protect Hinduism from being influenced by Islam but they wound up doing precisely the opposite since many Hindus from the lower castes converted to Islam and other religions simply to be able to avoid the discrimination they faced as low caste Hindus.

The position of both Hindu and Muslim women was lower than that of men. Practices like female infanticide and Purdah were common. Aristocratic women of both religions were confined to their homes and women were usually not allowed to execute legal documents. In some ways, however, Muslim women were better off than their Hindu counterparts. For example, unlike Hindu women, Muslim women had the right to divorce their husbands in certain circumstances and they could inherit property.

Polygamy was common throughout the country although polyandry was practised in the South Indian matriarchal Hindu Nayar community. The usual age at which a woman got married was between 8 and 18 years.

Widow-remarriage was almost unheard of in Hindu society. A Hindu widow did not inherit her dead husband's property although she sometimes received an allowance. She was usually encouraged to commit Sati i.e. burn herself alive on her husband's funeral pyre and if she did not, she was either subjected to a life of unspeakable indignity and/or forced into a marriage with one of the men of her dead husband's family.

However, none of this stopped a few women from becoming tremendously powerful. For example, one of Emperor Jehangir's twenty wives, Mihrunissa who was known by the title *Noor Jehan*–Light of the World–was very influential in the Mughal Court. Imperial rescripts were sometimes issued in her name and Jehangir added her name to silver rupees.[16]

It was also during this period though that a general rule by which upper caste/class women had much less freedom than their lower caste/class counterparts became firmly established. Whether it was due to the Islamic veil or the Hindu Ghumgat, women–particularly those belonging to the societal elite–began to quite literally see nothing apart from the ground beneath their feet when they were not sequestered.

## 1.3 The Influence of the British

The British first came to India in 1600 as traders. It didn't take them very long to become rulers. Most of the legal principles which guide those in the Indian legal system today are of British origin. The Supreme Court pointed out in 2006 that it is regrettable that Indian lawyers quote Maxwell and Craies but do not refer to the Mimansa Principles of Interpretation which are said to have been laid down by Jamini in the 5th Century BC and were regularly referred to by the ancient jurists Vijnaneshwar and Jimutavahana. The Supreme Court said, "MPI is a part of that intellectual treasury, but it is distressing to note that apart from the reference to these legal principles in the judgement of Sir John Edge, the then Chief Justice of the Allahabad High Court, in Beni Prasaad v/s Hardai Devi, 1892, and once more by Justice Katju in a recent case, there has been almost no utilization of these principles in our own country."[17]

The Colonial legacy with respect to women's rights is inconsistent at best. The British, inter alia, introduced the concept of 'restitution of conjugal rights' to India which did–and still does–next to nothing to help women. During the Raj, it gave a woman who had left her husband two options, both of which were usually unsafe: to go back to him or to go to gaol. The British themselves abolished suits for the restitution of conjugal rights by Section 20 of the Matrimonial Proceedings and Property Act, 1970. However, the concept still exists in Indian Personal Laws. For example, the 1976 amendment of Section 9 of the Hindu Marriage Act, 1955 says:

> When either the husband or the wife has, without reasonable excuse, withdrawn from the society of the other, the aggrieved party may apply, by petition to the District Court, for restitution of conjugal rights and the Court, on being satisfied of the truth of the statements made in such petition and that there is no legal ground why the application should not be granted, may decree restitution of conjugal rights accordingly.
>
> Explanation: Where a question arises whether there has been reasonable excuse for withdrawal from the society, the burden of proving reasonable excuse shall be on the person who has withdrawn from the society.

Prior to the 1976 amendment, under Section 9 (2)–which the amendment deleted–nothing could be pleaded in response to a petition for the restitution of conjugal rights which was not grounds recognised by the law for judicial separation, nullity of marriage or divorce.

There has been a great deal of controversy in Independent India regarding the Constitutional validity of the restitution of conjugal rights.

In Sareetha v/s Vekatasubbaiah, 1983,[18] the High Court of Andhra Pradesh accepted the wife's argument that the Constitution confers on her 'a right of free choice as to whether, where and how her body is to be used for the procreation of children and also the choice of when and by whom the various parts of her body are to be sensed', and held that the restitution of conjugal rights offended Article 21 of the Constitution which recognises the right to privacy and liberty as well as Article 14 which recognises the right to equality. The High Court of Delhi, however, disagreed with this judgment in 1984.[19]

The question finally arose before the Supreme Court in Saroj Rani v/s Sudarshan Kumar, 1984,[20] in which Justice Mukherji held that the Section which dealt with the restitution of conjugal rights only induced the spouses involved to live together and that it did not violate Articles 14 and 21 of the Constitution.

Moving back to the British though, they tried to prevent Sati and female infanticide, but supported not only widow remarriage in general but also the practice of Karewa (practiced by some communities such as the Jats of the State of Haryana) in which the widow was, for all practical purposes, left with no choice but to marry a man from her dead husband's family so as to prevent land from being alienated.

The British brought a number of Indian social and legal practices within the framework of the legal system they introduced but an analysis of their laws shows that they brought in reform primarily in regard to physical violence against women. They tried to decrease female infanticide, banned Sati in 1829, and passed the Widow Remarriage Act in 1856 despite massive opposition from orthodox Hindus but left practices which made women vulnerable in the first place untouched.

There was almost nothing which was done for about thirty-five years after the 1857 Indian Mutiny against the British primarily because of a policy of non-interference which had been spelled out in the Queen's Proclamation of 1858. However, the British raised the age of consent in the Native Marriage Act partly in response to a widely publicised case in which an eleven-year-old girl–Phulmani Bai–died of sexual intercourse with her husband in 1891.

There was very little done during the Raj to change the existing socio-economic structure in terms of enabling women to inherit property or otherwise ameliorate their financial condition. The primary concern of the British lay in the realm of commercial and other secular law. Nonetheless, they introduced the divide between the public and private spheres of life which simply did not exist earlier. And then, they further sub-divided the personal/private sphere along religious lines. Some of the policies of the British were, in fact, specifically designed to 'divide and rule' and they contributed to the formation of religious divisions which exist in India to this day.

## INDEPENDENT INDIA

Former President K R Narayanan said, "Mahatma Gandhi had mobilized ordinary women in large numbers for the cause of our country's independence. 70000 of them participated in the Salt Satyagraha. He included women's upliftment in his Constructive Programme as an important point not only for their elevation but also for positive social change and attainment of independence," in his address on the eve of Republic Day in 2002.

There are a number of polices at the national level to help alleviate the position of women in Indian society. They include:

The National Policy on Empowerment of Women 2001
The National Health Policy adopted 2001
to increase women's access to basic health care
The National Agricultural Policy 2000
to improve their access to technology

A legal framework within which women's rights can be protected exists in India. Human rights jurisprudence has Constitutional status and a great deal of religious law was codified soon after India achieved independence. Parliament has also passed a number of Acts which, inter alia, specifically protect women's rights. These Acts include:

- The Hindu Marriage Act, 1955.
- The Hindu Adoptions and Maintenance Act, 1956.
- The Immoral Traffic Prevention Act, 1956.
- The Dowry Prohibition Act, 1961.
- The Medical Termination of Pregnancy Act, 1971.
- The Indecent Representation of Women Prohibition Act, 1986.
- The Commission of Sati Prevention Act, 1987.
- The National Commission for Women Act, 1990.
- The Prenatal Diagnostic Techniques (Regulation and Prevention of Misuse) Act, 1994.

In addition to this, other laws, such as Indian labour laws, contain provisions to ensure that women are not exploited in the workplace.

The problem in India usually isn't that the required laws don't exist at all. The problem is that laws do not and cannot operate in a vacuum, and a social, economic, religious and cultural structure in which they can operate is fragile if not non-existent. The laws themselves, too, are often full of loopholes and, due to illiteracy and poverty, a large majority of people do not know of their existence, much less of how to use them for their own benefit. The abundance of seemingly senseless technicalities beyond belief, millions of forms to be filled and procedures to be followed doesn't help either, even though endless procedures are not an Indian monopoly.

Although he could just as easily have been speaking about virtually any Indian legal procedure, Jeremy Blachman, an American lawyer, speaking of an uncontested divorce in New York which should be a simple matter once said, "It's a tremendously long and complicated process. I may be naive; but I don't understand quite why. I don't understand a lot of these legal processes, and why there are always so many forms to file and papers to sign and bureaucratic hurdles to go through. I understand society is complicated. But is part of it just lawyers making rules to give lawyers something to do and hours to bill? That's a cynical view, and I'm sure there are other reasons, but I don't know them."[21]

And, speaking of loopholes large enough to drive horse carriages right through, the Dowry Prohibition Act, 1961 made it a crime both to take and to give dowry, so people who were forced into giving a dowry, in a way, were also on the wrong side of the law while in the infamous Prevention of Domestic Violence Bill, 2002, the law didn't clearly define domestic violence itself so, had the bill been passed, its implementation would have been difficult if not next to impossible. It said:

> Domestic violence: For the purposes of this Act, any conduct of the respondent shall constitute domestic violence if he habitually assaults or makes the life of the aggrieved person miserable by

> cruelty of conduct even if such conduct does not amount to physical ill-treatment...

The problem was that no one knew what 'habitually' meant. Was it once a day? Once a week? On the first Tuesday of every year?*

I can't be certain but to my mind, it could well be that such problems in the law are what lead to disasters like the murder of Akku Yadav in August, 2004 where, as *The Week* reported, "The women of Kasturba Nagar in [the city of] Nagpur killed Bhalchandra Kalicharan alias Akku Yadav, who allegedly had raped more than twenty women. In what sociologists later called 'an outrage of justice', *they lynched him in a Courtroom.*"[22*]

The law, in itself, is nothing more than an instrument of social change. The Indian statesman, Jawaharlal Nehru once said, "Legislation cannot by itself normally solve deep-rooted social problems. One has to approach them in other ways too, but legislation is necessary and essential, so that it may give that push and have that educative factor as well as the legal sanctions behind it which help public opinion to be given a certain shape."[23]

Almost all of these 'deep-rooted social problems' find their roots in custom and/or religion. Sociologists like Bogardus and McIver have pointed out that 'people tend to abide by them if only because they are a part of their social heritage. Codified laws which suddenly prohibit a custom have not much chance of being welcomed. Custom when attacked attacks law in turn'. Considering this, it probably isn't too surprising that protective laws have not been very successful.

Also, the issues which face Indians are not identical to those faced in the West. For example the Right to Life debate is virtually non-existent in India. Abortion is legal and is regulated by the Medical Termination of Pregnancy Act, 1971. It is permitted up to twenty weeks and the husband's permission is not required. A woman can legally have an abortion if she is in danger of grave physical injury, if her mental health is in danger, or if the pregnancy is a result of contraceptive failure in a marriage or of rape, or if the child is likely to have physical or mental abnormalities.

Abortion is usually associated with shame and secrecy if the woman happens to be unmarried and even if the need for it arises as a result of being raped, the woman is usually nonetheless held responsible for becoming pregnant against societal norms.

Within a marriage, abortion often becomes necessary because of economic conditions and because contraceptives are simply not used. Husbands and in-laws also often pressurise women to have abortions either because they don't want a child at all or because they don't want a child of the sex of the foetus. Some women are forced to have abortions because of becoming pregnant during 'inauspicious' months. The third time a woman becomes pregnant, she is sometimes forced to abort the foetus because the number 3 is considered unlucky. Or, she could be made to do so if the breadwinner/head of the family has an accident during her pregnancy; it is considered to be a bad omen. And occasionally, women use abortion as an instrument to get revenge–one woman in a study said that she had an abortion to get back at her husband and mother-in-law for abusing her.[24]

The issue in India isn't quite as much abortion per se but the selective abortion of female foetuses. Parliament passed the Prenatal Diagnostic Techniques (Regulation and Prevention of Misuse) Act in 1994 to try to curb the practise of female foeticide but if the skewed sex-ratios in India are anything to go by, the Act has not been spectacularly successful.

In a recent survey, in Ludhiana, Punjab, 67.50% of farming respondents and 50% of non-farming respondents approved of sex selective abortions. And of these, 82.97% saw nothing wrong with female infanticide considering the prevalence of dowry, the expense of a marriage and the high cost of living.[25]

The flip side of the problem is that in areas where sex selective abortion is most practised, there is now a shortage of women for men to marry. The 'solution' has been the 'import' or trafficking of women from areas–primarily in North East India–where sex selective abortion is not as widely practised. These imported women are often referred to as *lesser wives* in North India where they are taken and are sometimes shared by more than one *husband* due to the huge scarcity of women. Some estimates say that this scarcity causes as many as five hundred women from the North Eastern State of Assam alone to disappear each year. Other places these *lesser wives* originally come from include poor areas in West Bengal and Bangladesh in the East, as well as the poverty-stricken areas in the Southern states of Tamil Nadu and Andhra Pradesh.

*(See 'Migration and Indirect Trafficking' on page 105.)*

Although there are 'surplus' women available in the East of the country mainly because traditions there have generally discriminated less against women, there are indications that this is now beginning to change. The census figures for Kolkata, for example, show that in 1991, there were at least 17 wards in the city with healthy sex-ratios including Gariahat (Ward 68) in which there were 1006 females for every 1000 males in 1991. The 2001 census figures told a very different story though: the ratio had changed to 916 females for every 1000 males.

Access to healthcare is virtually non-existent for many women and gender-budgeting is virtually an alien concept. In the 2006-2007 Budget, the allocation for the Reproductive and Child Project was reduced from 1814.27 crore INR to 1765.83 crore INR. And about 780 obstetricians (out of a total of about 22000 in India) exist to take care of about 650 million people in rural areas.[26] The practice of getting married young also means that girls become mothers far too early – according to the 2001 census, there were nearly three lakh girls below eighteen who had at least one child.

In spite of all of this, there are women who have defied societal norms. A friend of mine once gave me the (unpublished) memoirs of a Gujarati lady who lived to be 100 to read. Her name was Soonamai Desai and she died in 1983. She was the first woman corporator in Navsari in the State of Gujarat and travelled widely.[27]

I suppose a great deal depends on the individual woman and on the choices she makes for herself.

The women in my own family have each charted their own course, for the most part. My paternal grandmother, for example, was very concerned about family 'honour'. She continued to study after her marriage till she got a PhD in Education. She set up schools and was 'successful' by any standard.

Nonetheless, she wound up being murdered at home in 1997–she was stabbed, beaten *and* poisoned.

Considering that she had what few women (even today) have: the financial ability to walk out, one would have imagined that, with her education, she would not have allowed herself to remain in what was obviously an unsafe environment for her. She seems to have considered image and prestige more important than her own safety though.

Nonica Datta who teaches history at Delhi University said that 1947, 1984, and 2002 were, for her, 'moments frozen in history as tombstones in a graveyard'. Unfortunately, many of us have such moments. Datta went on to say, "There are many unrecorded, unuttered histories of violence and fear–an amazing seamless continuity without rupture."[28]

### *Sometimes, the truth ultimately emerges. Usually, it doesn't*

Apart from the fact that women in all strata of society often say nothing of being abused, placing their own happiness and safety much lower than things like family prestige and the 'welfare' of their children–without realising that their children's welfare is closely connected to their own–the fact of the matter is that even if women do speak out against abuse, there is rarely anyone to listen. And there is almost never anyone who both can *and* will do something to help make a tangible difference.

## NOTES

1. Manu IX. 3.
2. This was first published in *In Shades of Grey;* catharticnemesis.blogspot.com; July 2005.
3. This is an excerpt from an article that was first published in *In Shades of Grey;* catharticnemesis.blogspot.com; in February, 2006.

   **The Vedas:**

   1. Rig Veda: Hymns of Praise
   2. Yajur Veda: Formulae for the performance of sacrifices (yajna)
   3. Sama Veda: Melodies to be sung during worship and Yajna

4. Atharva Veda: Magic formulae largely outside the scope of Yajna

**Each Veda has four Parts:**

1. Sanhitas: metrical hymns (mantras)
2. Brahmanas: prose explaining the hymns
3. Aranyakas: 'forest books'/treatises for hermits and saints
4. Upanishads/Vedanta: philosophical treatises

The Aranyakas and Upanishads are sometimes considered appendices of the Brahmanas

**Supplementary literature related to the Vedas:**

The six Vedangas (sometimes considered Smriti) expound the sciences required to understand and apply the Vedas. They are:

1. Kalp (ritual) Srauta, Grihya, Dharma and Sulba by various sages
2. Siksha (pronunciation/phonetics) of Panini
3. Vyakaran (grammar) of Panini
4. Nirukti (etymology) of Yaska
5. Chandas (metre) of Pingalacharya
6. Jyotishi (astronomy/astrology) of Garga

The four Upavedas (usually considered Smriti) deal with the four traditional arts and sciences:

1. Ayurved (medicine)
2. Gandharvaved (music and dance)
3. Dhanurved (warfare)
4. Shilpaved (architecture)

4. Art and science of law; *www*.hinduonnet.com/thehindu/br/2002/09/24/stories/2002092400040300.htm.
5. Sen, Amartya; The Argumentative Indian; Penguin; 2005.
6. Manu IX. 18.
7. Other books written in the period of the Sutras include:

**Itihas:** histories or epics viz. the Mahabharata, Valmiki-Ramayana, Yogavasishtha, Harivamsa

**Agama:** mainly theological philosophy dealing with knowledge (Jnan), ritual (Kriya), concentration (Yoga), worship (Charya) and is of three kinds:

1. Sakta Agamas or Tantras which glorify Devi (Goddess)
2. Vaishnava Agamas or Pancharatra Agamas which glorify Lord Vishnu

3. Saiva Agamas which glorify Lord Shiva
4. Sakta Agamas or Tantras which glorify Devi (Goddess)

**Puran:** history, legends and myths about Gods, sages and kings freely mixed. There are eighteen main Puranas and many subsidiary 'Upapuranas'. The main Puranas include Matsya Purana, Padma Purana, Naradiya Purana, Vishnu Purana, Varaha Purana, Vamana Purana, Bhavishya Purana, Brahma Purana, Shiva Purana, Devi Purana, Skanda Purana and Markandeya Purana.

**Sutra:** proverbs etc. c. 800 B.C. to 200 B.C. e.g. Ashtadhyayi composed by Panini, Naradbhakti Sutra, Sandilyabhakti Sutra;

1. Vritti: a short explanation of a sutra e.g. is Bodhayana's Vritti on the Brahma Sutra
2. Bhashya: an elaborate commentary on a Sutra e.g. Mahabhashya by Patanjali on the Vyakaran (grammar) Sutra of Panini
3. Tippani: Less orthodox than Vritti, it explains difficult words and phrases in the original sutra. e.g. are Kaiyata's Tippani on the Mahabhashya of Patanjali
4. Varttika: a critical analysis of a Bhashya e.g. Varttika of Katyayana on Panini's Sutra

Darshana constitute the six schools of Hindu philosophical thought.

1. Yoga by Patanjali
2. Nyaya by Gautama
3. Vaiseshika by Kanada
4. Sankhya by Kapila
5. Purva Mimamsa by Jaimini
6. Uttara Mimamsa or Vedanta by Badarayana or Vyasa

8. Section 3 (g); The Hindu Marriage Act, 1955: Degrees of prohibited relationship–Two persons are said to be within the 'degrees of prohibited relationship' if;
   (i) one is a lineal ascendant of the other; or
   (ii) one was the wife or husband of a lineal ascendant or descendant of the other; or
   (iii) one was the wife of the brother or of the father's or mother's brother or of the grandfather's or grandmother's brother or the other; or
   (iv) the two are brother and sister, uncle and niece, aunt and nephew or children of brother and sister or of two brothers or of two sisters.

'Relationship' includes:

(i) a relationship by half or uterine blood as well as by full blood;

(ii) an illegitimate blood relationship as well as legitimate;

(iii) a relationship by adoption as well as by blood.

9. Section 5; The Hindu Marriage Act, 1955: A marriage may be solemnized between any two Hindus, if the following conditions are fulfilled, namely:

   (i) neither party has a spouse living at the time of the marriage;

   (ii) at the time of the marriage, neither party:

      (a) is incapable of giving a valid consent of it in consequence of unsoundness of mind or

      (b) though capable of giving a valid consent has been suffering from mental disorder of such a kind or to such an extent as to be unfit for marriage and the procreation of children or

      (c) has been subject to recurrent attacks of insanity or epilepsy

   (iii) the bridegroom has completed the age of twenty one years and the bride the age of eighteen years at the time of the marriage

   (iv) the parties are not within the degrees of prohibited relationship unless the custom or usage governing each of them permits of a marriage between the two

   (v) the parties are not Sapindas of each other, unless the custom or usage governing each of them permits of a marriage between the two

   (vi) (Omitted)

10. First published in *In Shades of Grey*; catharticnemesis.blogspot.com; January 2006.

11. Manu IX.72

12. Shakuntala was the daughter of Kanva. Dushyant had come to visit him when he was away and fell in love with her. They got married and he gave her his ring. Shakuntala, however, incurred the wrath of the Sage Durvasas who cursed her–she was to lose Dushyant's ring and he was to forget her till he saw the ring. So, when she went to him (having, by then, lost the ring), he didn't recognise her. However, the God Indra took pity on her; he gave her refuge and years later, when the ring was found in a fish, he helped Dushyant go to her.

13. Bhag. Pur. I.4.25 (900 CE).
14. Rajagopalachari C (trans.); Tirukkural c. 100 AD; Bharatiya Vidya Bhawan; 2002.
15. Manu VIII. 416.
16. Richards, John; The Mughal Empire; Cambridge; South Asian Ed.; 1993.
17. This judgment was delivered by Justice Ashok Bhan and Justice Katju on 29.9.2006 in Ispat Industries Ltd. *v* CEGAT, Mumbai. In this case, the Bench referred to the Gunapradhan Axiom which states that if a word or sentence purporting to express a subordinate idea clashes with the principal idea, the former must be adjusted to the latter or must be disregarded altogether.
18. AIR 1983 AP 356.
19. Harvinder Kaur *v* Harmandar Singh, AIR 1984 Del 66.
20. AIR 1984 SC 1562.
21. http://jeremyblachman.blogspot.com/
22. *www*.the-week.com/24aug29/currentevents_article6.htm.
23. Statement of Objects and Reasons; The Dowry Prohibition (Amendment) Act, 1984.
24. Visaria, Ramchandran et al; Abortion in India; EPW; November 20, 2003.
25. Walia, Ajinder; Female Foeticide in Punjab: Exploring the Socio-economic and Cultural Dimension; Idea, a social issues journal, Vol. 10, No. 1.
26. Sharma, Benita; Budgets and the Invisible Woman; The Times of India; 22.3.2006.
27. I was intrigued by her life and also by her description of social life in general, the difference between the India she grew up in and the one she died in, and the way in which her story ties up with 'standard' history.

    For example, she spoke of meeting Madam Cama in Paris and of how the lady had made arrangements for what should be done if she died there as she expected to since, at the time, she doubted that the British would give her permission to return either to England or to India because of her Nationalist activities. As it turned out, the British did allow Madam Cama to return to her homeland and she died on Indian soil but I hadn't known anything at all about the French funeral arrangements. She ended the memoir by saying, "So now my life is not only in its evening–it is decidedly night and as I look back, with a few blinding spots which have hit me hard enough to make my head reel; life, fate, destiny –call it what you will–has been good to me and it is in this mood that I await the coming of a stage of life called death but which could be but another phase of life with some impatience and great curiosity." *

28. Datta, Nonica; You Have Options; Tehelka; 20.1.2007.

# PART - II

## VIOLENCE

*Opening the door on the subject of violence against the world's females is like standing at the threshold of an immense dark chamber vibrating with collective anguish, but with the sounds of protest throttled back to a murmur. Where there should be outrage aimed at an intolerable status quo there is instead denial, and the largely passive acceptance of 'the way things are'.*
*– Charlotte Bunch*[1]

Violence against women is inextricably linked to issues of gender equality and gender mainstreaming (which calls for the systematic incorporation of gender issues throughout *all* Governmental institutions and policies).[2] The preamble to the 1993 UN Declaration on the Elimination of Violence against Women clearly locates the roots of gender-based violence in 'historically unequal power relations between men and women, which have led to domination over and discrimination against women by men and to the prevention of the full advancement of women, recognising that violence against women is one of the crucial social mechanisms by which women are forced into a subordinate position compared with men'.[3]

Violence against women encompasses but is not limited to physical, sexual and psychological violence, firstly, occurring within the family, secondly, occurring within the general community and thirdly, perpetrated or condoned by the State.[4]

The UN Declaration on the Elimination of Violence against Women defines 'violence against women' as 'any act of gender-based violence that results in or is likely to result in, physical, sexual or psychological harm or suffering to women, including threats of such acts, coercion or arbitrary deprivation of liberty, whether occurring in public or in private life'.[5]

And in *Broken Bodies, Shattered Minds*, a 2001 Amnesty International publication,[6] the organisation observed that 'without exception women's greatest risk of violence comes not from 'stranger danger' but from the men they know, often male family members or husbands... what is striking is how similar the problem is around the world' in reference to a study[7] conducted by Johns Hopkins University. It continued, saying that violence is 'a truly global phenomenon and while the figures may vary in different countries, the suffering and its causes are similar throughout the world'.

A number of other studies have also come to similar conclusions and have said that their own homes are one of the most unsafe places for women to be in although they are, in contrast, one of the safest places for men to be in. Comparatively speaking, it has been easier to combat violence which occurs within the general community than to combat that which occurs within the family because traditionally, what happens behind closed doors is considered to be 'private' and quite simply beyond the purview of the law.

The approach has changed and now, 'the human right to a private and family life is of special importance, but cannot be tolerated to condone private conduct within families in which one partner enforces dominance by violence over the other. The key human rights principle is that violence deliberately directed against any other person is never a purely private matter'.[8]

That is, however, not to say that violence occurring in other spheres is any less important. Violence occurring within the general community includes rape, sexual abuse, sexual harassment and intimidation at work, in educational institutions and elsewhere, trafficking in women and forced prostitution.[9]

And as for violence perpetrated or condoned by the State, apart from unusual situations such as those seen during the riots in Gujarat, there is also an underlying violence seen in normal everyday life such as that which is seen in the treatment sometimes meted out by the police to women in their custody.

According to 'Crime Clock 2005' of the National Crime Records Bureau which lists crimes reported under the Indian Penal Code, in 2005, there was:

- One case of cruelty by a husband and his family every 9 minutes.
- One molestation every 15 minutes.
- One rape every 29 minutes.
- One sexual harassment case every 53 minutes.
- One dowry death every 77 minutes.

And not all acts of violence fit into neat little pigeon holes. For example, the cases of crimes against women which dominated the news in January and February 2004 were the Jyoti Chandra case[10] where a woman and her four-year-old daughter were brutally assaulted for a dowry, the case of a twelve-year-old girl who was shackled by her father for four years–in the pictures I saw, her legs seem to have become bowed possibly because of a lack of exercise, the Bijal Joshi rape case[11] where the victim was gang-raped by several men including her boyfriend and later committed suicide before the authorities really did anything about it, and a case in which a man cut off a female relative's nose apparently to uphold his honour.*

I get a lot of mail–most of which is far from pleasant–about violence against women from people I don't know and I'm usually left stunned by how impractical they are. One which I received on November 30, 2005, for example, said:

> Violence against women is definitely on the rise. But to counter force you need a deterrent force. A modern educated woman who thinks that an ideal body would be 5 foot 5 inches height and 40 kg weight with a waistline of 22 inches would obviously be in no position to defend herself against an 80 kg man. Why do some of the women's magazines keeping publishing articles on slimming showing pictures of anorexic models. This mindset has to be

> changed. Women should aim to be healthy and strong and assertive. The recent experience of Ms Neha Kubadia is really shocking. Men will never understand what she had to go through unless someone makes them go through the same experience. You are only penning your protest. Why don't you prove your assertiveness through action? *If a man ran a car over a woman thrice why don't you run a car over me, a man, thirty times? And if a girl survived it surely I will. Let us see if you have the guts to do it. Else your feminism is all sham.**

I read it at 1:48 a.m., was exhausted, and had no desire to reply to the sender who somehow managed to cram two very different contentions into one mail. The first, I couldn't agree more with–no one relishes being bombarded by supermodels who are almost always either genetic accidents or have eating disorders and, in an ideal world, one shouldn't be forced to deal with images of them all the time. The second contention, however, left me speechless. Drive over him thirty times? I've heard people say *Facta non Verba* often enough but I doubt drawing the line at murder speaks badly of anyone.*

Incidentally, Neha Kubadia was a 23-year-old woman who was engaged to get married to a Prakash Parekh aged twenty-seven on December 5, 2005. However, as the *Times of India* reported, "He asked his fiancée whether she would give up her life for him. She had no doubts about it and to prove it, she stepped out of his car to lie down on the road as asked. He promptly drove the car over her."[12]

Bizarre? The changing face of violence against women? An aberration? Or the norm nowadays?*

For years, women's activists have been fighting for women's rights using stereotypes–the five-year-old who's been gang-raped, the virtuous wife who's been murdered by her husband–that somewhere along the line, it seems to have been forgotten that women are human. They make mistakes just like men. And like men, they do stupid things every once in a while. Women are not saints and they're not Goddesses but that doesn't mean that they should lose their rights. It doesn't make it acceptable for society to refuse to protect their rights.*

We should move beyond the stereotypes and–at least begin to–see violence against women in more 'ordinary' scenarios where the women who have to deal with violence or discrimination are those whom one interacts with everyday, where there are subtleties and nuances involved, where in order to be able to see the need for protection, it isn't necessary to paint pictures of stereotypes who, in all likelihood, are in the minority. To be able to see shades of grey, if you will.*

## FEMALE FOETICIDE AND INFANTICIDE

Traditionally, girls have been considered a liability and the requirement to provide them with a dowry on marriage, a burden. The killing of female infants is not a new problem in India. Reflections of the practice can be seen in scriptures as old as the Vedas.

> Hence, they reject a female child when born, and take up a male.
> [Taittirya Samhita VI.5.10.3]
>
> Let a female child be born somewhere else; here, let a male child be born.
> [Atharva Veda VI.2.3]

Millions of families–rich and poor–solved the *problem* by simply killing their daughters: they gave female infants grains of uncooked rice to choke them or smothered them to death–methods varied in different parts of the country and among different castes. During the Raj, the British tried to curtail the practice by monitoring pregnancies and registering births. They weren't very successful. There was apparently not one girl born in the Royal House of the Raja of Porbandar for a hundred years in the 19th Century.

New technology has also created an allied problem – female foeticide. The decision to abort a female foetus or to murder a female child is not a result of poverty or illiteracy, as one would like to believe. Studies have repeatedly shown that some of the most affluent states in the country (and some of the richest neighbourhoods where highly educated people live) have the most abnormal sex-ratios.

The child sex-ratio in one of the richer states, Maharashtra, for example, was 946 females to 1000 males in 1991. By 2001, it declined significantly: the overall ratio was 917:1000 in the whole state, it was 906:1000 in one of the state's main cities (Pune), and it was 898:1000 in the capital city of Mumbai.

Indian women have the right to abortion under the Medical Termination of Pregnancy Act provided that the decision is not based on the sex of the foetus. Parliament also enacted the Prenatal Diagnostic Techniques Act in 1994–which, inter alia, requires sonography machines to be registered–to try to prevent female foeticide.

> The Prenatal Diagnostic Techniques (Regulation and Prevention of Misuse) Act, 1994 provides 'for the regulation of the use of Prenatal Diagnostic Techniques for the purpose of detecting genetic or metabolic disorders or chromosomal abnormalities or certain congenital malformations or sex-linked disorders and for the prevention of the misuse of such techniques for the purpose of prenatal sex determination leading to female foeticide'.

The Act provides for:

- The regulation of genetic counselling centres, genetic laboratories and genetic clinics[13]
- The regulation of Prenatal Diagnostic Techniques[14]
- The obtaining of the written consent of a pregnant woman and the prohibition of communicating the sex of foetus[15]
- The prohibition of sex determination[16]
- The establishment of the Central Supervisory Board:[17]
  - (a) to advise the Government on policy matters relating to use of Prenatal Diagnostic Techniques.
  - (b) to review implementation of the Act and the rules made under it, and to recommend changes in the Act and its rules to the Central Government.
  - (c) to create public awareness against the practice of prenatal determination of sex and female foeticide.
  - (d) to lay down a code of conduct to be observed by persons working at Genetic Counselling Centres, Genetic Laboratories and Genetic Clinics.
  - (e) to perform any other functions as may be specified under the Act.

- The appointment of Appropriate Authorities:[18]
  - (a) to grant, suspend or cancel the registration of a Genetic Counselling Centre, Genetic Laboratory or Genetic Clinic.
  - (b) to enforce the standards prescribed for a Genetic Counselling Centre, Genetic Laboratory or Genetic Clinic.
  - (c) to investigate complaints of the breach of the provisions of this Act or the rules made under it and to take immediate action.
  - (d) to seek and consider the advice of the Advisory Committee on applications for registration and on complaints for suspension or cancellation of registration.
- The establishment of an Advisory Committee for each Appropriate Authority to aid and advise the Appropriate Authority in the discharge of its functions.
- The registration of Genetic Counselling Centres, Genetic Laboratories or Genetic Clinics[19] and the cancellation and suspension of such registration.
- The prohibition of advertisement relating to prenatal determination of sex and punishment for contravention.[20]

The Act specifies offences under it and the punishments for those offences. Every offence under the Act is cognizable, non-bailable and non-compoundable.[21] Notwithstanding anything in the Indian Evidence Act, 1872, the Courts are to presume, unless the contrary is proved, that a pregnant woman has been compelled by her husband or relatives to undergo a prenatal diagnostic technique and such persons are liable for the abetment of the offence.[22]

No suit, prosecution or other legal proceeding lies against the Central or the State Government or the Appropriate Authority or any officer authorised by the Central or State Government or by the Authority for anything which is in good faith done or intended to be done in pursuance of the provisions of this Act.[23]

The Central Government may make rules for carrying out the provisions of this Act.[24] The Board may, with the previous sanction of the Central Government, by notification in the Official Gazette, make regulations not inconsistent with the provisions of this Act and its rules.

The Act has, however, barely made a dent; sex-ratios in India are as skewed as ever as can be seen in the following table which shows figures drawn from the official census.

| *Year* | *Female: Male Sex-Ratio* | |
|---|---|---|
| | *Universal* | *Children* |
| 1901 | 972:1000 | |
| 1951 | 946:1000 | |
| 1961 | 941:1000 | 976:1000 |
| 1971 | 930:1000 | 964:1000 |
| 1981 | 934:1000 | 962:1000 |
| 1991 | 929:1000 | 945:1000 |
| 2001 | 933:1000 | 927:1000 |

(Incidentally, healthy/normal sex-ratios show more women than men.)

Although the 2001 census shows an increase in the number of females per thousand males, this has been attributed to factors such as migration; the child sex-ratio tells another story. A study of the sex-ratios at birth reveals the prevalence of female foeticide.

It is commonly believed to be about 952:1000 but some estimates in 1998 placed it at 900:1000.

## HONOUR KILLINGS

Honour killings in India are, for the most part, a result of allegations of infidelity–in which women are killed by their marital families–or else, a result of an intimate relationship which is considered illicit–usually an adulterous relationship–or deemed 'unsuitable'–usually an inter-caste marriage after which the woman, and occasionally her husband and possibly, his family are killed by her natal family (or vice versa if it's the man's family which is doing the killing).

In one case decided in September 2006 where the accused were convicted and sentenced to death by a Fast Track Court, Sushma–the woman involved–came from a North Indian Brahmin family. She married Prabhu Nochil, a South Indian neighbour against her parents' wishes in October 2003. The result was that on the night of May 17, 2004–when she was out visiting relatives–her brother Dilip Tiwari along with two of his friends entered the Nochil household, hacked her husband Prabhu, his father, Krishnan, a thirteen-year-old cousin and a neighbour to death. They also stabbed Prabhu's twenty-year-old sister, Deepa and mother, Indira and left them for dead. Sushma was seven months pregnant at the time.[25]

Justice Markandey Katju had made the following observations shortly before this (on July 7, 2006) in the judgment he wrote in another case involving honour killings–Lata Singh v/s State of Uttar Pradesh and Another–on behalf of a Bench of the Supreme Court comprising Justice Ashok Bhan and himself:

> "This case reveals a shocking state of affairs. There is no dispute that the petitioner [woman] is a major and was at all relevant times a major. Hence she is free to marry anyone she likes or live with anyone she likes. There is no bar to an inter-caste marriage under the Hindu Marriage Act or any other law. Hence, we cannot see what offence was committed by the petitioner, her husband or her husband's relatives."

He added that the Supreme Court found it necessary to make some general comments on the matter since several such instances had been coming to its knowledge of harassment, threats and violence against young men and women who marry outside their caste.

> "The nation is passing through a crucial transitional period in our history, and this Court cannot remain silent in matters of great public concern, such as the present one.
>
> The caste system is a curse on the nation and the sooner it is destroyed the better. In fact, it is dividing the nation at a time when we have to be united to face the challenges before the nation unitedly. Hence, inter-caste marriages are in fact in the national interest as they will result in destroying the caste system. However, disturbing news is coming from several parts of the country that

> young men and women, who undergo inter-caste marriage, are threatened with violence or violence is actually committed on them. In our opinion, such acts of violence or threats or harassment are wholly illegal and those who commit them must be severely punished. This is a free and democratic country, and once a person becomes a major he or she can marry whosoever he/she likes. If the parents of the boy or girl do not approve of such inter-caste or inter-religious marriage the maximum they can do is that they can cut off social relations with the son or the daughter, but they cannot give threats or commit or instigate acts of violence and cannot harass the person who undergoes such inter-caste or inter-religious marriage. We, therefore, direct that the administration/police authorities throughout the country will see to it that if any boy or girl who is a major undergoes inter-caste or inter-religious marriage with a woman or man who is a major, the couple are not harassed by any one nor subjected to threats or acts of violence, and any one who gives such threats or harasses or commits acts of violence either himself or at his instigation, is taken to task by instituting criminal proceedings by the police against such persons and further stern action is taken against such persons as provided by law.
>
> We sometimes hear of 'honour' killings of such persons who undergo inter-caste or inter-religious marriage of their own free will. There is nothing honourable in such killings, and in fact they are nothing but barbaric and shameful acts of murder committed by brutal, feudal minded persons who deserve harsh punishment. Only in this way can we stamp out such acts of barbarism."

Nonetheless, in case after case, those who have committed honour killings have usually been held guilty of having committed culpable homicide and not of having committed murder if at all they have been convicted of any offence.

In Muniandi v/s State, 1992,[26] a brother stabbed his younger sister (whom he had brought up) for bringing dishonour to their family by marrying her sister's husband as his second wife. The Court reasoned that since he had only stabbed her once, he could not have intended to cause her death.

An accused who struck his sister once with a fatal blow the intention of obstructing her marriage was held to be guilty of culpable homicide not amounting to murder in Gulzar Hussain v/s State of Uttar Pradesh, 1992,[27]-the reasoning here was that he stuck her only once even though there was nothing to stop him from continuing to do so.

And when it comes to adultery, real or suspected:

> A husband who saw a neighbour steal out of his house and found his wife adjusting the folds of her Sari inside, and who then killed his wife by striking her twelve times with a sickle was held not to be guilty of murder but only of culpable homicide in Mudaiah v/s State, 1992.[28]

> A husband whose wife had disclosed having committed adultery and who had had a fight with his wife the previous night was held to be entitled to the benefit of having been subjected to grave and sudden provocation when he was tried for killing his wife with a carpenter's chisel in State of Karnataka v/s R. Varadraju, 1995.[29]

> Similarly, a husband who found his wife and neighbour in a compromising position and who then shot both of them to death was held to have been subjected to grave and sudden provocation in Ajit Singh v/s State of Punjab, 1989.[30]

Also, a father who killed his neighbour and his young daughter on finding out that they had been intimate was held to be guilty of culpable homicide and not of murder in Rizayat Ali v/s State of Uttar Pradesh, 2000.[31]

## DOMESTIC VIOLENCE

> "Violence against women in general, and domestic violence in particular, serve as essential components in societies which oppress women, since violence against women not only derives from but also sustains the dominant gender stereotype and is used to control women in the one space traditionally dominated by women, the home."
>
> – *The Special Rapporteur on Violence against Women*[32]

Domestic violence is one of the few phenomena which cuts across every imaginable cultural, political, socio-economic, ethnic, religious and educational boundary, and, absurdly enough, not only appears to be directly proportional to a woman's education but also prevails among the so-called elite of society, and among the well-educated: in one case–

Marepally Venkatta v/s State of Andhra Pradesh, 2002 [33]–a scientist killed his wife by inserting mercury into her vagina; she died forty-four days later.

India's Vision 2020 Report has said that the Vision 'must have special focus on bridging the existing gaps in the various levels of development and endeavour its best to fulfil the Constitutional commitment of raising the status of the vulnerable groups vis-à-vis the rest of the society. Increasing gender equity is an important challenge of the coming years. The UNDP's gender development index ranks India 108 among 174 countries in terms of gender equity. It is no coincidence therefore that countries ranking highest on this index are among the most prosperous in the world. Gender equity and social development are inseparably interlinked. Reducing the disparity in nutritional, literacy and educational levels between the sexes is essential for realization of the country's full potential.'

However, recognising that unless specific remedial action is taken, higher economic growth and better education in themselves will not eliminate and may even aggravate gender-based inequalities, fighting gender-based violence has become a priority for Governments and international organisations all over the world even though, for much of history, many forms of violence such as domestic violence were not only ignored but also legally condoned.

In the West, women were considered dead in the eyes of the law after marriage and in some cases their husbands were held liable for crimes committed by them (753 BC during the reign of Romulus in Rome).*

The Church played an important role in establishing the husband's authority. In the 1400s Friar Cherubino of Siena wrote the Rules of Marriage that sanctioned wife-beating: husbands were advised to be abusive to save the souls of their wives; while in the 1500s, the Church issued a Household Ordinance during the reign of the Russian Tsar Ivan the Terrible that described when and how a man might most effectively beat his wife for disciplinary purposes. He was legally allowed to kill his wife although she was not allowed to kill him.*

And although it would now be considered kidnapping, under English law that prevailed till 1973, husbands could legally stop their wives from leaving abusive situations and sue those who helped their wives to leave, while in Colonial America, husbands were allowed to beat their wives as long as they didn't disturb public peace i.e. they could not be violent towards their wives on Sundays or after 8:00 p.m.*

Throughout the ages there have, however, been both men and women who have stood up for women's rights and a great deal of their work has been through literature, even though much of it was written by men for men and almost completely ignores women unless their inclusion is unavoidable.

Take Agamemnon, for example. According to Homer he was the King of Mycenae but other sources say that he was the King of Argos. He was the leader of the Greek forces at Troy and there is no dearth of material on him. There were, however, at least four women–his wife, Clytemnestra, his daughters, Electra and Iphigenia and his war prize, the doomed prophetess, Cassandra–who played a part in his life and it isn't half as easy to find material on them unless it relates directly to Agamemnon himself.[34] In fact, if memory serves me, I don't think that Homer–who has written a whole epic about the Trojan War–even mentions Iphigenia by name in it although it was only by sacrificing her that the Greeks managed to sail to Troy in the first place; it is Euripides who wrote about her.

> *I am myn owene womman, wel at ese, I thank it God, as after myn estat, Right yong, and stonde unteyd in lusty leese, Withouten jalousie or swich debat. Shal noon housbonde seyn to me 'chek mat!' For either they ben ful of jalousie, Or maisterfull, or loven novelrie.*
>
> *– Criseyde*

That is not to say that women were always sidetracked or treated harshly–Chaucer's Criseyde unequivocally, and 'to the delight of feminists everywhere', declared that she was her own woman.[35] And in the *Parlement of Foules*, the poet left the Formel Eagle to choose her own mate.

Feminist works are not a new creation either. In 1405 itself, Christine de Pisan wrote *The Book of the City of Ladies* (translated by Earl Jeffrey Richards) in which she accused men of cruelty.

Mary Wollstonecraft wrote *A Vindication of the Rights of Women* in 1792 supporting better treatment of and education for women, and John Stuart Mill wrote *The Subjection of Women* in 1861. A few years later, Francis Power Cobbe published *Wife Torture in England* (1878) documenting about 6000 assaults over a three year period on women who had been left blind, burnt, maimed and dead.*

Things have, however, changed a great deal in Europe and in most of the Western world.

It is now accepted that 'domestic violence may be perpetrated by spouses, lineal ascendants and descendants and the lateral branch of the family up to the IV degree whether they are related by blood, marriage, fosterage or adoption, or by intimate partners or legal guardians. The spectrum of domestic violence (which, incidentally, has a high level of recidivism) may include psychological, physical, sexual, financial and emotional abuse which may manifest itself as physical injury, the deprivation of food, money or other resources, intimidation, humiliation and degradation, and may result in anhedonia, pain, exhaustion, isolation, alienation, depression, fear, and decreased levels of self-esteem, productivity and attentiveness.

Today in Europe, 'Article 2 of the EC Treaty states that the European Community shall have as its task equality between men and women and Article 13 states that without prejudice to the other provisions of the (same) Treaty and within the limits of the powers conferred by it upon the Community, the Council, acting unanimously on a proposal from the Commission and after consulting the European Parliament, may take appropriate action to combat discrimination based on sex, racial or ethnic origin, religion or belief, disability, age or sexual orientation.

Domestic violence proceedings can be made speedy, and various injunctions which (depending on the country) may include Non-Molestation Orders and Occupation Orders can be obtained by victims. The Power of Arrest may be attached to an injunction if it is shown that the perpetrator has used violence or has threatened to do so and may do so again.

The legal nature of a Complaint may make those who are aware of an offence liable to be sanctioned if they do not report it to the authorities. Due to this, in practice, doctors who provide medical assistance to victims of domestic violence have a legal obligation to notify not the police but the public prosecutor's office directly (except in the UK where the police undertakes the investigation). The public prosecutor then conducts a suo moto investigation into the incident(s). The British Government, for example, explicitly says, "The NHS has a particular contribution to make in domestic violence, not only because of the impact on victims' health, but also because the NHS may be the first contact point with professionals who can recognise and intervene in the situation."

The consent of victims is no longer essential to initiate action against perpetrators, and various advertising campaigns have been conducted to make people aware that 'the police will seek out men who abuse their partners and arrest them, even if the victim refuses to make a statement or give evidence'.[36] The penalties are higher if the victim has special needs such as those of being pregnant, handicapped or disabled.

Taking into consideration high stress-levels, judicial reconciliation has been made available to deal with domestic violence: the perpetrator receives psychological therapy at a public hospital (for as long as councillors think is necessary) and promises not to repeat his behaviour. Penal sanctions are suspended for a period that may vary between three and four years (depending on the country). The councillors report the perpetrator's progress to the judge and if it is unsatisfactory, the judicial reconciliation will end and penal sanctions will resume as they have a retrospective effect. These provisions, however, do not apply to guardians, foster parents, and minders.

Shelters, which provide a witness status to their guests, are set up by the State as well as other NGOs such as the Church and women's rights NGOs to protect victims of domestic violence. There is also an option to provide them with immediate interim shelter (for 48 hours) even before a medical examination by the coroner.

The first modern women's shelter (which was established in Chiswick, England in 1971 by Erin Pizzey) developed out of an advice centre for women and their children. Since then, the movement for shelters has grown and in 1986, the European Parliament's Committee on Women's Rights and Equal Opportunities recommended that one shelter should be available for every 10000 people.

The Commission has been conducting programmes and funding projects to raise awareness about violence and trafficking, to prevent them and to support victims. These include Daphne (2000-2003) and Daphne II (2004-08).[37] The financial framework for the Daphne Programme was €20 million for the first phase and €50 million for the second phase. The programmes have tried to contribute towards ensuring a high level of physical and mental protection for children, young persons and women against violence (including sexual exploitation) by preventing violence and by providing support to victims especially in order to prevent their re-exposure to violence. They have also tried to promote closer co-operation between Member States and harmonise responses to these crimes although the principle of subsidiarity requires Member States to take measures to fight violence individually.'[38]

Indian women, however, do not receive such protection.[39]

A husband who struck his wife on her head with a ploughshare causing her to lose consciousness and then, believing her to be dead, who then tried to create the impression of her having committed suicide by hanging herself, hanged her from a beam thereby actually causing her to die by strangulation was held to be guilty of causing grievous hurt and not of committing murder in Palani Goundan, 1919.[40]

And, more recently, in Brushava Bartha v/s State, 1988,[41] a husband who killed his wife by striking her on the head with the blunt side of an axe was held to be guilty of culpable homicide not amounting to murder.

Indian society makes domestic violence invisible and leaves it cocooned in feelings of guilt and embarrassment. Unfortunately, this attitude which makes domestic violence an invisible factor in India's social fabric vitiates not only societal responses to the issue but also institutional responses. A UN report found that some 70 per cent of Indian women believe that wife-beating is justified under certain circumstances such as refusing to have sex or for not preparing food on time.

In fact, in Ghansham v/s State of Maharashtra, 1996,[42] it was held that a husband who killed his wife for refusing to have sex with him was not guilty of murder. The Court held that he was only guilty of culpable homicide since he did not intend to kill her; he had acted out of sheer frustration.

It doesn't help that abusers typically isolate their victims from friends, family and anything that resembles a support system either, or that abusers tend to become violent if they find evidence of their victims seeking assistance.[43*]

According to the National Crime Records Bureau, there were 155553 crimes committed against women in 2005 and 68810 of them were related to domestic violence.

Half the women killed in India are killed in their bedrooms.[44]

## Cruelty

Cruelty in the Indian legal system is basically defined as a form of marital cruelty and it is spoken of in Section 498 A of the Indian Penal Code and Section 113 A of the Indian Evidence Act. Both these Sections are amendments which were introduced in 1983.

> Section 498 A, Indian Penal Code: Whoever being the husband or relative of the husband of a woman subjects such woman to cruelty shall be punished with imprisonment for a term which may extend to three years and shall also be liable to fine.

Under these two Sections, cruelty means:

- any wilful conduct which is of such nature as is likely to drive a woman to commit suicide or to cause grave injury or danger to life, limb or health (whether physical or mental) of the woman.
- harassment of the woman where such harassment is with a view to coercing her or any person related to her to meet any unlawful demand for any property or

valuable security or is on account of failure by her or any person related to her to meet such demand.

The offence under Section 498 A is cognizable and non-bailable, and cannot be settled privately. For the police to be able to act, information relating to the commission of an offence under the Section should be given to the officer in charge of a police station by the victim, a person related to her by blood, marriage or adoption, or any one of certain specified Public Officers.

The Constitutional validity of Section 498 A was upheld in Krishan Lal v/s Union of India, 1994.[45] The judgement said that a husband and his relatives who subject a wife to cruelty form a class unto themselves. As such, the classification is reasonable and does not violate the right to equality enshrined in Article 14 of the Constitution.

The corresponding provision in the Evidence Act states that a Court may presume, having regard to all the circumstances of a case, that the suicide of a married woman has been abetted by her husband or by her in-laws if it is shown that she committed suicide within seven years of getting married or that she had been subjected to cruelty by her husband or by her in-laws.

> *A stone keeps a knife in good form and a beating keeps a woman in good form.*
>
> – *Assamese proverb*

A large number of people associate Section 498 A of the Indian Penal Code exclusively with Indian anti-dowry laws and allegations of the Section being misused are rampant.

However, a Tata Institute of Social Sciences study in 1999 indicated that few women's organisations recommend recourse to Section 498 A, IPC as a first resort and that the number of such cases is miniscule in comparison to the prevalence of domestic violence. However, such studies have done little to stop a large spectrum of people ranging right from husbands and their families to some members of the judiciary from voicing their concerns and complaints.*

There seem to be two sides to the story: one is that Indian society is patriarchal and public attitudes are firmly in favour of men and wives are usually held responsible for marital problems as the following statement in a report prepared by the legal adviser to the Delhi Commissioner of Police in November 2000 shows: "...the reasons for disharmony between the wife and the husband arise only when either the wife is reluctant/ refuses to adjust herself in the family circumstances or if the husband feels reluctant to accommodate his wife either on account of unnecessary interference by the parents of the wife or non-cooperative attitude of the wife."*

It would be hard for anyone to deny that domestic violence is rampant–any given day's edition of a local newspaper would probably report at least two cases of women who've been killed or burned to death by it. And those are just the most extreme cases. No one really knows how many instances of domestic violence go completely unnoticed.

It seems faintly ridiculous to me to render useless one of the few laws which exist to combat it. This, however, is precisely what the (all male) Malimath Committee suggested in a way by recommending that such complaints be made bailable and compoundable. The committee produced a six-hundred-page report which, for some reason, excluded not only any discussion on the issue of violence against women but also excluded any inputs either from victims of marital cruelty or from those working in the field.[46*]

Some of its reasoning seems to have been encapsulated in 16.4.4 of the report which says: "A less tolerant and impulsive woman may lodge an FIR even on a trivial act. The result is that the husband and his family may be immediately arrested and there may be a suspension or loss of job. The offence alleged being non-bailable, innocent persons languish in custody. There may be a claim for maintenance adding fuel to fire, especially if the husband cannot pay. Now the woman may change her mind and get into the mood to forget and forgive. The husband may also realize the mistakes committed and come forward to turn over a new leaf for a loving and cordial relationship. The woman may like to seek reconciliation. But this may not be possible due to the legal obstacles. Even if she wishes to make amends by withdrawing the complaint, she cannot do so as the offence is non-compoundable. The doors for returning to family life stand closed. She is thus left at the mercy of her natal family."*

But the other side of the story is that there is abuse of the law although the extent to which such abuse takes place has never been firmly established.[47] There are unscrupulous women who use Section 498 A for their own ends but women are also often encouraged by lawyers and/or the police etc. to say that the violence they face is related to demands for dowry so that their complaints are taken 'seriously'.

And that is ironical because the Section itself was not designed exclusively in reference to dowry problems: in itself, it is meant to deal with cruelty in general although what does and does not constitute cruelty is open to debate: it was held that a husband who had committed bigamy and whose first wife (living separately) had had to struggle for existence and who had ultimately committed suicide was not guilty of cruelty towards his her (his first wife) in Supchand v/s State of Maharashtra, 1995.[48] (Incidentally, bigamy is supposed to be a criminal offence.)

*Alone Together*
*As we walk into our room,*
*A cold fear sweeps over me;*
*Wondering what you will do,*
*Now that we are all alone.*
*You could not speak earlier:*
*We were in company. And*
*Lost in my thoughts, I looked on*
*With a smile as you played the*
*Quintessential gentleman,*
*Only wishing that the truth*
*Was not so far removed from*
*Reality. And as I*
*Now look around the room, the*
*Contempt your conduct inspires*
*In me for you continues*
*To steadily increase. The bed,*
*Standings few feet away*
*From me, looks inviting.*
*I Think of how much I long to*
*Lie down on it, and feign sleep.**

Nonetheless, Section 498 A is, in a way, in favour of women. Close on its heels came two amendments to the Dowry Prohibition Act of 1961–in 1984 and 1986–which have made dowry giving and taking cognizable offences. Those accused under both these laws are not assumed to be innocent until proven guilty; contrary to other laws, the accused are, in theory, required to prove that they have not committed a crime although in practice that isn't always quite how it works.*

Tilting the balance in favour of women has often been useful since previously, women could not meet the burden of proof quite simply because marital violence usually occurred behind closed doors and that being the case, in the absence of independent witnesses, there was no easy way to prove cases beyond all reasonable doubt as is required by criminal law.*

The problem, however, has been that there is no mechanism to ensure that women don't lie. The law against perjury is virtually non-functional in India and there are no deterrents to ensure that complaints made under this Section are genuine.*

In December 2003, the Minister of State for Home Affairs, I D Swami said, "There is no information available with the Government to come to the conclusion that many families in India are suffering due to exaggerated allegations of harassment and dowry cases made by women against their husbands and other family members involving them in criminal misappropriation and cruelty."[49*]

The statement is probably not entirely true although cases of abuse of Section 498 A may simply be isolated ones and are not part of a general trend. The answer though doesn't lie in making the law bailable and compoundable but in amending it so that bonafide and malafide complaints can be separated.*

## Dowries and Dowry Deaths

The 'dowry system is not only responsible for snuffing out lives of our women at a very young age but is also primarily responsible for the growing incidence of female foeticide in the country'.[50]

Under the Dowry Prohibition Act, 'dowry' means any property or valuable security given or agreed to be given either directly or indirectly:

1. by one party in a marriage to the other party
2. by the parents of either party to a marriage or any other person, to either party to the marriage or to any other person at or before or at any time after the marriage but it does not include Mahr in the case of persons to whom the Shariat applies.

In Appasaheb v/s State of Maharashtra, 2007 the Supreme Court interpreted dowry very narrowly: it confined itself to the letter or the law instead interpreting the law liberally (as it has often done). It held that 'a demand for money on account of some financial stringency or for meeting some urgent domestic expenses or for purchasing manure cannot be treated as a demand for dowry. Giving or taking of property or valuable security must have some connection with the marriage of the parties and a co-relation between the giving or taking of property or valuable security with marriage of parties is essential'.[51]

The system of paying dowries has existed in India since ancient times. It was banned in 1961 by Parliament. Agreements to give or to take dowries are void and giving, taking, demanding and advertising of dowries are all punishable offences.

However, there was a great deal of controversy surrounding the Act–the passing of the Dowry Prohibition Act is in fact one of only three occasions in the history of Independent India which has required a Joint Session of both Houses of Parliament to be held. (The two other Joint Sessions which have been held have involved discussions about the nationalisation of banks in 1978 and the prevention of terrorism in 2000.) At the time, it was felt that 'a law which makes the practice punishable and at the same time ensures that any dowry, if given, enures for the wife's benefit would go a long way towards educating public opinion and eradicating the evil'.[52]

The Act was amended in 1984 and 1986 to make it more effective. Amendments notwithstanding, the Act has been anything but effective. On the contrary, the practise of giving dowries is now entrenched in growing consumerism and is closely associated with the increasing incidence of female foeticide and infanticide. To borrow a phrase from Mohan Rao,[53] what we now have is *Karva Chauth Capitalism*–a conjunction of consumerism, anti-feminism and Hindutva at a time of globalisation'.

The Dowry Prohibition (Maintenance of Lists of Presents to the Bride and Bridegroom) Rules were introduced in 1985, on the same day as the Dowry Prohibition (Amendment) Act, 1984 came into force, to try to control the prevalence of the custom.

These Rules direct that:

1. The list of presents which are given at the time of the marriage to the bride shall be maintained by the bride.
2. The list of presents which are given at the time of the marriage to the bridegroom shall be maintained by the bridegroom.
3. Each list of presents:
   (a) shall be prepared at the time of the marriage or as soon as possible after the marriage
   (b) shall be in writing
   (c) shall contain:
      (i) a brief description of each present
      (ii) the approximate value of the present
      (iii) the name of the person who has given the present and
      (iv) where the person giving the present is related to the bride or bridegroom, a description of such relationship
4. Each list shall be signed by both the bride and the bridegroom. If either of them is unable to sign, they–or whichever one of them cannot sign, as the case may be–may affix their thumb impressions instead of their signatures after having the list read out to them and obtaining the signature on the list of the person who has so read out the particulars contained in the list.

What, if any, difference the rules have made though is questionable; dowry deaths are rampant.

Traditionally, killing a woman is a minor crime and has been equated with stealing grain in ancient Hindu legal texts. Dowry deaths are now dealt with in Section 304 B of the Indian Penal Code and Section 113 B of the Indian Evidence Act. Both these Sections are amendments which were introduced in 1986.[54]

**Section 304 B,** Indian Penal Code:

> Where the death of a woman is caused by any burns or bodily injury or it occurs in other abnormal circumstances within seven years of her marriage, and it is shown that she was harassed or subjected to cruelty for or in connection with any demand for dowry by her husband or his relative(s), such death shall be called a 'dowry death' and the husband or his relative(s) shall be deemed to have caused the death. They shall be punished with imprisonment for a term which shall not be less than seven years but which may extend to imprisonment for life.

Speaking of the situation in the State of Karnataka, V. Janardhan, Deputy Director, Prosecution said, "Of the contested cases, ten per cent are found to be cases filed on frivolous grounds and those in which the harassment charge is not proved properly. It is only in fifteen per cent of the contested cases that conviction takes place."[55]

Sometimes, contesting parties 'compromise' with each other and witnesses, including members of the victim's natal family, become hostile to the prosecution. One of the most abhorrent (and unfortunately, common) forms of 'compromise' involves the dead woman's sister getting married to the husband (who agrees not take a dowry considering his having committed murder). It's a compromise which works out for both families: the husband and his relatives get a replacement (and evade gaol-time) and the women's family is spared the expense of getting a daughter married. I can't imagine what it must feel like to marry a man who you know has murdered your sister though.

Also, there is invariably a lack of evidence in such cases which doesn't help at all in getting convictions. The judiciary has, however, been trying to deal with this by interpreting existing laws innovatively.

In August 2006, the Bombay High Court held that, given the heinous nature of the crime and the difficulty in proving it, an accused who has been charged with murdering his wife in a dowry-related case can also simultaneously be charged with abetting her suicide.

And in October, 2006, the Supreme Court said, "The inmates of a house cannot get away by simply keeping quiet and offering no explanation on the supposed premise that the burden to establish its case lies entirely upon the prosecution and there is no duty at all on the accused to offer any explanation."[56]

Speaking of dowry deaths, on August 21, 2006, a Bench of the Supreme Court comprising Justice S.B. Sinha and Justice Dalveer Bhandari said, "To our information in no other civilized country similar problem of this magnitude exists. This is indeed a slur on our great heritage, ancient culture and civilization. Once a serious crime is committed, detection is a difficult matter and still more difficult is successful prosecution of the offender. The criminal is a member of the family; other members of the family are either guilty associates or silent but conniving witnesses. In any case, the shackles of the family are so strong that truth may not come out of the chains. Perhaps, to meet a situation of this kind, the Legislature must be enacted under Section 304 B of IPC and Section 113 B of the Evidence Act." (In this case, the deceased, Sanju Kumari, was murdered on the day of Chhath Puja in November, 1993–her husband, Ram Badan Sharma and father-in-law offered her Prasaad laced with poison. They had earlier demanded a colour TV, a motor cycle and 20000 INR in cash.)

Governments have been taking measures to try to curb the menace though many of these measures don't seem particularly useful. The Women and Child Welfare Department in the State of Uttar Pradesh, for example, asked each of its married officials who joined service on or after March 31, 2004 to give a declaration to their respective appointing authorities that they had not taken any dowry.[57]

### Dying Declarations

Dying declarations are written or verbal statements made by people before they die.[58] These declarations are covered by Section 32 (1) of the Indian Evidence Act which says that statements, written or verbal, of relevant facts made by a person who is dead, are themselves relevant facts when the statement is made by the person as to the cause of her death or as to any of the circumstances of the transaction which resulted in her death, in cases in which the cause of her death comes into question.

Unlike in English law, such statements need not be made under 'a settled and hopeless expectation of death'. They are relevant whether or not the declarant is, at the time when they are made, under the expectation of death, and whatever may be the nature of the proceeding in which the cause of death comes into question. All that is required is for the person who has made them to have died. If this doesn't happen and the person survives, the statement should be used in accordance with Section 157 of the Evidence Act and/or Section 164 of the Criminal Procedure Code.

**Section 157** of the Evidence Act says:

> In order to corroborate the testimony of a witness, any former statement made by such witness relating to the same fact at or about the time when the fact took place or before any authority legally competent to investigate the fact, may be proved.

And **Section 164** of the Criminal Procedure Code deals with how a Metropolitan Magistrate or Judicial Magistrate may record a confession or statement.

In Autar Singh v/s The Crown, 1923,[59] it was held that Section 32 (1) of the Evidence Act deals only with dying declarations. However, this decision was reversed in Inayat Khan v/s the Crown, 1934.[60]

Today, Pakala Narayan Swami v/s King Emperor, 1939,[61] is one of the leading cases as far as dying declarations are concerned. Lord Atkin explained the Section as follows:

> "The statement may be made before the cause of death has arisen or before the deceased has any reason to anticipate being killed. The circumstances must be circumstances of the transaction; general expressions indicating fear or suspicion whether of a particular individual or otherwise and not directly related to the occasion of death will not be admissible. 'Circumstances of the transaction' is a phrase no doubt that conveys some limitations. It is not as broad as in the analogous use in 'circumstantial evidence' which includes evidence of all relevant facts."

In this case, it was held that statements made by the deceased saying that he was going to the place where he was killed, and narrating whom he was going to meet and why he was doing so were included in the circumstances of the transaction.

As with any piece of evidence, there are various factors which must be considered:

- the relevancy and admissibility of the evidence
- how reliable it is
- how much weight/importance should be attached to it.

A person who makes a dying declaration is obviously not available for cross-examination later on. To deal with the problems which this presents, Section 158 of the Indian Evidence Act says:

> Whenever any such statement is proved, all matters may be proved either in order to contradict or to corroborate it or in order to impeach or confirm the credit of the person by whom it was made, which might have been proved if that person had been called as a witness and had denied upon cross-examination the truth of the matter suggested.

A conviction based on an uncorroborated dying declaration was held to be legal in Emperor v/s Kunwarpal Singh, 1948,[62] although such a declaration is not proof of the truthfulness of its contents. It is, however, recognised that as a general rule people do not lie in dying declarations for fear of divine punishment and a desire to have their killers punished. There are no procedures in the law which speak of how a dying declaration should be recorded but there are a number of judgments regarding how it should be treated. Some of these judgments speak of:

- the language of the declaration
- when it may be made
- by whom it may be recorded
- the state of mind of the declarant
- the state of body of the declarant

A dying declaration recorded in the language of the declarant acquires added strength and reliability although it cannot be discarded solely for the reason of having been recorded in another language.

As far as when the statement is made is concerned, it was held in Sharad v/s State of Maharashtra, 1984,[63] that 'there is no universal cut and dried formula'. In this case, the letters of a woman to her natal family about being abused by her in-laws were proved as a dying declaration–she died four months after sending the letters. Justice Fazal Ali said that 'where death is a logical consequence of a continuous drama long in process and in a way a finalé to the story, the statement regarding each step directly connected with the end of the drama would be admissible because the entire statement would have to be read as an organic whole and not torn from the context'.

In Laxman v/s State of Maharashtra, 2002,[64] it was held that the declarant should be in a fit state of mind in the opinion of the person who records the statement.

And in Jayaraj v/s State of Tamil Nadu, 1976,[65] Justice Sarkaria observed that 'when the deponent was in severe bodily pain, the brevity of his statement was an index of its being true and free from the taint of tutoring' while in State of Rajasthan v/s Teja Ram, 1999,[66] the Court refused to rely on a dying declaration by a victim who had sustained a brain injury.

Dying declarations may be recorded by anyone and proved in the same manner as other facts and documents.[67] They cannot be discarded merely because of not being in question and answer form.[68] However, if they are oral, the exact words of the declaration should be reproduced.

If a declarant makes more than one dying declaration, the circumstances in which they have been made should be considered in case they are inconsistent. This often happens in the case of victims of dowry harassment: they keep changing their statements depending on a variety of factors ranging from whether or not their in-laws are within earshot to not wanting to embarrass their marital and/or natal families.

In Harjit Kaur v/s State of Punjab, 1999,[69] the Supreme Court held that when more than one dying declaration has been made, just because the first one is not proper–and it is shown that at the time that it was made, the declarant was not a free person–the others should not be automatically rejected.

The judiciary is not always as sensitive as that to the fact that victims of violence often make inconsistent statements though as Supreme Court lawyer Rakesh Shukla has pointed out citing the case of Aruna Kumari.[70]

> "Aruna gave two dying declarations–one saying that her burns were the result of an accident and another that she had attempted suicide due to harassment, thus bringing it within the ambit of a 'dowry death'. Even though harassment for dowry was established in Aruna's case, the Court disbelieved the second declaration, observing that a woman being harassed for dowry could also die accidentally. So, the Court acquitted the husband and in-laws of the offence of dowry death."[71]

### The Domestic Violence Act, 2005

The Protection of Women against Domestic Violence Act, 2005 came into force in October 2006. The Act attempts to provide for effective protection of the rights (guaranteed by the Constitution) of women who are victims of violence of any kind occurring within the family.

It entitles a large number of women to legal protection including:

- wives and women who are or have been in a relationship in the nature of marriage with the perpetrator.
- women in conditions where both parties have lived together in a shared household and are related by consanguinity, marriage or adoption.
- women who are family members, living together as a joint family; sisters, widows, mothers, single women or living with the perpetrator of violence.

Thus, the 'aggrieved person' may be any woman who is or has been, in a domestic relationship–i.e. has lived together in a shared household–with the perpetrator and who alleges to have been subjected to any act of domestic violence by the perpetrator. The aggrieved person and the perpetrator may be related by consanguinity, marriage or through a relationship in the nature of marriage, adoption or may be family members living together in a joint family.

The perpetrator may be 'any adult male person who is or has been, in a domestic relationship with the aggrieved person and an aggrieved wife or female living in a relationship in the nature of a marriage may also file a complaint against a relative of the husband or the male partner'.

The definition of domestic violence includes actual abuse as well as the threat of abuse whether it is physical, sexual, verbal, emotional or economic abuse. The Domestic Violence Act has also made marital rape an offence for the first time.

Protection officers to help victims, to facilitate their obtaining medical aid, legal aid and a safe shelter are to be appointed in districts. They are to file complaints which are to be taken forward by a service provider whose responsibility it is to actually fight the case.

The Act also speaks of marital or relationship counselling. Magistrates are to appoint counsellors to resolve problems in a constructive, stress-free atmosphere. In case a compromise is reached, a Memorandum of Understanding is to be drawn up and countersigned by a magistrate, and a violation of the Memorandum is to result in punishment by imprisonment or by a fine being levied or by both.

The first case under the domestic violence act was filed in Tirunelveli, Tamil Nadu. According to media reports, the police arrested Joseph from Melapalayam after his wife, Benedict Mary, filed a complaint against him on Saturday, October 29, 2006.[72] She was a school teacher and her husband, allegedly, an alcoholic. The couple seem to have had similar issues earlier as well and a police inspector apparently had brokered a 'reconciliation' between the two which appears not to have worked.

The first ruling under the Domestic Violence Act, made in May 2007, was in a case heard in New Delhi. It required a Dr Amitava Mukherjee to pay his live-in partner 150000 INR for walking out on her after having promised to marry her. The lady concerned first met him in 1999 when he was working as the country director of Action Aid India and lived with him between 2003 and 2006 in New Delhi and in Bangkok where he had arranged to have her work with UNESCAP. City Magistrate

Jagdish Kumar said that Dr. Amitava Mukherjee and the lady lived together in a shared household and that Dr. Mukherjee had 'admitted her as his wife and applied Sindoor in her Maang. He held that this constituted emotional abuse.[73]

**Children and Domestic Violence[74]**

The effects of domestic violence are not confined to its victims. Apart from the fact that children may try to intervene to protect adult victims (thus putting themselves in danger), children who witness domestic violence are more likely than others to develop psychological and social problems including stress-related disorders such as PTSD.

Children who have been exposed to domestic violence may be fearful and angry, and exhibit (both as children and as adults) internalized and externalized behavioural problems including withdrawal, hostility and substance dependency. Their relationships may also reflect violence learned or seen at home.

Describing violence against women as 'the most atrocious manifestation of the systemic discrimination and inequality against women', Former UN Secretary-General Kofi Annan said that it 'is also damaging to society as a whole. It can prevent women from engaging in productive employment, and girls from attending school. It makes women more vulnerable to forced and unprotected sex, which plays a key role in the spread of HIV/AIDS. It takes a deep and enduring toll on the entire family, including and especially the next generation.'[75]

The reported instances of violence against children in the form of acts and omissions which endanger their physical or emotional health, well-being and development have also increased over the last few decades.

The primary forms of violence and abuse against children are neglect, exploitation and physical, sexual or emotional abuse, and they can have devastating consequences for victims both immediately and in the long-term.

There has been little research in the field in India. However, in England, the Teen Abuse Survey of Great Britain 2005 conducted by the NSPCC revealed that a third of teenage girls experienced or witnessed domestic violence at home but more than half of them did not consider this–hitting, screaming and shouting–to be domestic violence. 43% of teenagers thought that it was acceptable for a boyfriend to become aggressive and over 40% of all girls said that they would consider giving a boy a second chance if he hit them.

**Attitudes towards Domestic Violence**

The general awareness about domestic violence in Europe appears to be high; only 4% of Europeans said that they had never heard of domestic violence against women in the 1999 Eurobarometer Survey conducted by the EU Commission. The survey also divulged that 62% of Europeans considered domestic violence against women to be 'unacceptable in all circumstances and always punishable by law', 32% considered it 'unacceptable in all circumstances but not always punishable by law', 2% said that it was 'acceptable in certain circumstances' and, thankfully, only 0.7% believed that it was 'acceptable in all circumstances'.[76]

In India, on the contrary, the police often refuse to accept complaints of domestic violence from women, and occasionally, they broker 'reconciliations' which, not too surprisingly, rarely last.

Men are, however, generally treated much more sympathetically (usually at the expense of women). Kalindi Mazumdar illustrated the attitude of the police with a case in which a man went to the police to complain about his wife doing no housework and spending her time in bed. The Duty Officer summoned the wife (who could barely walk or talk) to the police station. She was running a temperature and the wounds caused by a Caesarean which she had just undergone had not yet healed. Nonetheless, the Duty Officer told her that hers was not a serious problem at all and that she should resume her household duties.

"A dominant trait in the police is their absence of respect, in fact, their undisguised contempt for women," according to Mazumdar although, of course, not all police personnel are unsympathetic and insensitive towards women.

Domestic violence is, however, almost always acceptable to all Indians–it's part of our culture. And that being the case, few women can afford to speak out against being abused. To fight back and to fail is unthinkable. And failure is not unlikely considering that, as Nonica Datta pointed out, "Never before did the home and the public connive in violence as insidiously as they do in our time. Never before was violence celebrated and normalised as it is now in this new millennium."[77] Sometimes, silence makes sense.

> ***Memory***
>
> *The Girl in Hyacinth Blue. There were those who called her 'Morning Shine'. She sits by a window with sunlight gently sweeping over her. Her serenity as the world passes by her seems overwhelming. Can anyone ever do that in real life?*
>
> *Blood seeping on to the floor; thicker than water, it does not spread out only to merge again and form grotesque but interesting patterns as it spills over. Distorted reflections make their appearance in water like that. Hoping to be able to decipher a meaning which, in your heart, you know doesn't even exist in the strange aberrations strewn on the dark black granite around you, you stare at them for what seems like an aeon and thank God for them. You do not want to see reality: it is too bleak. Hallucinations and lies are your respite from pain. Anything seems easier than the truth, and almost everything is.*
>
> *The patterns look like modern art if you stretch your imagination far enough except for the fact that you're certain that they've been randomly created by a lunatic. You can almost hear his raucous laughs echoing in the background.*
>
> *They don't stop and you begin to realize that it isn't your imagination playing tricks at all. You have to go back and face them: after all, they personify what your life has become. 'The Girl in Hyacinth Blue' never was anything more than a story. There still is blood mixed with water on the bathroom floor as you begin to make your way towards the door.*

## SATI

'Sati' means the burning or burying alive of:

- any widow along with the body of her deceased husband or any other relative, or with any article, object or thing associated with the husband or such relative.

- any woman along with the body of any of her relatives, whether or not such burning or burying is claimed to be voluntary on the part of the widow or the woman.[78]

On one level Sati is simply the 'logical' culmination of the Hindu belief of one's having the same partner in every life as is reflected in the traditional indissolubility of marriage. At another level though, it is little more than (yet) another mechanism with which to control women.

The British had abolished Sati in 1829 itself. However, there are cases which are still occasionally reported. One such case in the village of Deorala in the State of Rajasthan on September 4, 1987 sparked massive protests from women's activists (among others) and an Act was subsequently passed to try to prevent the practice.

In this case, a young Rajput woman named Roop Kanwar committed Sati. The whole village participated in the act, she was turned into an object of worship and, at the time, the State did not stop any of what was happening. What was particularly shocking though was that there were reports not only of her being forced to commit Sati but also of her trying to get off the burning pyre (in vain); she was pushed back on to it.

Sati is widely seen as a manifestation of the *true Hindu spirit*. A large number of people display feelings of contempt and disdain for the Act prohibiting it since they believe that it infringes on tradition and on religious injunctions. A few call the activists who pushed for the Act to be passed *female eunuchs*, *promiscuous* and *immoral* among other things. Some worship the women who commit Sati as 'Sati Mata'. And most, even if they do not actively support the practice, have a great deal of respect for those women who do commit Sati.

### *The Commission of Sati (Prevention) Act, 1987*

This Act was passed 'to provide for the prevention of the commission of Sati and its glorification'. It makes not only the commission of Sati itself an offence but also says that it is an offence to glorify Sati,[79] to abet the commission of Sati[80] and to attempt to commit Sati.[81]

The Commission of Sati (Prevention) Act gives detailed definitions of the acts which are contemplated by the terms 'glorification' and 'abetment' although these definitions are not exhaustive.

The abetment of Sati includes:[82]

- any inducement to a widow or woman to get her burnt or buried alive along with the body of her deceased husband or with any other relative irrespective of whether she is in a fit state of mind or is labouring under a state of intoxication or stupefaction or other case impeding the exercise of her free will.
- making a widow or woman believe that the commission of Sati would result in some spiritual benefit to her or her deceased husband or relative or the general well being of the family.
- encouraging a widow or woman to remain fixed in her resolve to commit Sati and thus instigating her to commit Sati.
- participating in the procession in connection with the commission of Sati or aiding the widow or woman in her decision to commit Sati by taking her along with the body of her deceased husband or relative to the cremation or burial ground.
- being present at the place where Sati is committed as an active participant to such commission or to any ceremony connected with it.
- preventing or obstructing the widow or woman from saving herself from being burnt or buried alive.
- obstructing or interfering with the police in the discharge of its duties of taking any steps to prevent the commission of Sati.

The glorification of Sati includes:[83]

- the observance of any ceremony or the taking out of a procession in connection with the commission of Sati.
- the supporting, justifying or propagating the practice of Sati in any manner.

- the arranging of any function to eulogise the person who has committed Sati.
- the creation of a trust or the collection of funds or the construction of a temple or other structure or the carrying on of any form of worship or the performance of any ceremony there with a view to perpetuate the honour of or to preserve the memory of a person who has committed Sati.

The Act itself specifies punishments, provides for the appointment of Special Public Prosecutors and for the establishment of Special Courts to try offences under it. An appeal lies as a matter of right from any judgment, sentence or order, not being an interlocutory order, of a Special Court to the High Court both on facts and on law.

Collectors and District Magistrates have wide powers to prevent the commission of offences relating to Sati. And all officers of Government are required and empowered to assist the police in the prevention of Sati. No suit, prosecution or other legal proceeding lies against the State Government or any officer or authority of the State Government for anything which is done in good faith.

The Commission of Sati (Prevention) Act, 1987 has also amended the Representation of the People Act, 1951 by disqualifying those convicted for an offence involving Sati, and making the propagation of the practice or the commission of Sati or its glorification illegal.[84]

One of the main problems proving that an act of Sati has in fact taken place is that even if people from the neighbourhood/village admit that a woman has burnt herself on her husband's funeral pyre–which they usually don't admit to–it's extremely difficult to prove that the woman was forced to do so, and if she wasn't *forced*, for all practical purposes, her death *isn't* considered to be Sati which is an offence–it's simply a case of suicide for which no one is responsible.

The difference created between *voluntary* and *involuntary* Sati is treacherous and it shouldn't exist. While there are those who believe that love can make persons not want to live without their partners, I have trouble accepting the theory that a woman who has an alternative would *choose* to allow herself to be burnt alive. If not anything else, it's probably one of the most gruesome and painful ways in which to die. History is, however, replete with examples of women who killed themselves when their husbands/lovers died, women whose death was attributed to unrequited love, (Rajput) women who committed suicide en masse by consigning themselves to flames to avoid being captured and dishonoured by the enemy–they committed Jauhar–and women who supposedly died of broken hearts. And literature has even more of them.

Juliet, Shakespeare's famous heroine, for example, wound up stabbing herself. The question, however, is precisely what choice any of these women had–or in Juliet's case, the girl had; she was about thirteen years old in the play. She was not a virgin when she killed herself, and had she actually gone ahead and married her official fiancé, he would almost certainly have killed her himself once he discovered the fact. Such killings were legal at the time in Italy; they involved honour, after all. And as John Sutherland commented in his book *Henry V, War Criminal?*, "In Verona, as Shakespeare's audience would have thought, the bloodstained sheets would have had to be outside the bedchamber window after the bridal night. And, if not one kind of blood, it would have to be another." In the circumstances, stabbing herself was probably the most practical thing for Juliet to do. *Was she forced to do it? No. Did she have a choice? Not really ...she seems not to have had any viable alternatives. And, this way, she managed to retain some sort of 'control' over her own life and her own body.*

I believe that a very similar situation exists with women today who supposedly *choose* to commit Sati or otherwise harm themselves. They simply don't have other viable options. If they choose to live, they are more than likely to be subjected to lives of humiliation and indignity. Among other things, Indian widows are traditionally forced to wear only white, shave their heads and keep from adorning themselves with any sort of jewellery. The traditions aren't as strictly enforced today as they once were but the abuse of widows–who are often neither literate nor financially independent and therefore completely dependant on their abusers–is widespread and is often so cruel that it is unspeakable.

There is no doubt in my mind that death is often preferable in a society which has no use or value for widows. And if tradition provides them with a socially acceptable way to kill themselves (which is also not against their religious beliefs), it's obvious why Sati would seem attractive to women who have nothing but years of misery before them, and know it. That certainly doesn't mean that women killing themselves by committing Sati or otherwise *choose* to do so.

In an unequal society, consent has to be looked at in the socio-cultural context in which it is given. And I don't believe that the *consent* of a person who is not in a strong–or at least equal–position can ever be true, free or voluntary. My own opinion is that such *consent* which is almost always obtained through the 'encouragement' of trusted family members among others is not consent at all, and it should not be considered as such.

The law recognises that consent should be treated cautiously in other scenarios. *Section 111* of the Evidence Act, for example, says that 'where there is a question as to the good faith of a transaction between parties, one of whom stands to the other in a position of active confidence, the burden of proving the good faith of the transaction is on the party who is in a position of active confidence'.

**Illustration:**

(b) The good faith of a sale by a son just come of age to a father is in question is a suit brought by the son. The burden of proving the good faith of the transaction is on the father.

The recognition of the need to treat consent cautiously does not really find its way into the realm of women's rights though.

## WITCH KILLINGS

Britain passed a Witchcraft Act in 1735. The last person to be tried under it was Helen Duncan, a Spiritualist from Edinburgh, Scotland who claimed to be able to summon the dead. Despite her frequently challenged authenticity, she was tried for witchcraft and although she wasn't burnt at the stake, she was sentenced to nine months in prison. Initially, she was charged with vagrancy, and then with conspiracy and finally, with witchcraft. She was accused of the exercise of human conjuration that 'through the agency of Helen Duncan spirits of dead persons should appear to be present'.*

The year was 1944 and Britain was in the throes of World War II. Churchill, who was the Prime Minister at the time, was furious as he asked: "What was the cost of a trial in which the recorder [junior magistrate] was kept busy with all this obsolete tomfoolery?" in a memo. Over half a century has passed since then, and Britain hasn't had any more witch trials but witch-hunting is still prevalent in various other parts of the world including in some Indian states such as Assam, Bihar, Madhya Pradesh, Gujarat, Rajasthan, Andhra Pradesh and Maharashtra.

Between 1991 and 2000, over 522 cases of witch-hunting were registered in Bihar alone. The Prevention of Witch Practices Act was passed in undivided Bihar in 1999 to protect those accused of being witches but it has had little effect. Social activists say that legislation alone is unlikely to do much to help solve the problem unless there is a change in the attitudes of the people.

It is time to re-open witch trials–only this time round, with those who hunt 'witches' being the ones to be prosecuted to the fullest extent that the law permits. One of the difficulties in prosecuting those responsible for killing 'witches' has been the lack of evidence. For example, it was held that an acquittal was inevitable in Pritam Nath v/s State of Punjab, 2002[85]–in this case, a woman was allegedly tied to a tree and beaten by Sadhus with Trishuls and Chimtas (three-pronged spears and tongs). The problem was that there was just one witness: her husband and the Court held that his evidence was not reliable since, in spite of the fact that there were burns on the body, there were no ligature marks which proved that she had been tied to the tree.

Witch-hunts are not a tribal phenomenon although there are many who would like to believe that they are, just they find it convenient to believe that crimes against women take place primarily among the poor and the uneducated.*

What's frightening though is that nowadays, being branded a witch is often just a device for people to settle disputes including property arguments and to ensure that women do not stand up for their political and other rights.*

Dev Nathan and Govind Kelkar's research has shown that 'where women's position in control of the economy is stronger, the ideological struggle is more intense and women alone are the carriers of evil; and conversely, where women's economic position is weaker, the ideological struggle is less intense and women and men can both be the carriers of evil'.

In February 2004, for example, sixty-year-old Chokli Ratansinh Kanasia of Jambusar village under Devagadh Baria Taluka had to flee to Vadodara in the State of Gujarat after relatives branded her a witch and alleged that her black magic made people sick and killed cattle. The reason: she had a discoloured eye.[86]

Recalling individual stories seems pointless though: there are so many of them and all of them are so similar in their burden that they often sound the same. Persecution and torture; sometimes it's due to Shamans who encourage such acts and due to genuine ignorance and superstition while at other times, it's due to the need for a 'socially acceptable' method to keep women from asserting their rights.*

Nathan and Kelkar maintain that 'the categorisation of women and men into witches and witch-finders respectively was an essential part of the process of establishing the authority of men'–women are far less likely to rebel if the consequences of not conforming to societal expectations, challenging the status quo or asserting their own individuality (among other things) are severe.

The persecution of so-called witches ranks among the most ignored crimes against women in Indian society today. And until attitudes do change, India will continue to have the 'dubious distinction of being a Nuclear Power engulfed in Black Magic frenzy'.[87*]

## MODESTY AND OBSCENITY

In 1946, George Mikes, a writer of Hungarian origin who studied law, wrote, "Continental people have sex life; the English have hot water bottles," in *How to be an Alien* and, in a later book, he continued, "They think that the high circulation of porn magazines is a sign of high sexuality and not of high neurosis. ...England may be a copulating country but it is not an erotic country."[88] I suspect that exactly the same remarks could quite truthfully be directed at contemporary India.

> *Virility does not consist in feebleness of self-control and indulgence in illegitimate desire.*
>
> *- Tiru-Valluvar*[89]

Our laws seem to be outdated and our conceptions skewed. The Indian judiciary has spent a great deal of time trying to define what is modest and what is obscene, and in some cases, the lack of more appropriate laws has made it necessary for Courts to convict persons under archaic laws which deal with modesty or obscenity for acts which are clearly wrong and unacceptable but which cannot be considered to be illegal under any other provision of the law.

Another problem is that a large number of women have had modesty thrust on them in various forms–in Kashmir, the Dukhtaran-e-Miltat *encouraged* women to wear the veil while in many other parts of the country, colleges have adopted dress codes of varying degrees of severity. Some require women to wear Salwaar Kameezes, others prohibit jeans and sleeveless shirts, and one Mumbai college banned the colour red.

### Indecent Representation

Pornography is easily available in India (just as it is in the rest of the world). In fact, any discussion about the availability of pornography is ludicrous in the Age of Online Porn. And, whether or not one wants to admit it, it is closely linked to prostitution and to trafficking: 'today, the hunt for cheap, easy prey has been made significantly easier because the prowlers know exactly where to click'.[90]

Every once in a while, the Government or someone else–usually an over-the-top organisation rambling on about *Indian*

*Culture*–does make a bit of a noise about porn being viewed at cyber cafés or about obscenity in general; no. too surprisingly, it never amounts to much although they have managed to get pubs and clubs to close down early all over the country.

There are provisions in the Penal Code, the Information Technology Act and the Indecent Representation of Women Act to deal with porn and other forms of indecent representation though.

> Any book, pamphlet, paper, writing, drawing, painting, representation, figure or any other object, is deemed to be obscene under *Section 292* of the Indian Penal Code 'if it is lascivious or appeals to the prurient interest or if its effect (or where it comprises two or more distinct items, the effect of any one of its items) is, if taken as a whole, such as to tend to deprave and corrupt persons, who are likely, having regard to all relevant circumstances, to read, see or hear the matter contained or embodied in it.

***Under Section 292 (2), of the Indian Penal Code, whoever***

(a) Sells, lets to hire, distributes, publicly exhibits or in any manner, puts into circulation or for purposes of sale, hire, distribution, public exhibition or circulation, makes, produces or has in his possession any obscene book, pamphlet, paper, drawing, painting, representation or figure or any other obscene object whatsoever or

(b) Imports, exports or conveys any obscene object for any of the purposes aforesaid, or knowing or having reason to believe that such object will be sold, let to hire, distributed or publicly exhibited or in any manner put into circulation or

(c) Takes part in or receives profits from any business in the course of which he knows or has reason to believe that any such obscene objects are, for any of the purposes aforesaid, made, produced, purchased, kept, imported, exported, conveyed, publicly exhibited or in any manner put into circulation or

(d) Advertises or makes known by any means whatsoever that any person is engaged or is ready to engage in any act which is an offence under this Section or that any such obscene object can be procured from or through any person or

(e) Offers or attempts to do any act which is an offence under this Section, shall be punished on first conviction with imprisonment of either description for a term which may extend to two years, and with fine which may extend to two thousand rupees, and, in the event of a second or subsequent conviction, with imprisonment of either description for a term which may extend to five years, and also with fine which may extend to five thousand rupees.

*This Section does not extend to*

(a) Any book, pamphlet, paper, writing, drawing, painting, representation or figure
    - (i) the publication of which is proved to be justified as being for the public good on the ground that such book, pamphlet, paper, writing, drawing, painting, representation or figure is in the interest of science, literature, art or learning or other objects of general concern or
    - (ii) which is kept or used bonafide for religious purposes

(b) Any representation sculptured, engraved, painted or otherwise represented on or in
    - (i) any ancient monument within the meaning of the Ancient Monuments and Archaeological Sites and Remains Act, 1958 or
    - (ii) any temple or on any car used for the conveyance of idols or kept or used for any religious purpose.

And under *Section 293* which deals with the punishment of an act listed in Section 292, 'whoever sells, lets to hire, distributes, exhibits or circulates to any person under the age of twenty years any such obscene object as is referred to in the last preceding Section or offers or attempts so to do, shall be punished on first conviction with imprisonment of either description for a term which may extend to three years, and with fine which may extend to two thousand rupees, and, in the event of a second or subsequent conviction, with imprisonment of either description for a term which may extend to seven years, and also with fine which may extend to five thousand rupees.'

The Indian Penal Code does not define obscenity itself. In Ranjit D Udeshi v/s State of Maharashtra, 1965,[91] the Supreme Court, however, accepted the test formulated over a century ago in R v/s Hicklin, the case in which a bookseller was prosecuted for keeping and selling the supposedly obscene *Lady Chatterley's Lover*. Despite the furore which the book created when it was first published, by itself, it simply cannot be considered obscene by any contemporary standard and as such, the test in R v/s Hicklin, which quite simply fails either to recognise or to make provision for this change in the perception of obscenity, should not have been accepted.

### The Indecent Representation of Women Act

Parliament passed the Indecent Representation of Women (Prohibition) Act in 1986. It extends to the whole of India except the State of Jammu and Kashmir and is meant to 'prohibit indecent representation of women through advertisements or in publications, writings, paintings, figures'.

'Indecent representation of women' means the depiction in any manner of the figure of a woman; her form or body or any part thereof in such way as to have the effect of being indecent or derogatory to or denigrating women or as is likely to deprave, corrupt or injure public morality or morals.[92]

#### *Under this Act*

No person shall publish or cause to be published or arrange or take part in the publication or exhibition of any advertisement which contains indecent representation of women in any form.[93]

No person shall produce or cause to be produced, sell, let to hire, distribute, circulate or send by post any material which contains indecent representation of women in any form.

***However, this Act does not apply to***

(a) Any book, pamphlet, paper, slide, film, writing, drawing, painting, photograph, representation or figure
   (i) the publication of which is proved to be justified as being for the public good on the ground that such book, pamphlet, paper, slide, film, writing, drawing, painting, photography, representation or figure is in the interest of science, literature, art or learning, or other objects of general concern or
   (ii) which is kept or used bonafide for religious purposes.

(b) Any representation sculptured, engraved, painted or otherwise represented on or in:
   (i) any ancient monument or
   (ii) any temple or on any car used or the conveyance of idols or kept or used for any religious purpose
   (iii) any film to which the provisions of Part II of the Cinematograph Act, 1952 are applicable.[94]

Any Gazetted Officer authorized by the State Government may search any place in which he has reason to believe that an offence under this Act has been or is being committed and seize any material which he has reason to believe contravenes any of the provisions of this Act.[95]

The Act also provides for the punishment of offences under it with imprisonment of either description for a term which may extend to two years and with a fine which may extend to two thousand rupees, and with an enhanced punishment in the event of a second or subsequent conviction.[96]

Further, there is a provision in the Information Technology Act, 2000 which deals with the publishing of information which is obscene in electronic form. Apart from online porn, recently, a large number of men have been morphing photos of women who either dump them or simply reject their advances and posting them on the Net. There doesn't seem to be very much that can be done about it-once the photos are on the Net, the damage has usually already been done as far as the woman involved is concerned.

Moving away from relationships which have gone sour (assuming they existed in the first place) though, another form of indecent representation which has been much talked about is that which is on TV. Apart from a large number of PILs being filed against various actresses for wearing supposedly indecent clothes in performances, in January 2007, the Government temporarily banned the AXN Channel for showing supposedly indecent content.

While the judiciary has been trying to curtail instances of frivolous public interest litigation being filed by persons suffering from bouts of self-righteousness, the Government has increasingly been making forays into realm of morality although, as Jug Suraiya[97] pointed out, "A perverse politics of pornography seems to prevail. A State apparatus which cannot grant its citizens the most basic of life enhancing requirements -primary healthcare, education, gainful employment, safety from violence–shows compensatory zeal in protecting its people from the ill-effects of moral pollutants in their most ingenious of Avatars... even as the regular police turns a blind eye, or worse and acts as an accomplice to rape, murder torture and other obscenities of violence."

For my own part, I've never had a problem with explicit images–I remember going to museums as a child which left nothing to the imagination. There is, of course, a thin line which divides Art and Porn though and I'm not entirely certain where that line is.

In 19th Century France, there were huge outcries when certain paintings like *Le Dejuner sur l'Herbe*[98] by Edouard Manet were first exhibited. This painting included fully clothed men with one naked woman and another clothed one in a contemporary setting. The official Academy refused to exhibit the painting–although it may have been as scandalised by Manet's technique as by the content of his work–so the artist and some of his contemporaries set up a parallel exhibition where they exhibited their work.

Paintings which caused such a hue and cry usually contained depictions of nude women in contemporary settings, and, to make matters worse, the women were sometimes recognisable prostitutes. One critic even warned pregnant women not too look at a picture which he found unspeakably outrageous.

Similar standards seem to apply to contemporary Indian society–to be socially acceptable and to avoid being considered pornographic, a woman must belong to antiquity before she can be represented in the nude. And, if the controversy surrounding the paintings by M F Hussain of Hindu Goddesses and Bharat Mata–Mother India–in the nude is anything to go by, such a painting should not be a contemporary one if it is to be acceptable; vast numbers of people have said that Hussain's paintings have offended their cultural and religious sensitivities.

Even leaving aside the debate about the difference between nudity and nakedness in art, this can be confusing because traditionally, many of the images which define our culture are extremely explicit although those who speak against explicit contemporary imagery argue that it is different from traditional imagery (which they claim is a celebration of Kama and other Hindu ideals and beliefs).

In 2005, an Art Gallery in Mumbai exhibiting what were considered by some people to be explicit works of art was vandalised. Believing in artistic freedom, I think that should not have happened–I see nothing wrong in people expressing/ displaying sexuality and/or the unclothed human body particularly, if it is required to tell a story with a social message.

In Bobby Art International v/s Om Pal Singh Hoon, 1996,[99] the Supreme Court did not quash the certificate of exhibition of a film which told the story of a tribal girl–Phoolan Devi–whose being exposed to various forms of brutality shown in the film (including gang-rape) turned her into a dreaded dacoit known as the 'Bandit Queen'. The Court held that the film had to be judged in its entirety and that nakedness did not always arouse a baser instinct.

The problem, to my mind, crops up when people are forced, either directly or indirectly, to display/express/sell their own sexuality for any purpose including for monetary consideration.

Personally, I don't understand porn. Many of my male friends watch a lot of porn and what puzzles me is that these men are not socially-deviant. They are decent human-beings and it is quite simply not within the ethical and moral scope of their actions to treat the women in their lives badly or to be abusive towards them. They say that porn turns them on–I simply don't see the point. After all, even leaving aside ethical issues, there's a limit to what can be done and once it is done, porn becomes repetitive. And without some sort of emotional factor being involved, it's messy.

What particularly bothers me about pornography available today though is that the women in it are not human-beings; they are–as has often been observed–'three holes and two hands'. They have no value apart from the friction which those holes and hands are capable of producing.[100]

Some people oppose porn citing religious considerations and take the moral high ground while others speak of it as a manifestation of the growing equality between men and women. Although I appreciate that pornography raises questions of sexual ethics, neither of these arguments makes much sense to me.

Those who speak of religion usually speak of women in terms of their being asexual entities in need of perpetual protection and of their deserving to be virtually worshipped provided they are not promiscuous. It certainly isn't a view shared by pornographers but it is unrealistic nonetheless, it is patriarchal and, by implication, it denies that women are, first and foremost, simply human-beings.

And if the porn available in the market is anything to go by, pornography has got nothing to do with equality, modernisation or liberalisation. The images, for the most part, are images of callousness if not of outright cruelty. It's not consensual–there cannot be *consent* where there is no equality. At this point, I'm reminded of a feminist theory which was misinterpreted as *All Heterosexual Sex Is Rape*. That isn't what I'm saying - what I am saying is those who are not equal cannot negotiate as equals, and in an unequal society where women have less power than men their *consent*, such as it is, to being filmed in porn cannot and should not be considered to be true and voluntary consent.

In other contexts, the law recognises that if the relations subsisting between parties are such that one of them has the power to dominate the will of the other, that power may be used to obtain an unfair advantage over the other, and in such cases, it treats the 'consent' of the weaker party cautiously. For example, Sections 16 and 19 A of the Contract Act say that if consent to an agreement is given due to the exercise of undue influence, the resulting contract is voidable at the option of the party on whom such influence has been exercised. And, if the contract appears to be unconscionable, the burden of proving that consent to it has not been induced by undue influence lies on the party in a position to dominate the will of the other.

This understanding of the concept of consent in contract law does not influence the public perception of women who contract to act in porn despite the fact that, as a group, they are invariably in a much weaker position than those they negotiate with and they certainly do not have an equal–much less, a powerful–societal position.

I find it difficult to accept that most women in pornography *enjoy* it–an assertion I've heard from male friends who watch porn; I think that that's just what they've convinced themselves of so that they don't feel guilty.

I've never heard of a girl ever saying that she'd like to grow up and sell herself in any way.

And I do not believe that any woman would ever volunteer to do so if she thought she had a viable alternative.

Robert Jensen, a journalism professor in the University of Texas has pointed out that 'in a society where so many men are watching so much pornography that is rooted in the pain and humiliation of women, it is not difficult to understand why so many can't bear to confront it: Pornography forces men to face up to how they have learnt to be sexual. And pornography forces women to face up to how men see them'.[101]

## Sexual Harassment

The Indian Penal Code speaks of offences against the modesty of a woman in Sections 509 and 354.

**509.** Word, gesture or act intended to insult the modesty of a woman

Whoever, intending to insult the modesty of any woman, utters any word, makes any sound or gesture or exhibits any object, intending that such word or sound shall be heard or that such gesture or object shall be seen, by such woman or intrudes upon the privacy of such woman shall be punished with simple imprisonment for a term which may extend to one year or with fine or with both.

**354.** Assault or criminal force to a woman with intent to outrage her modesty

Whoever assaults or uses criminal force to any woman, intending to outrage or knowing it to be likely that he will thereby outrage her modesty, shall be punished with imprisonment of either description for a term which may extend to two years or with fine or with both.

The Courts of India have gone to almost absurd lengths to define what a woman's modesty is. This is probably best seen in the case of Major Singh v/s Rattan Singh, 1997,[102] where the accused was alleged to have fingered a six-month-old girl. The Court ultimately concluded that the six-month-old infant did in fact possess modesty and that he had outraged it.

Apart from illustrating the lengths to which the judiciary has gone to, the case also illustrates the need for the laws to be reformed–what the Major did was obviously wrong by any contemporary standard but there was no other provision of the law under which he could have been held accountable.

One of the main problems with the provisions governing rape is that they define rape extremely narrowly - to commit rape as defined by the Indian Penal Code, there must be penile-vaginal penetration. All other forms of penetration simply do not amount to rape.

The Supreme Court, however, finally defined what a woman's modesty is in March 2007. In a case where an accused, Ramkripal, had been convicted of rape but had pleaded for leniency saying that he was at worst guilty of outraging the modesty of the woman, Justices Arijit Pasayat and S.H.

Kapadia said, "The act of pulling a woman, removing her Saree, coupled with a request for sexual intercourse... would be an outrage to the modesty of a woman; and knowledge, that such modesty is likely to be outraged, is sufficient to constitute the offence." The Bench further held that a lack of protest on the woman's part cannot be used as a defence: "The culpable intention of the accused is the crux of the matter. The reaction of the woman is very relevant, but its absence is not always decisive."

In this case, the Bench did not allow the argument of the accused since it had already been proved that he had raped the victim: it held that penetration by itself is enough to constitute the offence of rape regardless of whether or not ejaculation has taken place.

Further, the Law Commission has recommended that the definition in Section 375 which deals with rape in the Indian Penal Code be amended to say:

*375. **Sexual Assault means***

- Penetrating the vagina (which term shall include the labia majora), the anus or urethra or any person with
  - * any part of the body of another person or
  - * an object manipulated by another person

  except where such penetration is carried out for proper hygienic or medical purposes.
- manipulating any part of the body of another person so as to cause penetration of the vagina (which term shall include the labia majora), the anus or urethra of the offender by any part of the other person's body.
- introducing any part of the penis of a person into the mouth of another person.
- Engaging in cunnilingus or fellatio.
- Continuing sexual assault as defined in the clauses mentioned earlier.

  Penetration to any extent is sufficient for the purposes of this Section although sexual intercourse by a man with his own wife is not sexual assault provided she is not less than sixteen years old.

In addition to this, there has been much lobbying to repeal or, at least, to amend Section 377 of the Indian Penal Code which was introduced by the British and says:

> Whoever voluntarily has carnal intercourse against the order of nature with any man, woman or animal shall be punished with imprisonment for life, or with imprisonment of either description for a term which may extend to ten years, and shall also be liable to fine.
>
> Explanation: Penetration is sufficient to constitute the carnal intercourse necessary to the offence described in this section.

In an old English case, it was held that an imputation of lesbianism is an imputation of unchastity within the Slander of Women Act, 1891,[103] and in a 1954 case, it was held that lesbianism might amount to cruelty to a husband.[104] Today, it may (being 'unreasonable' behaviour) constitute the basis for divorce.

In India, despite the fact that Section 377 of the Indian Penal Code makes homosexuality unlawful, this is one of the few provisions in the law under which paedophiles can be prosecuted. As such, it cannot be easily repealed. One suggestion has been to add a proviso which says that any such 'unnatural' act between consenting adults in private shall not be unlawful, but successive Governments have refused to make any change at all to the Section claiming that public morality is not ready to handle such a change. One of the primary manifestations of this provision, however, is that far from protecting anyone, it allegedly simply facilitates the extortion of money (by the police and others) from homosexual people on account of their sexuality.

In its 172nd Report, the Law Commission also suggested that a new Section-376E-be introduced to deal with Unlawful Sexual Contact.

There are several problems with sexual harassment. For one thing, it is extremely difficult to prove, and even worse, it can be difficult to recognise. I think that as one grows older, one develops a sixth sense which enables one to spot men who have the potential to be trouble and one learns to differentiate between things like simply being given a hug and having someone try to feel you over while giving you a hug, but it isn't something one instinctively differentiates between.

There are, apparently, two reasons why young women don't recognise sexual harassment: one is that they have never been in sexually abusive situations and therefore really don't have the emotional background to recognise what's happening and the other is that they simply do not want to know because that would mean that they would have to deal with the reality of being abused or harassed.

Another form of sexual harassment is street harassment although it's called Eve Teasing in India. Usually, it's mild but there are times when it can become frightening - eve teasers sometimes follow women for miles or become physically violent. Under the law, there isn't much that can be done about it unless the teasing involves 'outraging the modesty' of the woman involved or can be classified as being threatening.

One comment on street harassment I read (if memory serves me) on the HollaBackNYC website–a project which fights street harassment–pointed out that to be considered threatening, the harassment would have to be considered threatening by the police. And considering that 'the police' usually means 'men with guns', there is very little that they do find threatening. Consequently, even in the US, street harassment is not always taken seriously.

Recently, there have been attempts in India such as those made by the Blank Noise Project to fight Eve Teasing and raise awareness about it. Apart from organising marches and maintaining a website, one of the things the project did was collect the clothes which women teased were wearing when the teasing took place–the common perception is that if, as a woman, you are sexually harassed, you were wearing short clothes or somehow otherwise 'asking' for it. The clothes, however, came in all sizes: short, long, tight and loose, and showed, as they were intended to, that it really doesn't matter what you wear.

As a woman, you are vulnerable to harassment.

### *Sexual Harassment at Work*

The leading case on sexual harassment at the work-place is a Class Action by some social activists and NGOs: Vishakha v/s State of Rajasthan which was decided by a Bench of the Supreme Court comprising Justice Sujata Manohar and Justice B.N. Kirpal on August 13, 1997. The immediate cause for the filing of the writ petition was a brutal gang-rape of a social worker in a village in Rajasthan (which was dealt with in a separate criminal proceeding). This is a heavily edited excerpt of the Vishakha judgment:

> "With the increasing awareness and emphasis on gender justice, there is an increase in the effort to guard against such violations. The resentment towards incidents of sexual harassment is also increasing. The present petition has been brought with the aim of focussing attention towards this societal aberration, and assisting in finding suitable methods for the realisation of the true concept of gender equality; and to prevent the sexual harassment of working women in all work-places through the judicial process.
>
> Each such incident results in a violation of the fundamental rights of 'Gender Equality' and the 'Right of Life and Liberty'. It is a clear violation of the rights under Articles 14, 15 and 21 of the Constitution. One of the logical consequences of such an incident is also the violation of the victim's fundamental right under Article 19 (1) (g) 'to practice any profession or to carry out any occupation, trade or business'. Such violations, therefore, attract the remedy under Article 32 for the enforcement of these fundamental rights of women.

This Class Action under Article 32 of the Constitution is for this reason. A writ of mandamus in such a situation, if it is to be effective, needs to be accompanied by directions for prevention as the violation of fundamental rights of this kind is a recurring phenomenon. The fundamental right to carry on any occupation, trade or profession depends on the availability of a 'safe' working environment. Right to Life means life with dignity. The primary responsibility of ensuring such safety and dignity through suitable legislation, and the creation of a mechanism for its enforcement, is of the legislature and the executive. Apart from Article 32 of the Constitution of India, other provisions[105] also envisage judicial intervention for eradication of this social evil:

**Article 15** Prohibition of discrimination on grounds of religion, race, caste, sex or place of birth.

**Article 42** Provision for just and humane conditions of work and maternity relief.

**Article 51 A** Fundamental duties including that of every citizen to renounce practices derogatory to the dignity of women.

When, however, instances of sexual harassment resulting in violation of fundamental rights of women workers under Articles 14, 19 and 21 are brought for redress under Article 32, an effective redressal requires that some guidelines be laid down for the protection of these rights to fill the legislative vacuum. They would be treated as the law declared by this Court under *Article 141* of the Constitution.

HAVING REGARD to the definition of 'human rights' in the Protection of Human Rights Act, 1993[106] and TAKING NOTE of the fact that the present civil and penal laws in India do not adequately provide for specific protection of women from sexual harassment in work-places, and that the enactment of such legislation will take considerable time, it is necessary and expedient for employers in work-places as well as other responsible persons or institutions to observe certain guidelines to ensure the prevention of sexual harassment of women:

1. *Duty of the employer or other responsible persons in work-places and other institutions*

It shall be the duty of the employer or other responsible persons in work-places or other institutions to prevent or deter the commission of acts of sexual harassment and to provide procedures for the resolution, settlement or prosecution of acts of sexual harassment by taking all steps required.

## 2. *Definition*

For this purpose, sexual harassment includes such unwelcome sexually determined behaviour (whether directly or by implication) as:

(a) physical contact and advances

(b) a demand or request for sexual favours

(c) sexually coloured remarks

(d) showing pornography

(e) any other unwelcome physical verbal or non-verbal conduct of a sexual nature.

Where any of these acts is committed in circumstances in which the victim of such conduct has a reasonable apprehension that in relation to the victim's employment or work (whether she is drawing salary or honorarium or voluntary, whether in Government, public or private enterprise) such conduct can be humiliating and may constitute a health and safety problem.

It is discriminatory when the woman has reasonable grounds to believe that her objection would disadvantage her in connection with her employment or work including recruitment or promotion or when it creates a hostile work environment, or when adverse consequences might be visited on the victim if she does not consent to the conduct in question or raises any objection thereto.

## 3. *Preventive Steps*

All employers or persons-in-charge of work-places (whether in the public or private sector) should take appropriate steps to prevent sexual harassment. Without prejudice to the generality of this obligation, they should take the following steps:

(a) Express prohibition of sexual harassment as defined earlier at the work-place should be notified, published and circulated in appropriate ways.

(b) The rules/regulations of Government and Public Sector bodies relating to conduct and discipline should include rules/regulations prohibiting sexual harassment, and provide for appropriate penalties against the offender.

(c) As regards private employers, steps should be taken to include the aforesaid prohibitions in the Standing Orders under the Industrial Employment (Standing Orders) Act, 1946.

(d) Appropriate work conditions should be provided in respect of work, leisure, health and hygiene to further ensure that there is no hostile environment towards women at work-places and no female employee should have reasonable grounds to believe that she is disadvantaged in connection with her employment.

### 4. *Criminal Proceedings*

Where such conduct amounts to a specific offence under the Indian Penal Code or under any other law, the employer shall initiate appropriate action in accordance with law by making a complaint with the appropriate authority and shall ensure that victims or witnesses are not victimized or discriminated against whilst dealing with complaints of sexual harassment.

The victims of sexual harassment should have the option to seek transfer of the perpetrator or their own transfer.

### 5. *Disciplinary Action*

Where such conduct amounts to misconduct in employment as defined by the relevant Service Rules, appropriate disciplinary action should be initiated by the employer in accordance with those rules.

### 6. *Complaint Mechanism*

Whether or not such conduct constitutes an offence under law or a breach of the Service Rules, an appropriate complaint mechanism should be created in the employer's organization for the redressal of complaints made by victims. Such a complaint mechanism should ensure that the treatment of complaints is time bound treatment.

## 7. *Complaints Committee*

The complaint mechanism, referred to in (6) earlier, should be adequate to provide, where necessary, a Complaints Committee, a Special Counsellor and other support service, including the maintenance of confidentiality. The Complaints Committee should be headed by a woman and not less than half of its members should be women.

Further, to prevent the possibility of any under pressure or influence from senior levels, each such Complaints Committee should involve a third party, either an NGO or some other body which is familiar with the issue of sexual harassment.

The Complaints Committee must make an annual report to the concerned Government Department of the complaints received and of action taken by it.

The employer and person-in-charge will also report on the compliance with the aforesaid guidelines including on the reports of the Complaints Committee to the Government Department.

## 8. *Workers' Initiative*

Employees should be allowed to raise issues of sexual harassment at workers' meetings and in other appropriate fora and the issue should be affirmatively discussed in Employer-Employee Meetings.

## 9. *Awareness*

Awareness of the rights of female employees in this regard should be created, in particular, by prominently notifying the guidelines (and appropriate legislation when enacted on the subject) in a suitable manner.

## 10. *Third Parties*

Where sexual harassment occurs as a result of an act or omission by any third party or outsider, the employer and person-in-charge will take all steps necessary and reasonable to assist the affected person in terms of support and preventive action.

### 11. *Suitable Measures*

The Central/State Governments are requested to consider adopting suitable measures including legislation to ensure that the guidelines laid down by this order are also observed by the employers in Private Sector.

### 12. *Other Rights*

These guidelines will not prejudice any rights available under the Protection of Human Rights Act, 1993.

Accordingly, the Supreme Court directed these guidelines and norms to be strictly observed in all work-places for the preservation and enforcement of the right of working women to gender equality. They are binding and enforceable in law until suitable legislation is enacted to occupy the field. In laying them down to help deal with the prevention of sexual harassment at work-places the Supreme Court also referred to Constitutional provisions and India's obligations under various International Conventions which, inter alia, say:

**The Constitution of India**

Article 51 (d)

The State shall endeavour to foster respect for International Law and treaty obligations in the dealings of organised people with one another.

Article 253

Parliament has power to make any law for the whole or any part of the territory of India to implement any treaty, agreement or convention with any other country or countries or any decision made at any international conference, association or other body.

**The Beijing Statement**

Article 10

The objectives of the judiciary are:

- to ensure that all persons are able to live securely under the Rule of Law.

- to promote, within the proper limits of the judicial function, the observance and the attainment of human rights.
- to administer the law impartially among persons and between persons and the State.

**The Convention on the Elimination of All Forms of Discrimination against Women**

Article 11

1. State Parties shall take all appropriate measures to eliminate discrimination against women in the field of employment in order to ensure, on the basis of equality of men and women, the same rights, in particular:

   (a) The right to work as an inalienable right of all human-beings

   (f) The right to protection of health and to safety in working conditions, including the safeguarding of the function of reproduction.

   *The general recommendations regarding 'violence and equality in employment' in this context.*

   Equality in employment can be seriously impaired when women are subjected to gender-specific violence, such as sexual harassment in the work-place.

Sexual harassment includes such unwelcome sexually determined behaviour as physical contacts and advances, sexually coloured remarks, showing pornography and sexual demands, whether by words or actions. Such conduct can be humiliating and may constitute a health and safety problem; it is discriminatory when the woman has reasonable grounds to believe that her objection would disadvantage her in connection with her employment, including recruiting or promotion or when it creates a hostile working environment.

Effective complaints procedures and remedies, including compensation, should be provided.

States should include in their reports information about sexual harassment, and on measures to protect women from sexual harassment and other forms of violence of coercion in the work-place.

Article 24

State Parties undertake to adopt all necessary measures at the national level aimed at achieving the full realization of the rights recognised in the present Convention.

The Government of India ratified this Resolution on June 25, 1993 with some reservations. Nonetheless, it did not enact any legislation to prevent sexual harassment at the work-place.

## RAPE

Rape laws were overhauled after the decision of the Supreme Court in Tukaram and Another v/s State of Maharashtra–also known as the Mathura case–delivered on September 15, 1978. The case generated a great deal of outrage and the Indian Penal Code was amended as a result.

Since then, both the law itself and its interpretation have been becoming more stringent. In September 2004, Special District and Sessions Judge Renu Sharma in Shivpuri, Madhya Pradesh awarded separate sentences of rigorous imprisonment–the maximum being of ten years–to two persons for the rape of a eunuch in a landmark judgment.

*Section 375, Indian Penal CodeA man is said to commit 'rape' who except in the case hereinafter excepted, has sexual intercourse with a woman under circumstances falling under any of the five following descriptions:*

- *Against her will.*
- *Without her consent.*
- *With her consent, when her consent has been obtained by putting her in fear of death or of hurt.*
- *With her consent, when the man knows that he is not her husband, and that her consent is given because she believes that he is another man to whom she is or believes herself to be lawfully married.*
- *With or without her consent, when she is under sixteen years of age.*

*Explanation: Penetration is sufficient to constitute the sexual intercourse necessary to the offence of rape.*

*Exception: Sexual intercourse by a man with his wife is not rape as long as she is not under fifteen years of age.*

And marital rape is also viewed differently. Earlier, it was not recognised by the law either in England or in India since wives were deemed to have given their irrevocable consent to sexual relations at the time of marriage. The current position, however, is not the same. Although conjugal rights are still recognised, a husband cannot legally use force to enjoy/enforce them. The marital exemption to rape was abolished in England by R v/s R [1991] All 481. And in India, the 2005 Domestic Violence Act has recognised marital rape as a form of domestic violence for the first time.

Till October 2006, a man who convinced a girl to have sex with him by promising to marry her was not considered to be guilty of raping her[107] but this too has now changed– in October, 2006, a Bench of the Supreme Court comprising Justice A.K. Mathur and Justice Altamas Kabir changed the status quo by rejecting a plea of consensual sex and holding that a man who convinces an impressionable young girl to have sex with him by promising to marry her is guilty of rape.[108]

One problem though has been that the judiciary has often been willing to reduce the term of imprisonment of a rapist (or not punish him at all) if he has got married to or agreed to marry his victim. In Satendra Singh Kushwala v/s State of Bihar, 2003,[109] for example, the sentence of the accused was reduced from nine years to five years.

But, of course, this is a problem which crops up only if the case makes it to Court at all; police often hesitate to help victims. And once the case makes it to Court, the experience is usually traumatic for the victim. In Delhi Domestic Women's Forum v/s Union of India, 1995,[110] the Supreme Court pointed out the defects in the system by pointing out that 'firstly, complaints are handled roughly and are not given such attention as is warranted. The victims, more often than not, are humiliated by the police. They have also invariably found rape trials a bad experience and often say they consider the ordeal to be even worse than the rape itself.'

In this case, the Supreme Court laid down guidelines for the trial of rape cases. It directed that victims be provided with legal assistance from a person who would also guide them with regard to their obtaining other forms of assistance (such as medical aid). The police were directed to inform victims of the availability of such assistance and to provide it. They were also directed to inform victims of their right to representation before questioning them. These guidelines also provided for compensation to be paid to victims and for the maintenance of the anonymity of victims as far as necessary.

The Supreme Court has recognised a victim's right to compensation in other cases as well. In Chairman, Railway Board v/s Chandrima Das, 2000,[111] it awarded compensation to a woman who was gang-raped by Railway employees in a building belonging to the Railways. And in Bodhisathwa Gautam v/s Subhra Chakraborty, 1996,[112] the Supreme Court awarded interim compensation of 1000 INR per month to the victim till her charges of rape were decided by the Trial Court.

These are relatively recent developments though. In the Mathura case–Tukaram and Another v/s State of Maharashtra, 1978–two policemen apparently raped a teenaged orphan named Mathura in the police station they were attached to. The judgment was delivered by Justice Khosla. This is a heavily edited excerpt of it (with emphasis added in certain places).

> "Mathura is the girl who is said to have been raped. Her parents died when she was a child and she is living with her brother, Gama. Both of them worked as labourers to earn a living. Mathura used to go to the house of Nunshi for work and during the course of her visits to that house, she came into contact with Ashok, who was the sister's son of Nunshi and was residing with the latter.
>
> The contact developed into an intimacy; and Ashok and Mathura decided to marry.
>
> On March 26, 1972, Gama lodged a report at the Desai Gunj police station alleging that Mathura had been kidnapped by Nunshi, her husband Laxman and Ashok. The report was recorded by Head Constable Baburao at whose instance all the three persons complained against, as well as Mathura, were brought to the police station at about 9 p.m. and who recorded the statements of the two lovers. By then it was about 10.30 p.m. and Baburao told them to go after directing to Gama bring a copy of the entry regarding

the birth of Mathura recorded in the relevant register. Baburao then left for his house. At that time the two appellants–the accused policemen, Tukaram and Ganpat–were present at the police station.

After Baburao had gone away, Mathura, Nunshi, Gama and Ashok started leaving the police station. The appellants, however, asked Mathura to wait at the police station and told her companions to move out. The direction was complied with. Immediately thereafter, Ganpat took Mathura into a latrine situated at the rear of the main building, loosened her underwear, lit a torch and stared at her private parts. He then dragged her to a Chhapri which serves the main building as its back verandah. In the Chhapri he threw her on the ground and raped her in spite of protests and stiff resistance on her part. He departed after satisfying his lust and then Tukaram, the second appellant, who was seated on a cot nearby, came to the place where Mathura was and fondled her private parts. He also wanted to rape her but was unable to do so because he was in a highly intoxicated condition.

Nunshi, Gama and Ashok, who had been waiting outside the police station for Mathura, grew suspicious when they found the lights of the police station being turned off and its entrance door being closed from within. They went to the rear of the police station in order to find out what the matter was. No light was visible inside and when Nunshi shouted for Mathura there was no response. The noise attracted a crowd and some time later, Tukaram emerged from the rear of the police station and on an enquiry from Nunshi stated that the girl had already left. He himself went out and shortly afterwards Mathura also emerged from the rear of the police station and informed Nunshi and Gama that Ganpat had compelled her to undress herself and had raped her.

Nunshi took Mathura to Dr. Khume and the former told him that the girl had been subjected to rape. The doctor told them to go to the police station and lodge a report there.

Mathura was examined by Dr. Kamal Shastrakar at 8 p.m. on March 27, 1972. *The girl had no injury on her person. Her hymen revealed old ruptures. The vagina admitted two fingers easily.* There was no matting of the public hair. The age of the girl was estimated by the doctor to be between 14 and 16 years. A sample of the public hair and two vaginal smear slides were sent by the doctor in a sealed packet to the Chemical Examiner who found no traces of semen therein. The presence of semen was however detected on the girl's clothes and the pyjama which was taken off the person of Ganpat.

**The Learned Sessions Judge** found that there was no satisfactory evidence to prove that Mathura was below 16 years of age on the date of the occurrence. *He further held that she was 'a shocking liar' whose testimony 'is riddled with falsehood and improbabilities'*. But he observed that 'the farthest one can go into believing her and the corroborative circumstances, would be the conclusion that while at the Police Station she had sexual intercourse and that, in all probability, this was with an accused policemen.' He added however that there was a world of difference between 'sexual intercourse' and 'rape', and that rape had not been proved in spite of the fact that the defence version which was a bare denial of the allegations of rape, could not be accepted at its face value. He further observed: "Finding Nunshi angry and knowing that Nunshi would suspect some thing fishy, she (Mathura) could not have very well admitted that of her own free will, she had surrendered her body to a Police Constable. The crowd included her lover Ashok, and she had to sound virtuous before him. This is why - this is a possibility - she might have invented the story of having been confined at the Police Station and raped by one of the accused policemen.

**Mathura is habituated to sexual intercourse,** as is clear from the testimony of Dr. Shastrakar and one of the accused is no novice. He speaks of nightly discharges. This may be untrue, but there is no reason to exclude the possibility of his having stained his Paijamal with semen while having sexual intercourse with persons other than Mathura. The seminal stains on Mathura can be similarly accounted for. She was, after all, living with Ashok and was very much in love with him.

**The High Court** took note of the various findings arrived at by the Learned Sessions Judge and then itself proceeded to sift through the evidence bearing in mind the principle that a reversal of the acquittal would not be justified if the view taken by the Trial Court was reasonably possible, even though the High Court was inclined to take a different view of the facts. The High Court proceeded to observe that although the Learned Sessions Judge was right in saying that there was a world of difference between sexual intercourse and rape, he erred in appreciating the difference between consent and 'passive submission'.

In coming to the conclusion that the sexual intercourse in question was forcible and amounted to rape, the High Court remarked:

"Besides the circumstances that emerge from the oral evidence on the record, we have to see in what situation Mathura was at the time. Both the accused were strangers to her. It is not the case of the defence that Mathura knew both these accused or any of them since before the time of occurrence. It is, therefore, indeed, highly improbable that Mathura on her part would make any overtures or invite the accused to satisfy her sexual desire. Indeed it is also not probable that a girl who was involved in a complaint filed by her brother would make such overtures or advances. The initiative must, therefore, have come from the accused and if such an initiative comes from the accused, indeed she could not have resisted the same on account of the situation in which she had found herself especially on account of a complaint filed by her brother against her which was pending enquiry at that very police station. If these circumstances are taken into consideration it would be clear that the initiative for sexual intercourse must have come from the accused or any of them and she had to submit without any resistance... *Mere passive or helpless surrender of the body and its resignation to the other's lust induced by threats or fear cannot be equated with desire or will, nor can it furnish an answer by the mere fact that the sexual act was not in opposition to such desire or volition...* On the other hand, taking advantage of the fact that Mathura was involved in a complaint filed by her brother and that she was alone at the police station at the dead hour of night, it is more probable that the initiative for satisfying the sexual desire must have proceeded from the accused, and that victim Mathura must not have been a willing party to the act of the sexual intercourse. Her subsequent conduct in making a statement immediately not only to her relatives but also to the members of the crowd leaves no doubt that she was subjected to forcible sexual intercourse."

In relation to Tukaram, the High Court did not believe that he had made any attempt to rape the girl but took her word for granted insofar as he was alleged to have fondled her private parts after the act of sexual intercourse by Ganpat. It was in these premises that the High Court convicted and sentenced the two appellants.

***The Supreme Court held***

Her failure to appeal to her companions who were no others than her brother, her aunt and her lover, and her conduct in meekly following Ganpat and allowing him to have his way with her to the extent of satisfying his lust in full, makes us feel that the consent in question was not a consent which could be brushed aside as 'passive submission'.

Secondly, it has to be borne in mind that the onus is always on the prosecution to prove affirmatively each ingredient of the offence it seeks to establish and that such onus never shifts.

The circumstantial evidence available, therefore, is not only capable of being construed in a way different from that adopted by the High Court but actually derogates in no uncertain measure from the inference drawn by it.

In view of what we have said here, we conclude that the sexual intercourse in question is not proved to amount to rape and that no offence is brought home to Ganpat.

The High Court itself has taken note of the fact that in the First Information Report the girl had made against Tukaram serious allegations on which she had gone back at the trial and the acts covered by which she attributed in her deposition to Ganpat instead. Those allegations were that Tukaram who had caught hold of her in the first instance, had taken her to the latrine in the rear of the main building, had lit a torch and had stared at her private parts in the torch-light. Now if the girl could alter her position in regard to these serious allegations at will, where is the assurance that her word is truthful in relation to what she now says about Tukaram? We do not, therefore, propose to take the girl at her word in relation to Tukaram and hold that the charge remains wholly unproved against him.

The judgment of the High Court is reversed and the conviction recorded against as well as the sentences imposed upon the appellants by it are set aside."

There were several problems which the judgment highlighted including:

- the issue of consent
- the refusal to recognise that victims of violence rarely make consistent statements
- the reference to the girl's sexual history
- the reference to the two-finger test
- the question of on whom the burden of proof lies.

Some of these problems were dealt with by subsequent amendments in the law.

### Consent

The amended provisions which exist today in Section 376 of the Indian Penal Code and Section 114 A Evidence Act are a direct consequence of the outrage the Mathura judgment created.

***Section 376 of the Indian Penal Code says***

(1) Whoever, except in the cases provided for by subsection (2), commits rape shall be punished with imprisonment of either description for a term which shall not be less than seven years but which may be for life or for a term which may extend to ten years and shall also be liable to fine, unless the women raped is his own wife and is not under twelve years of age, in which case, he shall be punished with imprisonment of either description for a term which may extend to two years or with fine or with both although the Court may, for adequate and special reasons to be mentioned in the judgement, impose a sentence of imprisonment for a term of less than seven years.

(2) Whoever:

(a) being a police officer commits rape

(i) within the limits of the police station to which he is appointed or

(ii) in the premises of any station house whether or not situated in the police station to which he is appointed or

(iii) on a woman in his custody or in the custody of a police officer subordinate to him

(b) being a public servant takes advantage of his official position and commits rape on a woman in his custody as such public servant or in the custody of a public servant subordinate to him

(c) being on the management or on the staff of a gaol, remand home or other place of custody established by or under any law for the time being in force or of a woman's or children's institution takes advantage of his official position and commits rape on any inmate of such gaol, remand home, place or institution

(d) being on the management or on the staff of a hospital takes advantage of his official position and commits rape on a woman in that hospital

(e) rapes on a woman knowing her to be pregnant

(f) rapes on a woman when she is under twelve years of age

(g) commits gang-rape.

Shall be punished with rigorous imprisonment for a term which shall not be less than ten years but which may be for life and shall also be liable to fine although the Court may, for adequate and special reasons to be mentioned in the judgement, impose a sentence of imprisonment of either description for a term of less than ten years.

*Explanations*

- Where a woman is raped by one or more in a group of persons acting in furtherance of their common intention, each of the persons shall be deemed to have committed gang-rape within the meaning of Section 376 (2).

- 'Women's or children's institution' means an institution, whether called an orphanage or a home for neglected women or children or a widows' home or any other name, which is established and maintained for the reception and care of women or children.
- 'Hospital' means the precincts of the hospital and includes the precincts of any institution for the reception and treatment of persons during convalescence or of persons requiring medical attention or rehabilitation.

The offences specified in Section 376 of the Indian Penal Code are cognisable, non-bailable and non-compoundable. However, sexual intercourse by a man with his wife aged twelve or above twelve is non-cognisable, bailable and non-compoundable. All of the offences can be tried by a Court of Session.

The corresponding Section in the Evidence Act–114 A introduced in 1983–creates a presumption as to the absence of consent in certain prosecutions for rape. It says that in a prosecution for rape under Section 376 (2) of the Indian Penal Code–except in a case under Section 376 (2) (f)–where sexual intercourse by the accused is proved and the question is whether it was without the consent of the woman alleged to have been raped, if she states in her evidence before the Court that she did not consent, the Court shall presume that she did not consent.

Section 376 (2) (f), IPC has been excluded from the purview of Section 114 A of the Evidence Act since it deals with the consent a woman aged twelve or less which is anyway a crime under Section 375 of the Penal Code.

Also, Sections 376 A, 376 B, 376 C and 376 D[113] make provision for the following sexual offences:

- Intercourse by a man with his wife during separation without her consent.
- Intercourse not amounting to rape by a public servant with a woman in his custody.
- Intercourse not amounting to rape by a Superintendent of a gaol, remand home or other place of custody with a female inmate thereof.

- Intercourse not amounting to rape by any member of the management or staff of a hospital with any woman in that hospital.

The issue of consent has always been tricky not just in the legal arena but also in the social arena as is reflected in works of literature. For example, one of the central questions in *Tess of the d'Urbervilles* is whether or not she was raped. As John Sutherland said in *Is Heathcliffe a Murderer?*, "She who was seduced in 1892 is she who is raped in the permissive 1960s." This is how various commentators have described what happened to the heroine, Tess:

| | | |
|---|---|---|
| Seduction | 1932 | *The Oxford Companion to English Literature* |
| Seduction and rape | 1974 | *The Great Web* by Ian Gregor |
| Cunning seduction | 1984 | *The Oxford Companion to English Literature* |
| Seduction-cum-rape/virtual rape | 1993 | *The 1890s* edited by G.A. Cevasco |

The World's Classics editors used the ambiguous term *betrayed* and the non-felonious term *violated–violated,* as John Sutherland pointed out in his book, cannot land you a ten-year prison term, *rape* can.[114]

Thus, perceptions of what does and does not amount to rape have changed dramatically over time. This is also reflected in case law both in India and in other parts of the world, in definitions of rape and in the criteria which determine whether or not a woman has been raped.

In the Mathura case, the High Court spoke of Passive Consent which the Supreme Court refused to accept while in the US, the checklist developed by retired Air Force Lt. Col. Charles McDowell to determine whether or not a rape accusation is false made it virtually impossible for a woman in the US military to prove that she had been raped.[115]

However, in R v/s Z, 2000,[116] a man accused of rape said that he had obtained consent or, alternatively, that he believed that he had obtained consent. The testimony of four women who had earlier accused him of having raped them was used to rebut his defence even though he had been acquitted of having raped three of them. It was held that previous acquittals may be relevant in a subsequent case where the defendant is charged with rape. The House of Lords held that the principle of double jeopardy did not make relevant evidence inadmissible merely because it pointed towards the fact that the accused had previously been acquitted of a crime he was guilty of. The accused was in fact not placed in double jeopardy at all because the facts giving rise to the later prosecution differed from those in the earlier ones.[117]

And in 2005, a Court in Swansea told English women that Drunken Consent is consent while acquitting twenty-year-old Ryairi Dougal of raping a 21-year-old woman although that was probably understandable–the alleged victim admitted that she had been too drunk to remember whether or not she had consented to sex.[118]

**Sexual History**

Earlier, under Section 155 (4) of the Evidence Act which dealt with how the credit of a witness could be impeached, the adverse party or the party calling the witness (with the consent of the Court) could introduce the prior sexual history of the victim into evidence.

***Section 155 (4) read***

> When a man is prosecuted for rape or an attempt to ravish, it may be shown that the prosecutrix was of generally immoral character.

This Section was, however, repealed by the 2002 amendment of the Act and a proviso was added to *Section 144* which says:

> In a prosecution for rape or an attempt to commit rape, it shall not be permissible to put questions to the prosecutrix as to her general immoral character.

Both the National Commission for Women and the Law Commission in its 84th and 172nd Reports had recommended that this be done since:

- there is no connection between a woman's sexual history and her being raped
- unrestrained questioning leads to the reputation and self-respect of the victim being damaged and reduces her chances of marriage
- the victim's sexual history was used to demolish her testimony.

Prior to this, although the Supreme Court had held that although 'every latitude' should be given to the defence to test the veracity of the prosecutrix, it was the duty of the Court to ensure that a victim of a sex crime was not harassed or humiliated by the cross-examining lawyer.[119] However, there was not much that could be done to prevent the introduction of the victim's sexual history into evidence.

> *The eight following qualities are the characteristics of women: uttering lies, unsteadiness, deceit, stupidity, greed, impurity, wickedness and rashness.*
>
> *-Sukra [III.163]*

And for all practical purposes, a woman who was 'habituated' to sexual intercourse was less likely to see her rapist being punished and more likely to be accused of lying herself and/or of inflicting wounds on herself. Medical jurists like Modi, Lyon and Taylor virtually managed to construct a legal vagina as opposed to the real thing and, in the process, they made it ever more difficult to obtain convictions for rape. Pratiksha Baxi has described this as the 'medicalisation of falsity'. When it was discovered that the presence or absence of a hymen was not conclusive proof of virginity, jurists began differentiating between true and false virgins, and began to speak of how distensible the vaginal orifice is. Pipettes and other devices were inserted into women's vaginas and finally, there came the 'two-finger test'–if a woman's vagina admitted two fingers, she was assumed to be 'habituated to sexual intercourse' which was fine if she was married, but if she wasn't, it usually meant that her allegations of being raped wouldn't be believed.

### Technicalities

The procedural aspects of the law can sometimes be so technical that it is very easy for the prosecution to fail because of a technical snag. Even those laws which seem clear enough prima facie are sometimes interpreted extremely strictly.

For example, *Section 6* of the Indian Evidence Act speaks of those facts which are relevant because they form a part of the same transaction. It says:

> Facts which, though not in issue, are so connected with a fact in issue as to form part of the same transaction, are relevant, whether they occurred at the same time and place or at different times and places.
>
> **Illustration:**
>
> (a) A is accused of the murder of B by beating him. Whatever was said or done by A or B or the bystanders at the beating or so shortly or after it as to form part of the transaction, is a relevant fact.

'These facts are connected to each other in such a way that they may be referred to by a single legal name such as a crime or a contract. In a broad sense, a transaction is an act or a series of acts and the words which accompany those acts.'[120] The words–as can be seen from the illustration earlier–may be spoken by the person who has committed the act or by someone else: a bystander, in this illustration, for example.

It was under this Section that the exclamations of children at the time when their mother cried out for help as her husband pushed her into a room where he killed her were received through people who had heard them and were held to be a part of the same transaction in Sawaldas v/s State of Bihar, 1974.

And in Vinod v/s State of Uttar Pradesh, 1994, the facts that an accused had raped a woman, strangled her to death and then pleaded for forgiveness when he was caught while trying to run away were all held to be a part of the same transaction.

Thus, 'Res Gestae includes acts done from the inception of the principal act which constitutes the offence till the completion of the act. They grow out of the main fact, are usually contemporaneous with it and illustrate its character.' A subsequent narration of facts does not constitute Res Gestae.[121]

For example, the statement of a six-year-old girl to her mother about a rape she had been subjected to was held not to be a fact contemplated by this Section in Indu v/s State of Himachal Pradesh, 1989.

The test of whether or not a statement may be considered to be relevant under Section 6 is spontaneity i.e. the following questions should be answered in the affirmative:

- Is the even speaking for itself through the instinctive words of the participants or the witnesses?
- Are the facts speaking though the words of the speaker (as opposed to the speaker narrating the events later on)?

However, the judiciary has been becoming more active and sensitive to the needs of victims. Rohtas District and Sessions Judge Arun Kumar Srivastava, for example, completed a trial in five hours in 2006; he found the accused guilty of attempting to rape a five-year-old girl and sentenced him to rigorous imprisonment for five years. In this case, the victim and her eight-year-old brother had been on their way to collect grass for cattle when the incident occurred. The accused (Deo, aged 30) lured them to a secluded poultry farm with a five-rupee note and attempted to rape the girl there; villagers heard the children cry though and rescued them. Initially, both village elders and the Officer in Charge of the Police Station where the girl's father tried to lodge a complaint advised him to 'compromise'. Following his refusal to do so, the accused's uncle assaulted him. A complaint was then filed against both the accused and his uncle (for attempted rape and assault respectively).[122]

And in October 2006, Justices S.B. Sinha and Dalveer Bhandari of the Supreme Court held that Courts can alter police charges to convict an accused. The Bench said this in a case in which the accused (Tarkeshwar Sahu) dragged a twelve-year-old girl to a nearby house and attempted to rape her on July 18, 1998. He was caught by people who intervened on hearing the girl's cries and prevented the rape being committed. The problem was that police charged the accused under Sections 376 (rape) and 511 (an attempt to commit an offence punishable with life imprisonment) of the Indian Penal Code instead of charging him with attempted rape, and so, it appeared that he would evade punishment on account of a technicality. The Supreme Court, however, modified the charges by applying Section 222 of the Criminal Procedure Code and convicted the accused for kidnapping the girl and outraging her modesty under Sections 366 and 354 of the Indian Penal Code.[123]

The judiciary has also been trying to make the application of laws less technical and also to hasten the process of dispensing justice even though there are, obviously, times when there is little that the law, even at its most sensitive, can do to correct what has been done.

In January 2004, a thirteen-year-old girl was allegedly raped by two Sadhus: Baba Balak Das himself and Baba Omkar Yadav at the Matadev Ashram located near Bamaur (under Rannaud Police Station) in the State of Madhya Pradesh. She was offered Prasaad laced with sedatives by the supposed man of God, thirty-year-old Baba Balak Das when she had gone to deliver food to him and the other Sadhu at the Ashram (in whose agricultural fields her father, Dhooman Lodhi worked). According to a PTI report which appeared in the Indian Express,[124] she subsequently lost her eyesight because of some form of *medicine* she consumed to induce an abortion subsequent to the rape. The Superintendent of Police, Anshuman Yadav said that Balak Das had been arrested from Vichoniya village while Omkar Yadav was picked up from Aakoda village. I wouldn't dare to estimate how much consolation that was to the girl though.*

## PROSTITUTION AND TRAFFICKING

*Shall we accept the fact that certain women and children, primarily girls, often those who are most economically and ethnically marginalized, are treated as a lower class, whose purpose is to serve men sexually?*

*— Former Swedish Minister of Gender Equality, Margareta Winberg*[125]

A prostitute is a woman who offers her body to indiscriminate sexual intercourse, especially for hire.[126] To commit an act of prostitution, 'a woman should surrender her body for monetary consideration to someone who is not legally entitled to have sexual intercourse with her'.[127]

Prostitution shouldn't exist in an ideal society but the fact is that we don't live in a society which even remotely resembles a Utopian one, and as such, I believe that prostitution should be legalised since that would at the very least be a mechanism to afford some sort of protection to sex-workers who are, as a group, vulnerable to abuse and exploitation particularly since they are rarely accorded any sort of societal recognition or respect.*

I've been told by a close friend who used to work in an NGO which focussed on rescuing and rehabilitating prostitutes that the legalisation of prostitution works only in theory though; in practise, it does nothing but legalise the extremely exploitative sex industry, and make it far more difficult to prosecute pimps and traffickers.*

The willingness to treat prostitutes inhumanly isn't a problem that is limited to India though. In 2004, researchers in Africa and Cambodia were reportedly conducting experiments on prostitutes to determine if Gilead Sciences Inc.'s drug *Viread* could be used as an AIDS prevention pill. Some of the prostitutes involved were to take placebos while others were to take the drug to see which–if either–group contracted the HIV virus more readily.[128]

The Immoral Traffic (Prevention) Act, 1956 was enacted in pursuance of the International Convention signed at New York on May 9, 1950. Most of the provisions of this Act came into force on May 1, 1958.

The Immoral Traffic Prevention Act, 1986 which now governs prostitution does not make prostitution itself illegal. It makes a lot of the allied activities–such as trafficking and pimping–illegal but commercial sex workers are often treated like criminals with no rights nonetheless. Even as it stands today, the Act has failed in its objective–it tends to create human rights abuses and does little to prevent them.*

***Indian Courts have held that***

- Any person who keeps or maintains or acts or assists in the keeping and management of a brothel is liable to be punished.[129]

***Although***

- A solitary instance of prostitution in a place does not make the place a 'brothel'.[130]
- The residence of a single woman who practices prostitution for her own livelihood does not amount to a brothel.[131]

An order to a prostitute to remove herself from the limits of a busy city under the provisions of the Suppression of Immoral Traffic in Women and Girls Act, 1956, and the placing of restrictions on where she could live/move was held to be reasonable in State of Uttar Pradesh v/s Kaushalya, 1964.[132]

> *The false embrace of a woman who sells herself for money is like trying to find pleasure in the embrace of a dead body of an unknown person in a dark room.*
>
> *– Tiru-Valluvar c. 100 AD*

What I'd like to see is an Act which differentiates between prostitution and trafficking and ensures that prostitutes who are vulnerable enough as it is aren't further exploited. The Immoral Traffic Prevention Act might as well have made prostitution illegal since it criminalises the activities required to carry it out and does nothing to help prostitutes. It makes it illegal to solicit in public places, keep a brothel or allow premises to be used as a brothel.

In addition to this, the law punishes a person for living on the earnings of prostitution by saying that any person over the age of eighteen years who knowingly lives, wholly or in part, on the earnings of prostitution shall be punishable with imprisonment. If her partner, parent or adult child is dependent on her income for survival, they are liable to prosecution under Section 4 of the Immoral Traffic Prevention Act.

Prostitution is very closely allied with though not the same as trafficking which is prohibited by the Constitution. *(See page **Error! Bookmark not defined.** 6)* 'Traffic in human beings' means selling and buying of men and women like goods and includes immoral traffic in women and children for immoral or other purposes.'[133] The UN Protocol on Trafficking says that it involves the recruitment, movement or transportation of a person through force, deception fraud or violence into a site of exploitative work. Although not all trafficking is sex trafficking, the link between prostitution and trafficking is comparable to the link which existed between slavery in America and kidnapping in Africa.

There have been proposals to amend the Immoral Traffic Prevention Act. For example, it has been proposed to scrap Section 8 of the Act which deals with the offence of solicitation. However, the proposed amendments do not seem to recognise the difference between trafficking and prostitution.

What I find most disturbing is that some of the proposed amendments–Sections 5A, 5B and 5C–not only fail to segregate trafficking from sex work but in fact integrate the two. I think that that's a differentiation which should be made, and that the definition of pimps should be made wider. For example, it should include 'marriage-brokers' who arrange the kind of marriages where women are made *wives* but treated as unpaid servants by day and sex-slaves by night. As they stand right now, although the amendments might do a little good, they are far more likely to a lot of harm.'

The Supreme Court has held that 'it is the duty of the State and all voluntary non-Government organizations and public spirited persons' to come to the aid of sex workers and 'to retrieve them from prostitution, rehabilitate them with a helping hand to lead a life with dignity of their person'.[134]

Nina Shapiro pointed out in *The New Abolitionists,* "Freeing 'sex slaves' is now at the top of the human rights agenda."[135] In fact, in 2003, Bush became the first President to address the UN

General Assembly about the need to deal with the problem of trafficking although his words were eclipsed by his take on Iraq and the fact that the US doesn't have an impressive record as far as signing international human rights conventions–such as the Convention on the Elimination of All Forms of Discrimination against Women–is concerned.

However, pressure from the US seems to have prompted the Indian Government to support the Immoral Traffic Prevention Amendment Act, 2006 despite its flaws. The US passed the Trafficking in Victims Protection Act in 2000 under which there is provision for an annual evaluation of the anti-trafficking efforts of over a hundred and fifty countries and their classification into three tiers by a Task Force.

In *The Natashas,* Victor Malarek called them *Crocodile Tiers.* This is how they work: those countries that have met the minimum standards to fight trafficking are placed in Tier 1; those that have not yet done so but are making efforts in that direction are placed in Tier 2, while those that have neither met the minimum standards nor made significant efforts to do so are placed in Tier 3, and being placed in Tier 3 involves the withdrawal of US non-humanitarian, non-trade related aid as well as US opposition to non-humanitarian assistance from international financial assistance.

One of the main problems with these Tiers has been that determining which Tier a country belongs to appears to involve political and other considerations. Lisa Thompson of the Initiative against Sexual Trafficking, a coalition headed by the Salvation Army, has (among others) said that the tiers shouldn't be used to manipulate political debates or international relationships. There have been many indications that this is precisely what has been happening though.

India was placed in Tier 2 in 2006. USAID, which sits on the Task Force, has an explicit policy of refusing funds to HIV/AIDS or anti-trafficking projects to 'organisations advocating prostitution as an employment choice or which advocate or support the legalisation of prostitution'.[136]

There are some provisions in the Indian Penal Code to try to curb trafficking and prostitution. They include:

| Section | |
|---|---|
| 366 | Kidnapping, abducting or inducing a woman to compel her marriage, or in order that she may be forced or seduced to illicit intercourse or knowing it to be likely that she will be so forced or inducing, by means of criminal intimidation or of abuse of authority or any other method of compulsion, any woman to go from any place for any of the purposes mentioned earlier |
| 366 A | Procuration of a minor girl |
| 366 B | Importation of a girl from foreign country |
| 367 | Kidnapping or abducting in order to subject person to grievous hurt, slavery, or to unnatural lust |
| 372 | Selling a minor for purposes of prostitution or illicit intercourse with any person or for any unlawful and immoral purpose |
| 373 | Buying a minor for purposes of prostitution, or illicit intercourse with any person or for any unlawful and immoral purpose |

The punishment for each of these offences is imprisonment of either description–simple or rigorous–for a term which may extend to ten years and, possibly, a fine. Also, it is enough if the accused knows that the woman involved is likely to be subjected to any of these offences for him to be guilty of having committed the offence itself.

None of these provisions which deal with prostitution in Indian Law expressly make prostitution illegal though. The result is that the Indian Government has been scrambling to amend the Immoral Traffic Prevention Act.

Victor Malarek has pointed out that 'what happens to most trafficked women whether they are tricked, abducted or willing is criminal. The level of physical violence and psychological intimidation used to control them is deliberate and extreme. It is meant to instil fear, destroy their will, and force them to comply.'[137]

And even assuming that they do 'consent' to being used as prostitutes, my own belief is that *consent* is inseparably entwined with *choice* and as such, that it exists only where viable alternatives exist. Giving in to the inevitable or the unavoidable gracefully is not the same as *consenting* to it.

What is most shocking though is that, in India, parents are often involved in trafficking. In the State of Andhra Pradesh, for example, the National Human Rights Commission estimates that parents may have sold their daughters into prostitution in as many as *eighty* per cent of child trafficking cases. A CNN IBN report on January 27, 2007 said that girls were sold for between twelve and fifteen thousand INR.

## Migration and Indirect Trafficking[138]

Women who have entered a society alien to them are especially vulnerable to being subjected to exploitation and violence since they often do not know their rights and even if they do, they may not know how to protect themselves.

'Mass migrations due to poverty, pauperisation and prejudice ensure that rootlessness, ethnic tensions and violent lawlessness are a feature of nearly every city of the developed democratic world,'[139] and one of the manifestations of this phenomenon is that those who are violent at home now have access to a market of both women who are illegally trafficked and women who migrate, whether or not legally, to India primarily from Bangladesh and other neighbouring countries.

Moreover, women who migrate to marry 'threaten' the local women, particularly those who are already married, because their husbands may divorce them in favour of (younger) migrants thus often leaving them in poverty after decades of marriage.

Both human rights law and (the majority position in) refugee law now acknowledge State responsibility for human rights violations such as family violence which has become one of the most visible (and prolific) emerging bodies of refugee case law.[140]

*(See 'lesser wives' on page 17.)*

## NOTES

1. Bunch, Charlotte; The Intolerable Status Quo: Violence Against Women And Girls; www.unicef.org/pon97/women1.htm.
2. Flessas, Panagiotis; Gender Equality as 'practice': towards an emerging European Liberalism; POROS EU Law Seminar; May 24, 2005.
3. This is from an essay on 'Domestic Violence against Women and Children in the European Union' written under the guidance of Yannis Boudouris.
4. Article 2; The Declaration of the Elimination of Violence Against Women, 1993.
5. Article 1; The UN Declaration on the Elimination of Violence against Women.
6. ACT 40/001/2001.
7. Ending Violence against Women was based on over 50 population surveys and was published in early 2000.
8. Cook, Dickens, Fathalla; Reproductive Health And Human Rights: Integrating Medicine, Ethics And Law; Oxford; 2003.
9. Article 2; The Declaration of the Elimination of Violence Against Women, 1993.
10. http://timesofindia.indiatimes.com/articleshow/425247.cms.
11. www.gujaratsamachar.com/gsa/20040201/eng/gujarat/news2.html.
12. http://timesofindia.indiatimes.com/articleshow/1307459.cms.
13. Section 3; The Prenatal Diagnostic Techniques Act, 1994.
14. Section 4; The Prenatal Diagnostic Techniques Act, 1994.
15. Section 5; The Prenatal Diagnostic Techniques Act, 1994.
16. Section 6; The Prenatal Diagnostic Techniques Act, 1994.
17. Sections 7 and 16; The Prenatal Diagnostic Techniques Act, 1994.
18. Section 17; The Prenatal Diagnostic Techniques Act, 1994.
19. Section 18; The Prenatal Diagnostic Techniques Act, 1994.
20. Section 22; The Prenatal Diagnostic Techniques Act, 1994.
21. Section 27; The Prenatal Diagnostic Techniques Act, 1994.
22. Section 24; The Prenatal Diagnostic Techniques Act, 1994.
23. Section 31; The Prenatal Diagnostic Techniques Act, 1994.
24. Section 32; The Prenatal Diagnostic Techniques Act, 1994.

25. Three get Death in Honour Killings Case; The Times of India; 9.9.2006.
26. 1992 CrLJ 2954 (Mad).
27. AIR 1992 SC 2027.
28. 1992 CrLJ 502 (Karn).
29. 1995 CrLJ 1429 (Karn).
30. AIR 1991 SC 1738.
31. 2000 CrLJ 3055 (All).
32. http://web.amnesty.org/library/index/ENGIOR410042004.
33. 2002 CrLJ 3625 (AP).
34. While sailing for Troy, the Greeks somehow managed to offend the Goddess of the Hunt: Artemis (Diana). In her anger, Artemis kept the Greek fleet in the bay of Aulis and prevented it from sailing to Troy, and so, in order to appease her, the prophet Calchas advised Agamemnon to sacrifice his daughter Iphigenia to the Goddess.

    Agamemnon followed the advice but he was not honest about his intention to sacrifice Iphigenia: he told both his daughter and his wife Clytemnestra whose name means 'praiseworthy wooing' that he intended to get her to marry the famous warrior Achilles. It was only much later that they realized what he'd actually planned and not too surprisingly, both Clytemnestra and Achilles objected to the plan, but Agamemnon–true to his name which means 'very resolute'–did not change his mind.

    Iphigenia too initially pleaded for her life saying, "... to gaze upon the light is man's most cherished gift; that life below is nothingness, and whoever longs for death is mad. Better live a life of woe than die a death of glory! (Iphigenia to Agamemnon, Euripides, Iphigenia in Aulis 1250) while Clytemnestra asked Agamemnon: "...suppose you sacrifice the child, what prayer will you utter, when it is done? What will the blessing be that you will invoke upon yourself as you are slaying our daughter?" (Euripides, Iphigenia in Aulis 1185).

    The interesting thing about Iphigenia's story is that there are two versions: in one she is actually killed while being sacrificed but in the other, the Goddess Artemis transported her to Taurus, a city on the Black Sea where she was to serve as a priestess and she replaced Iphigenia herself with an animal which was sacrificed.

In the process, although the Greek fleet managed to sail to Troy, Iphigenia was lost to her mother. And while Agamemnon went on to win the battle of Troy, and bring home Cassandra whose name means 'she who entangles men', one of the daughters of the king and queen of Troy, as a concubine, Clytemnestra had an affair with Aegisthus.

When Agamemnon returned to Mycenae from the Trojan War, Cassandra saw the danger he was in since she had been given the gift of prophecy by the God Apollo who had wanted to seduce her. However, when she refused his advances he deprived her of the power of persuasion and so she was unable to convince anyone of what she saw. As a result, her prophecy was ignored by Agamemnon and both she herself and Agamemnon were murdered by Clytemnestra and her lover Aegisthus. In his play, The Libation Bearers (c. 460 BCE) Aeschylus says that Clytemnestra later used the sacrifice of Iphigenia to justify the murder of Agamemnon even though Iphigenia may not actually have died.

Some sources say that she served as the priestess at the Temple of Artemis at Taurus where she had to perform barbaric customs such as sending strangers to be butchered at the Goddess' altar. However, she firmly believed that it was the people who were in the wrong and she said, "Men of this country, being murderers, impute their sordid practice to divine command. That any god is evil I do not believe." (Euripides, Iphigenia in Tauris 390).

Aegisthus then ruled Mycenae with Clytemnestra until both of them were murdered seven years later by Agamemnon's son Orestes who was helped by his sister Electra. The Erinyes or Furies followed Orestes everywhere he went after his having killed his mother right up to the time he sought judgment and was subsequently acquitted for the crime at the Aeropagus in Athens. In addition to killing Clytemnestra and her lover Aegisthus, Orestes is also said to have helped his sister Iphigenia escape more than twenty years after she was sacrificed to Diana.*

35. Davis Kirsten; The Development of Criseyde in Troilus and Criseyde.
36. Metropolitan Police Service-Domestic Violence Advertising Campaign; www.Met.Police.Uk/Dv/.
37. Gender Mainstreaming and Gender Based Violence and Trafficking in Women; The Daphne Programmes; europa.eu.int/

comm/employment_social/gender_equality/gender_mainstreaming/violence/domestic_violence_en.html; europa.eu.int/scadplus/leg/en/lvb/l33062.htm; europa.eu.int/scadplus/leg/en/lvb/l33299.htm.

38. Saikia, Nandita; 'Domestic Violence against Women and Children in the European Union'; POROS Project; 2006.
39. Report of the Committee on India Vision 2020, Planning Commission, Government of India (December, 2002); Statement referred to in reply to Rajya Sabha starred question no. 230 for 17.12.2003 regarding amendments in sections 406 and 498 A of the IPC.

    http://164.100.24.219/annex/200/AS230.htm; In India, Domestic Violence Rises with Education by Swapna Majumdar (WeNews, June 11, 2003); Domestic abuse hits India's elite by Geeta Pandey (BBC, May, 30 2003); Private Concerns in Public Discourse by Nandita Bhatla and Anuradha Rajan (EPW, April 26, 2003); Dowry Laws by Nandita Saikia (Panorama, A TakingITGlobal online publication, Jan 31, 2005); India: Report of the Malimath Committee on Reforms of the Criminal Justice System: Some observations by Amnesty International (September, 19 2003).

    http://web.amnesty.org/library/index/engasa200252003.
40. (1919) 42 Mad 547 (FB).
41. 1988 CrLJ 1916 (Ori).
42. 1996 CrLJ 27 (Bom)
43. A few websites such as that of WADV and the American Bar Association therefore provide information to battered women on just how to cover their tracks on the Internet while seeking online assistance.
44. President K.R. Narayanan's Address On The Eve Of Republic Day, 2002.
45. 1994 CrLJ 4372 (P&H) (FB).
46. Batra, Bikram J; Misuse of 498 A – Much Ado About Nothing?; Aawaaz; March 2004; www.indiatogether.org/2004/mar/law-sect498a.htm.
47. Kishwar, Madhu; Laws against Domestic Violence: Underused or Abused?; Manushi; Issue No. 120, September-October 2000; www.indiatogether.org/manushi/issue120/domestic.htm.
48. 1995 CrLJ 3939 (Bom).

49. Statement referred to in reply to Rajya Sabha starred question no. 230 for 17.12.2003 regarding amendments in Sections 406 and 498 A of the IPC http://164.100.24.219/annex/200/AS230.htm.
50. President K.R. Narayanan's Address On The Eve Of Republic Day, 2002.
51. Mahapatra, Dhananjay; Dowry gets a New Definition, Thanks to SC; The Times of India; 15.1.2007.
52. Statement of Objects and Reasons; The Dowry Prohibition Act, 1961.
53. Rao, Mohan; Karva Chauth Capitalism; The Times of India; 26.10.2006.
54. Deshpande, Swati; Court can Frame Accused on Two Counts; The Times of India; 14.8.2006.
55. www.hindu.com/2006/11/13/stories/2006111308210500.htm.
56. Mahapatra, Dhananjay; Kin of the Accused must be Quizzed: SC; The Times of India; 16.10.2006.
57. Letter (No. 2729/60-3-06/6 AQ/2000 dated 2.9.2006 as reported in www .hindustantimes.com/news/5922_1820131,0015002500000005.htm.
58. Sant Gopal v State of Uttar Pradesh, 1995 CrLJ 312 (All).
59. (1923) Lah 451.
60. (1934) 16 Lah 589.
61. AIR 1939 PC 47.
62. 1948 All 122.
63. AIR 1984 SC 1622.
64. 2002 CrLJ 4095.
65. AIR 1976 SC 1519.
66. AIR 1999 SC 1773.
67. Narpat Singh v State of Rajasthan, 1990 CrLJ 2720 (Raj.)
68. State of Karnataka v Shariff, AIR 2003 SC 1074.
69. AIR 1999 SC 2571.
70. Nallam V Stayanandham v The Public Prosecutor, AP 2004 (2) SCALE 659.
71. Shukla, Rakesh; Multiple testimonies by victims of gender violence; Info Change News & Features, September 2006; www.infochangeindia.org/analysis139.jsp.

72. First case under domestic violence Act filed; The Times of India; 29.10.2006.

73. Mahapatra, Dhananjay; In First Domestic Violence Ruling, man to pay Rs. 1.5 Lakh; The Times of India; 23.5.2007.

74. Saikia, Nandita; 'Domestic Violence against Women and Children in the European Union'; POROS Project; 2006.

75. Former UN Secretary-General Kofi Annan's message on the International Day for the Elimination of Violence against Women observed on 25.11.1005; www.un.org/News/Press/docs/2005/sgsm10225.doc.htm

76. Saikia, Nandita; 'Domestic Violence against Women and Children in the European Union'; POROS Project; 2006.

77. Datta, Nonica; You Have Options; Tehelka; 20.1.2007.

78. Section 2; The Commission of Sati (Prevention) Act, 1987.

79. Section 2; The Commission of Sati (Prevention) Act, 1987.

80. Section 4; The Commission of Sati (Prevention) Act, 1987.

81. Section 3; The Commission of Sati (Prevention) Act, 1987.

82. Section 4; The Commission of Sati (Prevention) Act, 1987.

83. Section 2; The Commission of Sati (Prevention) Act, 1987.

85. 2002 CrLJ 3772 (SC).

86. timesofindia.indiatimes.com/articleshow/425550.cms.

87. In the name of the witch and Stop the Witch-Hunt; www.frontlineonnet.com/fl1723/17230870.htm,www. infochangeindia.org/Womenlstory.jsp?recordno=74& section_idv=1.

88. Mikes, George; How to be a Brit; André Deutsch; 1984 (They fail to see why sweating topless waitresses should put you off food and sex at one and the same time... They are misled by their noble democratic principles which proclaim that justice must not only be done but must be seen to be done. They think that it applies to the female organ, too. It must not only be there; it must be seen to be there.)

89. Rajagopalachari C (trans.); Tirukkural c. 100 AD; Bharatiya Vidya Bhawan; 2002.

90. Malarek, Victor; The Natashas; Arcade Publishing; 2003.

91. AIR 1965 SC 881.

92. Section 2; Indecent Representation of Women (Prohibition) Act, 1986.

93. Section 3; Indecent Representation of Women (Prohibition) Act, 1986.
94. Section 4; Indecent Representation of Women (Prohibition) Act, 1986.
95. Section 5; Indecent Representation of Women (Prohibition) Act, 1986.
96. Section 6; Indecent Representation of Women (Prohibition) Act, 1986.
97. Suraiya, Jug; Risque and Porn: Can I& B tell the difference?; The Times of India; 21.1.2007.
98. Exhibited at the Salon des Refuses; 1863.
99. (1996) 4 SCC 1
100. Jensen, Robert; Cruel to be Hard: Men and Pornography; Sexual Assault Report; January/February 2004.
101. Jensen, Robert; Cruel to be Hard: Men and Pornography; Sexual Assault Report; January/February 2004.
102. AIR 1997 SC 1906.
103. Kerr v. Kennedy [1942] 1KB 409.
104. Spicer v. Spicer [1954] 1 WLR 1051.
105. Constitutional Provisions

     **Article 15.** Prohibition of discrimination on grounds of religion, race, caste, sex or place of birth:

     (1) The State shall not discriminate against any citizen on only of religion, race, caste, sex, place of birth or any of them.

     (3) Nothing in this article shall prevent the State from making any special provision for women and children.

     **Article 42.** Provision for just and humane conditions of work and maternity relief:

     The State shall make provision for securing just and humane conditions of work and for maternity relief.

     **Article 51A.** Fundamental duties:

     It shall be the duty of every citizen of India: (a) to abide by the Constitution and respect its ideals and institutions; (e) to promote harmony and the spirit of common brotherhood amongst all the people of India transcending religious, linguistic and regional or sectional diversities; and to renounce practices derogatory to the dignity of women.

**Article 51.** Promotion of international peace and security:

The State shall endeavour to (c) foster respect for international law and treaty obligations in the dealings of organised people with one another.

**Article 253.** Legislation for giving effect to international agreements:

Parliament has power to make any law for the whole or any part of the territory of India for implementing any treaty, agreement or convention with any other country or countries or any decision made at any international conference, association or other body.

**Seventh Schedule; List I, Union List 14.** Entering into treaties and agreements with foreign countries and implementing of treaties, agreements and conventions with foreign countries.

106. 'Human rights' are defined in the Protection of Human Rights Act, 1993 as those rights relating to life, liberty, equality and dignity of the individual guaranteed under the Constitution or embodied in the International Covenants–i.e. the International Covenant on Civil and Political Rights and the International Covenant on Economic, Social and Cultural Rights adopted by the General Assembly of the United Nations on the 16th December, 1966–and enforceable by Courts in India.

107. Jintu Das v State of Assam, 2003 CrLJ 1411 (Gau)

108. Mahapatra, Dhananjay; Sex with Girl on False Promise of Marriage is Rape: SC; The Times of India; 3.10.2006.

109. 2003 CrLJ 392.

110. (1995) 1 SCC 14.

111. AIR 2000 SC 988.

112. (1996) 1 SCC 490.

113. **376A. Intercourse by a man with his wife during separation:** Whoever has sexual intercourse with his own wife, who is living separately from him under a decree of separation or under any custom or usage without her consent shall be punished with imprisonment of either description for a term which may extend to two years and shall also be liable to fine.

**376B. Intercourse by public servant with woman in his custody:** Whoever, being a public servant, takes advantage of his official position and induces or seduces, any woman, who is in his custody as such public servant or in the custody of a public servant subordinate to him, to have sexual intercourse with him, such sexual intercourse not amounting to the offence of rape, shall be punished with imprisonment of either description for a term which may extend to five years and shall also be liable to fine.

**376C. Intercourse by superintendent of jail, remand home, etc.:** Whoever, being the superintendent or manager of a jail, remand home or other place of custody established by or under any law for the time being in force or of a woman's or children's institution takes advantage of his official position and induces or seduces any female inmate of such jail, remand home, place or institution to have sexual intercourse with him, such sexual intercourse not amounting to the offence of rape, shall be punished with imprisonment of either description for a term which may extend to five years and shall also be liable to fine.

*Explanation 1*—"Superintendent" in relation to jail, remand home or other place of custody or a women's or-children's institution includes a person holding any other office in such jail, remand home, place or institution by virtue of which he can exercise any authority or control over its inmates.

*Explanation 2*—The expression "women's or children's institution" shall have the same meaning as in Explanation to sub-section (2) of section 376.

376D. Intercourse by any member of the management or staff of a hospital with any woman in that hospital:

Whoever, being on the management of a hospital or on the staff of a hospital takes advantage of his position and has sexual intercourse with any woman in that hospital, such sexual intercourse not amounting to the offence of rape, shall be punished with imprisonment of either description for a term which may extend to five years and shall also be liable to fine.

*Explanation*—The expression "hospital" shall have the same meaning as in Explanation to sub-section (2) of section 376.

114. Sutherland, John; Is Heathcliffe a Murderer?; Oxford University Press; 1996.

115. Lydersen, Kari; www.alternet.org/rights/19134/; July 2004; Alter Net.

116. (2000) All ER 385.

117. On a slightly different note, Ann Ming–the mother of a woman whose daughter, Julie, had been murdered at 22–made legal history in September 2006 by having William Dunlop, the man

who murdered her daughter, retried even though he had earlier been formally acquitted.

118. www.telegraph.co.uk/news/main.jhtml?xml=/news/2005/11 24/npubs124.xml
119. State of Punjab v Gurmit Singh, AIR 1996 SC 1393.
120. Ratanlal and Dhirajlal; The Law of Evidence; Wadhwa; 21st Edition.
121. Ratanlal and Dhirajlal; The Law of Evidence; Wadhwa; 21st Edition.
122. No Fast Track Court This but the Fastest; The Times of India; 21.10.2006.
123. Court can alter police charges to convict accused; The Times of India; 12.10.2006.
124. 19.1.2004
125. Farley, Melissa; action.web.ca/home/catw/readingroom.shtml?x =81265;January 2006.
126. Razia v State of Uttar Pradesh, AIR 1957 All 340.
127. Emperor v Lalya Bapu Jadhav, AIR 1929 Bombay 266.
128. www.cp.org/english/online/full/health/040714/x071432A. html;
129. State of Rajasthan v Mst.Wahida, 1981 Rajasthan Criminal Cases 42.
130. Sushila v State of Tamil Nadu, 1982 CrLJ 702 (Madras).
131. Ratnamala; AIR 1962 Madras 31.
132. AIR 1964 SC 416.
133. Raj Bahaduar v Legal Remembrancer, AIR 1953 Cal 522.
134. Gaurav Jain vs. Union of India; AIR 1997 SC 3021
135. www.seattleweekly.com/features/0434/040825_news_slavery. php
136. Kapur, Ratna; Long Way to Go; Times of India; 8.1.2007.
137. Malarek, Victor; The Natashas; Arcade Publishing; 2003.
138. Saikia, Nandita; 'Domestic Violence against Women and Children in the European Union'; POROS Project; 2006.
139. Keane, John Keane; Reflections On Violence; Oxford; 1996.
140. Anker, Deborah E.; Refugee Law, Gender, And The Human Rights Paradigm; Harvard Human Rights Journal; Volume 15 Spring 2002.

# PART - III

## PROTECTION

*Men who do or at least are capable of doing no end of mischief, are let loose, and the innocent women shut up in the Zenana.*
*– Rokeya Shekhawat Hossain*

In her book, *The Nine Parts of Desire*, Geraldine Brooks said that in Islamic countries, women were believed to have been given nine parts of desire while men were given just one; they therefore had to be controlled. In the West, however, women were deemed to be too *pure* to have sexual desires; *they* therefore had to be protected from the uncontrolled lust of men. Either way, as she pointed out, women wound up with the short end of the stick.

> *What is 'immorality' other than pretence with which to qualify one's prejudice against another?*
> *– zipsix.com*

By and large, the average Indian man–and society in general, for that matter–divides women into two groups: sluts and sisters. There's very little middle ground.

As far as the judiciary is concerned, its perception of women in general while not being blatantly discriminatory has usually been Victorian; although the judiciary has taken some extremely progressive steps to realise women's rights, it has often seen women as pure or impure, chaste or unchaste. And the average Indian woman is considered pure, unblemished and in need of protection. She 'occupies a respected position in society as a mother, a wife, companion and a social worker'.[1]

In an unequal society, I suppose women do need protection but if the past has taught us anything, it's that it's all too easy for protection to turn into control.

Illustrating the connections between '(actual) violence and (ostensible) protection' is the Pune Hysterectomies Scandal; hysterectomies were routinely performed on the female inmates of an institution for mentally-disabled women in the city of Pune.[2]

The logic was that the performance of hysterectomies was the only *solution* which could kill two birds with one stone: it ensured that the staff didn't have to deal with the hygiene of the women when they had their period–mentally-disabled or not, menstruating women are considered impure and cannot traditionally enter kitchens etc.–*and* it *protected* the women from unwanted pregnancies (even though it did nothing to protect them from unwanted sexual abuse).

Even if protection is available, it isn't always easy to access. The formal legal system is difficult to deal with even at the best of times. And the 'protection' it provides is sometimes rather distasteful even if it is effective.

For example, one of the defences open to women who kill violent husbands is Battered Women's Syndrome but to avail of this defence, the woman involved first has to prove that she was so psychologically affected at the time that she was incapable of rational thought. I find that particularly unpalatable since, by extension, it means that the woman has to demean/ degrade herself before she becomes worthy of either understanding or sympathy.

Suzanne Levitt, a legal theorist, has suggested that Battered Women's Syndrome be interpreted differently: the woman involved did not react to violence with violence because of being a psychological wreck devoid of reason, but because reason dictated that she do what she had to do to survive. It's an interpretation I'd like to see applied.

We've already firmly established a society in which the 'sanctity of marriage' and the 'welfare of the family' (and its 'honour') take precedence over the happiness and safety of women. The average Indian woman might need to be either dead or dying before she receives societal support; she shouldn't also have to be demented before she is able to receive justice from Courts.

## CONSTITUTIONAL PROVISIONS

The Constitution of India came into force in 1949. It contains a number of Articles which speak of women's rights. However, it recognises pre-constitutional laws provided that they (like post-constitutional laws) do not violate or infringe on any of the Fundamental Rights listed in Part III of the Constitution.[3]

One of the main problems which this recognition of pre-constitutional laws has created in the legal arena when it comes to the prevention of discrimination against and the protection of women within the family is that is ensures the existence and recognition of 'Personal Laws' in India which the British 'respected' during the Raj so as not to 'antagonise' Indians.

For the most part, the laws which the British enacted are designed to operate in the public sphere and deal with matters such as trade and commerce.

Personal Laws, on the other hand, are basically laws which operate in the private domain, govern personal relationships and are, by and large, based on religious considerations. They were first recognised by the British in Warren Hastings' Judicial Plan of 1772. All of the (then newly constituted) Diwani Adalats or Civil Courts were given instructions which said that 'in all suits regarding inheritance, marriage, caste and all other religious usages or institutions, the laws of the Koran with respect to the Mohametans, and those of the Shaster with respect to the Gentoos, shall invariably be adhered to'.

The concept of Personal Laws is not unique to India–they were also seen in Europe after the fall of the Roman Empire till about the 10th Century AD during which time, each tribe–such as the Visigoth, Lombard and Burgundian–retained its own Tribal Law.[4]

The root of the division between private religious laws and public secular laws is probably the separation of different spheres of life recognised in the West–such as that between the Church and the State–which is alien to ancient Indian jurisprudence and philosophy.

After achieving independence, different states have treated Personal Laws differently but they have almost always been upheld. In 1952, the Bombay High Court held them to be immune from Constitutional challenge on the ground that they violate the right to equality.[5]

Although Article 44 of the Constitution envisages the formulation of a Uniform Civil Code to apply to all Indians,[6] such a Code is nowhere near coming into being. And, as Indira Jaisingh has pointed out, "Since the participation of women in the public domain is low in this region, the consequences of this division between the two domains [public and private] have been devastating for women's rights."[7]

The Supreme Court has on a number of occasions spoken of the importance of having a Uniform Civil Code. In the Shah Bano case, Chandrachud CJ said that it would help the cause of national integration by removing disparate loyalties to laws which have conflicting ideologies.

However, in general, the judiciary seems to have avoided subjecting Personal Laws to the test of being compatible with fundamental rights. For example, when a question arose in the Mary Roy case regarding the Travancore Christian Succession Act which allowed the daughter to inherit a maximum amount of 5000 INR and left the rest of the estate to the son, the Supreme Court side-stepped the question by saying that there was no need to answer it since the Act had anyway been repealed by the entry into force of the Indian Succession Act.[8]

In a case filed by Madhu Kishwar,[9] the Supreme Court upheld a Tribal Law which prevented tribal women from inheriting land. The argument in favour of the prohibition was that if tribal women married non-tribal men, it would lead to alienation of tribal land and ultimately, to the erosion of the identity of the tribe.

And when a woman named Githa Hariharan tried to make an investment in the name of her son in a national bank, she found that she could not do so because of a provision in the

Hindu Minority and Guardianship Act which says that the mother is the natural guardian only 'after the father'. The Supreme Court did not remedy the inequality in the provision; it interpreted the provision to mean 'in the absence' of the father.[10]

## Fundamental Rights

Part-III of the Constitution of India lists several fundamental rights which the State is obliged to respect and from which it cannot derogate.

These fundamental rights have often been compared to the Magna Carta–the Charter of Liberties of Henry II–and although they are enforceable, much like the Magna Carta, the mere fact that they exist does not mean much.

Gurney Champion felt so strongly about this lack of enforcement and implementation that in *Justice and the Poor in England* he drafted a bill to amend one of the greatest assertions of the Magna Carta:

> To no man will we deny, to no man will we sell or delay, justice or right
>
> *unless he happens to be poor.*[11]

> It isn't be too much of a stretch to change the 'amendment' to
>
> *unless she happens to be female.*

However, Justice Krishna Iyer had stated that Human Rights Jurisprudence has Constitutional status in India in the late 1970s itself (in the Sunil Batra case), and in the 1997 Vishakha case, the Supreme Court observed that 'the meaning and content of the fundamental rights guaranteed in the Constitution of India are of sufficient amplitude to encompass all the facets of gender equality including the prevention of sexual harassment or abuse.'

### *Equality*

Anatole France once commented that the law, in its majestic equality, forbids not only the poor but also the rich from sleeping under bridges and begging in streets. The interpretation and the understanding of the concept of equality have themselves changed since the time he made that remark though.

Equal justice is a concept which can easily trace its origins to early Anglo-Saxon jurisprudence, and the equal treatment of equals is one of the fundamental principles of the Indian legal system today (although that doesn't mean that equals are actually treated equally).

The right to equality is defined in *Article 14* of the Constitution.

> The state shall not deny to any person equality before the law or the equal protection of the laws within the territory of India.

**Article 15** speaks of non-discrimination.

> Prohibition of discrimination on grounds of religion, race, caste, sex or place of birth
>
> (1) The State shall not discriminate against any citizen on only of religion, race, caste, sex, place of birth or any of them.
>
> (3) Nothing in this Article shall prevent the State from making any special provision for women and children.

And **Article 16** provides for the equality of opportunity to all citizens in matters of public employment.

The phrases *equality before the law* and *equal protection of the law* have both been used in the Universal Declaration of Human Rights, 1948. The first is of British origin while the second appears in the American Constitution.

In E.P. Royappa v/s State of Tamil Nadu,[12] Justice Bhagwati explained the concept of equality as Article 14 of the Constitution contemplates it as follows:

> "Equality is a dynamic concept with many aspects and dimensions and it cannot be 'cribbed, cabined and confined' within traditional and doctrinaire limits. From a positivistic point of view, equality is antithetic to arbitrariness. In fact, equality and arbitrariness are sworn enemies; one belongs to the rule of law in a Republic while the other, to the whim and caprice of an absolute monarch."

The Supreme Court struck down the regulations which Air India had created in regard to pregnancy and retirement in Air India v/s Nargesh Meerza, 1981.[13] Regulation 46 provided that an air hostess would retire from the service of the corporation as soon as any of the following happened:

- she attained the age of thirty-five years
- she married (if the marriage was within four years of service) or
- she became pregnant.

The Court held that the termination of service on pregnancy was unreasonable and arbitrary, that it interfered with and diverted the ordinary course of human nature, that it was an insult to Indian womanhood and that it violated Article 14.

In Revathi v/s Union of India, 1988,[14] Section 198 (2) of the Criminal Procedure Code and Section 497 of the Indian Penal Code which disqualify a wife from initiating criminal prosecution against her adulterous husband and prevent the prosecution of an adulterous wife were challenged. However, the Supreme Court held that these Sections do not violate the right to equality and that they do not discriminate against women; they are not designed to enable spouses to use the provisions of criminal law against each other.

### *Freedom*

Articles 19 to 22 of the Indian Constitution deal with the right to freedom.[15] There are a number of different rights which are listed in these Articles and not all of them are available to persons who are not citizens of India. Also, none of these rights is absolute.

**Article 19** Protection of certain rights regarding freedom of speech etc.

1. All citizens shall have the right
   (a) to freedom of speech and expression
   (b) to assemble peaceably and without arms
   (c) to form associations or unions

(d) to move freely throughout the territory of India

(e) to reside and settle in any part of the territory of India

(f) —repealed—

(g) to practise any profession, or to carry on any occupation, trade or business.

These freedoms are subject to the restrictions specified in Article 19 (2) which basically says that the State may make a law to impose reasonable restrictions in the interest of the sovereignty and integrity of India, the security of the State, friendly relations with foreign States, public order, decency or morality, or in relation to contempt of Court, defamation or incitement to an offence, or in the interest of the general public or for the protection of the interests of any Scheduled Tribe, or to prescribe professional or technical qualifications necessary to practise any profession or carry on any occupation, trade or business.

The Supreme Court held that the right of movement of prostitutes may be restricted on the ground of public health and in the interest of public morality in State of Uttar Pradesh v/s Kaushalya, 1964.[16]

The right of working women against sexual harassment at their workplaces was dealt with in Vishakha v/s State of Rajasthan, 1997,[17] under Articles 14, 19 and 21 of the Constitution which speak of equality, freedom and liberty respectively. In this case, the Supreme Court observed that 'at the Fourth World Conference on Women in Beijing, the Government of India made an official commitment, inter alia, to formulate and operationalise a national policy on women which will continuously guide and inform action at every level and in every sector, to set up a Commission for Women's Rights to act as a public defender of women's human rights, and to institutionalise a national level mechanism to monitor the implementation of the Platform for Action'.

The 1995 Beijing UN Women's Conference which recognised 'violence against women' as a critical area of concern, acknowledged that violence against girls 'begins at the earliest stages of life and continues unabated throughout their lives', and reaffirmed commitments to the equal rights and inherent human dignity of women and men enshrined in the Charter of the United Nations and other international human rights instruments such as the 1979 Convention on the Elimination of All Forms of Discrimination against Women and the 1989 Convention on the Rights of the Child.[18]

### *Life and Liberty*

The Right to Life and Liberty is contained in **Article 21**.

> No person shall be deprived of his life or personal liberty except according to the procedure established by law.

The interpretation of the this right was broadened a great deal in the 1978 Maneka Gandhi case[19] in which it was held that Article 21 contemplates reasonableness, a just and fair procedure, and the concept of natural justice. In subsequent decisions, the Supreme Court went on to say that the Right to Life includes not just the right to be alive but also the right to live with human dignity.

Article 21 is now understood to include a number of rights not expressly mentioned in it including:

- the right to a clean environment
- the right to privacy
- the right to medical aid
- the right to education

In the State of Maharashtra v/s Madhulkar Narain, 1991,[20] the Supreme Court upheld the right of a prostitute to privacy. In this case, a Police Officer went to the home of a prostitute in uniform and demanded sexual intercourse with her. When she refused, he tried to force her to submit to him.

But in Ms X v/s Mr Z, 2002,[21] it was held that the right to privacy does not exist in respect of what is contained in a public document.

In this case for the dissolution of a marriage, the husband involved alleged that his wife had aborted a child who had been conceived as a result of an adulterous relationship. (The wife had also alleged that her husband had committed adultery and that he had been cruel to her.) He wanted a DNA test using slides which had been preserved at AIIMS to be performed to ascertain the paternity of the foetus. The Supreme Court held that, considering the circumstances, the wife could not claim that her privacy would be affected since the foetus was no longer part of her body.

The Punjab and Haryana High Court, however, held that the performance of a Virginity Test on a woman is a violation of her privacy in Surjit Singh Thind v/s Kanwaljit Kaur, 2003.[22]

**The Right to Die**

In P. Rathiram v/s Union of India, 1994,[23] a Division Bench of the Supreme Court held that a person has the Right to Die and declared that Section 309 of the Indian Penal Code (which makes an attempt to commit suicide an offence) to be unconstitutional.

This decision was, however, overruled in Gian Kaur v/s State of Punjab, 1996,[24] in which the Supreme Court held that the Right to Life does not include the Right to Die.

In the Gian Kaur case, the in-laws of a woman who had committed suicide because of being harassed, inter alia, claimed that they could not be guilty of abetting her suicide since the act of committing suicide was itself not an offence. In a unanimous decision, the Supreme Court overturned the decision given in the P Rathinam case. It held that any aspect of life which makes it dignified may be read into Article 21 of the Constitution but no right that extinguishes life is contemplated by the Article. Suicide was therefore declared to be incompatible and inconsistent with the Right to Life as it is understood under the Constitution.

***The Right against Exploitation***

This right is spoken of in Articles 23 and 24 which prohibit trafficking, Begar–a form of bonded labour–and the employment of children in factories although none of these prohibitions prevents the State from imposing compulsory service for public purposes.

**Article 23** Prohibition of traffic in human-beings and forced labour:

(1) Traffic in human beings and Begar and other similar forms of forced labour are prohibited and any contravention of this provision shall be an offence punishable in accordance with law.

(2) Nothing in this Article shall prevent the State from imposing compulsory service for public purposes, and in imposing such service, the State shall not make any discrimination on grounds only of religion, race, caste or class or any of them.

*(See 'Trafficking and Prostitution' on page 127.)*

In Gaurav Jain v/s Union of India, 1997,[25] the Supreme Court observed that 'women found in the flesh trade should be viewed more as victims of adverse socio-economic circumstances than as offenders in our society. Prostitution in Five Star Hotels is a licence given to persons from the higher echelons. The commercial exploitation of sex may be regarded as a crime but those trapped in custom-oriented and gender-oriented prostitution should be viewed as victims of gender vulnerability'.

Condemning the practice of initiating women as Devdasis, Jogins or Venkatasins–a practice which usually, inter alia, involves dedicating the eldest girl of a family to a temple as an offering to the deity or to redeem a pledge–which is prevalent in the states of Maharashtra, Karnataka and Andhra Pradesh, the Supreme Court said that 'the pursuit of customary beliefs traps women into this glorified self-sacrifice and ultimately leads to prostitution in temples and charitable institutions which is a crime against humanity, a violation of human rights and of the Human Rights Act. The practice is void under Article 13 of the Constitution and is punishable under the law. Fundamentalists and proponents of the practice are Constitutional criminals'. In this case, the Supreme Court also referred to the UN Declaration on the Rights of the Child, 1959 and emphasised the need to find ways in which to rehabilitate prostitutes and their children.[26]

## *Remedies*

The Universal Declaration of Human Rights says that individuals should have recourse to redressal at appropriate national fora. The Indian Constitution provides for this in Articles 32 and 226. Further, Articles 141 says that the law declared by Supreme Court is binding on all Courts and Article 142 deals with the enforcement of decrees and orders.

**Article 32** Remedies for enforcement of fundamental rights:

(1) The right to move the Supreme Court by appropriate proceedings for the enforcement of the rights conferred by this Part [i.e. Part III which deals with Fundamental Rights] is guaranteed.

(2) The Supreme Court shall have power to issue directions or orders or writs, including writs in the nature of habeas corpus, mandamus, prohibition, quo warranto and certiorari, whichever may be appropriate, for the enforcement of any fundamental right.

(3) Without prejudice to the powers conferred on the Supreme Court by clauses (1) and (2), Parliament may by law empower any other Court to exercise within the local limits of its jurisdiction all or any of the powers exercisable by the Supreme Court under clause (2).

(4) The right guaranteed by this Article shall not be suspended except as otherwise provided for by this Constitution.

**Article 226** Power of High Courts to issue certain writs

(1) Notwithstanding anything in Article 32, every High Court shall have powers, throughout the territories in relation to which it exercises jurisdiction, to issue to any person or authority, including in appropriate cases, any Government, within those territories directions, orders or writs, including writs in the nature of habeas corpus, mandamus, prohibitions, quo warranto and certiorari, or any of them, for the enforcement of any of the [fundamental] rights conferred by Part III and for any other purpose.

(2) The power conferred by clause (1) to issue directions, orders or writs to any Government, authority or person may also be exercised by any High Court exercising jurisdiction in relation to the territories within which the cause of action, wholly or in part, arises for the exercise of such power, notwithstanding that the seat of such Government or authority or the residence of such person is not within those territories.

(3) Where any party against whom an interim order, whether by way of injunction or stay or in any other manner, is made on, or in any proceedings relating to, a petition under clause (1), without

(a) furnishing to such party copies of such petition and all documents in support of the plea for such interim order and

(b) giving such party an opportunity of being heard

makes an application to the High Court for the vacation of such order and furnishes a copy of such application to the party in whose favour such order has been made or the counsel of such party, the High Court shall dispose of the application within a period of two weeks from the date on which it is received or from the date on which the copy of such application is so furnished, whichever is later, or where the High Court is closed on the last day of that period, before the expiry of the next day afterwards on which the High Court is open.

If the application is not so disposed of, the interim order shall, on the expiry of that period, or, as the case may be, the expiry of the said next day, stand vacated.

(4) The power conferred on a High Court by this Article shall not be in derogation of the power conferred on the Supreme Court by Article 32 (2).

**Article 141** says that 'the law declared by the Supreme Court shall be binding on all Courts within the territory of India'.

**Article 142** Enforcement of decrees and orders of Supreme Court and unless as to discovery, etc.

(1) The Supreme Court in the exercise of its jurisdiction may pass such decree or make such order as is necessary for doing complete justice in any cause or matter pending before it, and any decree so passed or orders so made shall be enforceable throughout the territory of India in such manner as may be prescribed by or under any law made by Parliament and, until provision in that behalf is so made, in such manner as the President may by order prescribe.

(2) Subject to the provisions of any law made in this behalf by Parliament, the Supreme Court shall, as respects the whole of the territory of India, have all and every power to make any order for the purpose of securing the attendance of any person, the discovery or production of any documents, or the investigation or punishment of any contempt of itself.

There are, of course, alternatives to litigation as well. One often sees them in rural India in various forms such as the Nyay Panchayat, an offshoot of the Village Panchayat, in which justice is administered primarily by village elders. It is traditional and has the potential to do much good. Over the last few decades, the State has been trying to revive it; the main arguments in its favour are that it brings justice to the doorstep of disputants, is cheap, avoids legal technicalities and is quick.

**Article 40** of the Constitution (contained in Part IV which lists the Directive Principles of State Policy), in fact, specifically directs the organisation of Village Panchayats.

> The State shall take steps to organize Village Panchayats and endow them with such powers and authority as may be necessary to enable them to function as units of self-Government.

There are also Caste Panchayats which exist although the Constitution doesn't say anything about them. The problem, however, with Panchayats in general is that they are often so entrenched in tradition that the decisions they come up with and the punishments they mete out are sometimes human rights violations in themselves.

For example, it is possible for a woman to commit adultery without sleeping with a man other than her husband under traditional Hindu laws. According to Manu, the ancient law-giver:

> He who addresses the wife of another man at a Tirtha, outside the village, in a forest, or at the confluence of rivers, must suffer the punishment for adulterous acts (Samgrahana).[27]
>
> When a woman, proud of her relations or abilities, deceives her husband with another man, the king should ensure that she be torn apart by dogs in place frequented by people.[28]

Earlier, if a husband accused his wife of infidelity she had to literally pass through fire and any burns which she sustained in the process were considered to be a sign of her guilt. This was based on Ram's conduct towards his wife, Sita as narrated at the end of the Ramayana. Sita, however, was protected by Agni, the God of Fire. As a general rule, mere mortal women receive no such protection.

And writing *Band Darwaza* in 1984, the author Lakshman Mane spoke of the traditional trial by ordeal for adultery in the Pardhi Tribe. The woman's ordeal is to pick up a coin from a vessel of boiling hot oil and the man's is to pick up a red hot iron axe from cowpat cinders and bring it to the Panches. But even in this, there exists blatant discrimination against the woman; the man's hands are covered with thick Dhatura leaves which protect them from being burnt. The woman is allowed no such protection. And once adultery is proved, the woman is punished.

| **The Act** | **The Punishment** |
|---|---|
| Adultery with her tongue i.e. by speaking inviting words/ (?) flirting | Branding her tongue with a burning incense stick |
| Adultery with her ears | Pouring hot oil into her ears |
| Adultery with her eyes | Branding her eyes and (?) possibly blinding her |
| Adultery by actually having extra-marital sex | Roasting her genitals 'like an egg plant' |

Alternatives to litigation don't always work out well for women.

However, there are also situations in which community-based initiatives can be more useful than the formal legal system. Take domestic violence, for instance. In some areas of West Bengal, for example, the Shalishi - of Persian origin - is used to mediate between the parties involved in a dispute with (ideally) unbiased but powerful Shalishidaars acting as mediators. The law is used as a framework within which the community (through Shalishidaars) intervene and negotiate with the perpetrators of the violence not just to punish them but also to get justice for victims.

The Shalishi has existed since Pre-Mughal times and with its informal set up, many people prefer it to formal legal avenues. It derives its legitimacy from traditional norms and value systems, and it attempts to ensure that the family remains intact while it dispenses justice. In doing so, the Shalishi may compromise on meting out a punishment to the culprit as the criminal system would do but at the end of the day, it seems to help ameliorate the condition of women and that is a kind of empowerment in itself.[29]

### The Directive Principles of State Policy

The Directive Principles of State Policy are listed in Part IV of the Constitution. The provisions contained in this Part are not enforceable by any Court, but the principles laid down in them are nevertheless fundamental in the governance of the country and it is the duty of the State to apply them in making laws.[30] And as Dr Ambedkar once pointed out, even though the Directive Principles of State Policy are not enforceable by Courts, if the Government does not follow them, it has to answer for not having followed them at the time of elections.

**Article 38** The State to secure a social order for the promotion of welfare of the people

(1) The State shall strive to promote the welfare of the people by securing and protecting, as effectively as it may, a social order in which justice, social, economic and political, shall inform all the institutions of the national life.

(2) The State shall, in particular, strive to minimize the inequalities in income, and endeavour to eliminate inequalities in status, facilities and opportunities, not only amongst individuals but also amongst groups of people residing in different areas or engaged in different vocations.

**Article 39** Certain principles of policy to be followed by the State

The State shall, in particular, direct its policy towards securing:

(a) that the citizens, men and women equally, have the right to an adequate means to livelihood

(b) that the ownership and control of the material resources of the community are so distributed as best to subserve the common good

(c) that the operation of the economic system does not result in the concentration of wealth and means of production to the common detriment

(d) that there is equal pay for equal work for both men and women

(e) that the health and strength of workers, men and women, and the tender age of children are not abused and that citizens are not forced by economic necessity to enter avocations unsuited to their age or strength

(f) that children are given opportunities and facilities to develop in a healthy manner and in conditions of freedom and dignity and that childhood and youth are protected against exploitation and against moral and material abandonment.

**Article 39 A** Equal justice and free legal aid

The State shall secure that the operation of the legal system promotes justice, on a basis of equal opportunity, and shall, in particular, provide free legal aid, by suitable legislation or schemes or in any other way, to ensure that opportunities for securing justice are not denied to any citizen by reason of economic or other disabilities.

**Article 40** The organisation of Village Panchayats

*(See page **Error! Bookmark not defined.**9.)*

**Article 41** The right to work, education and public assistance

The State shall, within the limits of its economic capacity and development, make effective provision for securing the right to work, to education and to public assistance in cases of unemployment, old age, sickness and disablement, and in other cases of undeserved want.

**Article 42** The provision for just and humane conditions of work and maternity relief

The State shall make provision for securing just and humane conditions of work and for maternity relief.

**Article 43** Living wage, etc. for workers

The State shall endeavour to secure, by suitable legislation or economic organisation or in any other way, to all workers, agricultural, industrial or otherwise, work, a living wage, conditions of work ensuring a decent standard of life and full enjoyment of leisure and social and cultural opportunities and, in particular, the State shall endeavour to promote cottage industries on an individual or co-operative basis in rural areas.

**Article 43A** The participation of workers in the management of industries

The State shall take steps, by suitable legislation or in any other way, to secure the participation of workers in the management of undertakings, establishments or other organisations engaged in any industry.

**Article 46** The promotion of the educational and economic interests of Scheduled Castes, Scheduled Tribes and other weaker sections

The State shall promote with special care the educational and economic interests of the weaker sections of the people, and, in particular, of the Scheduled Castes and the Scheduled Tribes, and shall protect them from social injustice and all forms of exploitation.

**Article 47** The duty of the State to raise the level of nutrition and the standard of living and to improve public health.

> The State shall regard the raising of the level of nutrition and the standard of living of its people and the improvement of public health as among its primary duties and, in particular, the State shall endeavour to bring about prohibition of the consumption except for medicinal purposes of intoxicating drinks and of drugs which are injurious to health.

A number of laws including those regulating labour have been passed by Parliament keeping these principles in mind. They include:

- The Employees State Insurance Act, 1948.
- The Equal Remuneration Act, 1976.
- The Factories Act, 1948.
- The Mines Act, 1952.
- The Maternity Benefits Act, 1961.

However, although there has been a huge shift in what is deemed to be politically-correct rhetoric, there has not really been a corresponding change in the ground realities seen in the lives of women.

### *International Relations*

**Article 51** The promotion of international peace and security

> The State shall endeavour to
>
> (a) Promote international peace and security
>
> (b) Maintain just and honourable relations between nations.
>
> (c) Foster respect for International Law and treaty obligations in the dealings of organised peoples with one another and
>
> (d) Encourage settlement of international disputes by arbitration.

To explain why International Law and treaty obligations have been mentioned separately, Alexandrowicz has suggested that, in this Article, *International Law* is restricted to Customary International Law.

**Customary International Law** is treated as a part of Indian law. Radhika Coomaraswamy has made a compelling argument saying that certain practises which violate women's rights violate peremptory jus cogens norms. She says that it is universally accepted today that an act of torture is a violation of jus cogens and some practices against women like Sati and honour killings amount to torture.

In the international arena, there have been a number of declarations and conventions made, and conferences held in regard to women's rights. They include:

- The Convention on the Elimination of All Forms of Discrimination against Women, 1979.
- The Nairobi World Conference, 1985.
- The UN World Conference on Human Rights, 1993.
- The UN Declaration on Violence against Women, 1993.
- The UN Commission on Human Rights, 1994.
- The Beijing Declaration and Platform for Action at the Fourth World Conference on Women, 1995.

However, they do not constitute legally binding treaties. "There is a wide gap between standards on women's rights and the reality on the ground," as Amnesty International has repeatedly pointed out. "Ensuring that the law is respected and implemented requires the hard work and advocacy of those who are committed to ensuring that violence is not inflicted on women and to promoting a holistic approach to the problem of violence against women and to solutions."[31]

**As far as treaties are concerned,** the Indian position has changed. Parliament can enact laws for whole or any part of India to give effect to an international treaty or covenant which India is a party to by virtue of Article 253 of the Constitution and earlier, unless this was done, Indian Courts would not apply the provisions of the treaty to any case.

In ADM Jabalpur v/s Shukla, 1976,[32] the Supreme Court held that the Universal Declaration of Human Rights, 1948, is not a part of Indian law and four years later, in Jolly Verghese v/s Bank of Cochin,[33] the Supreme Court observed that the signing of a covenant ignites legislative action at home but does not automatically make it a part of the corpus juris of India.

This position has, however, changed after the 1997 Vishakha[34] case in which the Supreme Court referred to Nilabati Behera v/s State of Orissa, 1993,[35] which had itself referred to a provision in the International Covenant on Civil and Political Rights 'to support the view taken that an enforceable right to compensation is not alien to the concept of enforcement of a guaranteed right as a public law remedy under Article 32 distinct from the private law remedy in tort'. The Supreme Court also referred to international covenants in the Vishakha case saying:

> "Independence of Judiciary forms a part of our Constitutional scheme. The International Conventions and norms are to be read into them in the absence of enacted domestic law occupying the fields when there is no inconsistency between them. It is now an accepted rule of judicial construction that regard must be had to International Conventions and norms for construing domestic law when there is no inconsistency between them and there is a void in the domestic law.
>
> In the absence of domestic law occupying the field, to formulate effective measures to check the evil of sexual harassment of working women at all work-places, the contents of International Conventions and norms are significant for the purpose of the interpretation of the guarantee of gender equality and the right to work with human dignity in Articles 14, 15, 19 (1) (g) and 21 of the Constitution [which deal with the fundamental rights of equality, non-discrimination, freedom and life] and the safeguards against sexual harassment implicit therein. Any International Convention consistent with the fundamental rights and in harmony with its spirit must be read into these provisions to enlarge the meaning and content thereof, and to promote the object of the Constitutional guarantee. This is implicit from Article 51 (c) and the enabling power of the Parliament to enact laws to implement International Conventions and norms by virtue of Article 253 read with Entry 14 of the Union List in Seventh Schedule of the Constitution [which speak of entering into treaties and agreements with foreign countries and implementing treaties, agreements and conventions entered into with foreign countries].

Article 73 also is relevant. It provides that the executive power of the Union shall extend to the matters with respect to which Parliament has power to make laws. The executive power of the Union is, therefore, available till the Parliament enacts laws to expressly provide measures needed to curb the evil."

**Fundamental Duties**

Fundamental Duties were added to the Constitution in 1976 by the 42nd Amendment and are contained in *Article 51 A.*

It shall be the duty of every citizen of India:

(a) to abide by the Constitution and respect its ideals and institutions, the national Flag and the National Anthem

(b) to cherish and follow the noble ideals which inspired our national struggle for freedom

(c) to uphold and protect the sovereignty, unity and integrity of India

(d) to defend the country and render national service when called upon to do so

(e) to promote harmony and the spirit of common brotherhood amongst all the people of India transcending religious, linguistic and regional or sectional diversities to renounce practices derogatory to the dignity of women

(f) to value and preserve the rich heritage of our composite culture

(g) to protect and improve the natural environment including forests, lakes, rivers and wild life, and to have compassion for living creatures

(h) to develop the scientific temper, humanism and the spirit of inquiry and reform

(i) to safeguard public property and to abjure violence

(j) to strive towards excellence in all spheres of individual and collective activity so that the nation constantly rises to higher levels of endeavour and achievement.

The Article was further amended later in regard to education. However, these duties cannot be enforced by writs. They can only be promoted by Constitutional methods and can be used to interpret ambiguous statutes. They are invoked through the argument that on the principle that citizens are obliged to perform these duties, the State should also perform them.[36] They have most often been invoked in environmental cases.

However, there are also cases in which fundamental duties have been referred to in reference to women, their rights and their ability to access justice.

In Usha Badri Poonawala v/s K Kurian Babu,[37] 2002, for example, Justice Chandrachud spoke of women's access to justice. In this case, it was held that defamation constitutes violence against women as contemplated by a notification dated October 10, 1994 issued by the Government of the State of Maharashtra in the exercise of the powers conferred on it by Section 46 of the Bombay Court Fees Act, 1959.

The notification was held to be 'designed to ensure that women subjected to violence and other situations envisaged in the notification have an efficacious remedy of access to justice for redressing their grievances. That being the beneficial object of the notification, the interpretation to be placed on the said notification must, therefore, be interpreted so as to advance and promote the object of ensuring that women who suffer from gender discrimination are not impeded in seeking access to justice by being required to pay, upfront, a substantial Court fee which few of the class can afford. The notification subserves a salutary object. The interpretation to be placed in the notification by the Court must, therefore, be one of width and amplitude'.

In coming to this decision, reference was made to the Declaration on the Elimination of Discrimination against Women, 1993 and the Beijing Platform for Action which, inter alia, says that Governments are to ensure that women have access to justice and to various Constitutional provisions.

These provisions include:

**Article 15**

(1) The State shall not discriminate against any citizen on grounds only of religion, race, caste, sex, place of birth or any of them.

(3) Nothing in this article shall prevent the State from making any special provision for women and children.

**Article 51 A (e)**

It shall be the duty of every citizen of India to promote harmony and the spirit of common brotherhood amongst all the people of India transcending religious, linguistic and regional or sectional diversities; ***to renounce practices derogatory to the dignity of women.***

Justice Chandrachud also pointed out that access to justice is an intrinsic part of the right to life recognised by Article 21 of the Constitution.

## EDUCATION[38]

*For most of history anonymous was a woman.*
*– Virginia Woolf*

Mark Twain is reported to have said that he wouldn't let schooling interfere with his education. Today, many Indian students, not having good academic facilities available, follow the same path or else, simply remain uneducated.

When India achieved Independence from the British in 1947, only 12% of Indians were literate. The aim of the British, as far as educating Indians was concerned was articulated by the architect of Colonial Britain's Educational Policy in India, Thomas Macaulay, in 1835 when he said, "We must do our best to form a class who may be interpreters between us and the millions whom we govern, a class of persons Indian in blood and colour, but English in taste, in opinions, words and intellect."

Since Independence, the Government of India has reaffirmed its commitment to education several times. However, literacy rates in India are extremely low, and unfortunately, they are even lower for women than they are for men. According to the census, literacy rates go up by approximately 10% every ten years with the 1991 census showing that there was then

52% of the population that had become literate. The spread of literacy in India is not uniform though: urban areas, men and the upper castes all have higher literacy rates than their counterparts.

In 1991, although the overall literacy rate was 52%, only 40% of women were literate. The gap between the percentage of men and women who are literate varies widely from state to state. In Kerela, for example, which has one of the highest literacy rates, the gap is only about 7% but in states like Bihar it is a whopping 30% or so. The country has seen a huge increase in the number of educational institutions: the number of universities has gone up from 19 in 1947 to 219 in 1997.

The Government also often provides free education at the primary level, but even so, less then 3% of India's population has academic education. Very often State Governments simply do not have adequate funds to accommodate all the children of the school-going age. There are, however, organizations, both national and international which support education in India. The World Bank's support of education in India, for example, focuses on not only primary education but also vocational and technical education and training.

But even so, few Indians get the opportunity to go to educational institutions at all. And among those who do get the chance to do so, there are always a number of questions about just what they are being taught at these institutes. The are several problems: outdated syllabi, exam systems that put incredible amounts of pressure on to students and textbooks that often give students rather warped views of the world around them. This includes not only doing such things as presenting students with texts that have strong gender biases, showing men as leading characters who are strong and women primarily as victims of abuse as Narendra Nath Kalia pointed out in 1988 in *Women and Sexism: Language of Indian School Textbooks*.

We have psychology textbooks which inform students that 'lower class parents are not good models for their children, do not inspire their children to achieve, and that they are much more strict. Further they are not so affectionate towards their children as those from the middle and upper classes.' And to explain the concept of obsessions, the same textbook cites only two obsessions: 'A person may all the time be thinking of poisoning his wife or beating her with a hammer.'*

What bothers me is not so much the lack of information but the abundance of incorrect information. A lady I once interviewed for a *Times News Network* article who'd written a textbook on sociology defended the section on prostitution (which I found infuriating) in her book by telling me that prostitution is a social necessity and that it helps to decrease the number of rapes of 'other women'. Personally, I believe that prostitution *is* usually rape and I am always amazed by the fact that pimps etc. who've raped dozens of prostitutes are often awarded lighter punishments than those men who rape just one supposedly 'good' housewife, but that's another story.

Leaving that contention aside for the moment, what is pertinent here is that, as award-winning journalist Victor Malarek pointed out in *The Natashas*, there is no biological imperative which requires men to have sex with any particular frequency.

There is something wrong with the ethics and the morality of men who commit rape–and the existence of prostitution certainly isn't going to fix whatever it is that's wrong.

However, to continue with the same example, when you have textbooks which tell you otherwise, you grow up with the understanding that prostitution is normal, that it's acceptable for a man to use a woman to satisfy his own desires whether or not she wants to be so used, and, in the ultimate analysis, that women exist for men to use and abuse.

**Semantics**

The language used to speak of violence against women and women's rights should be rethought. The terms we use define how we perceive the women involved, and how we perceive them determines whether or not we, as a society, afford them any form of protection or relief.

Consider the use of the term *habitué* to describe a woman who has been subjected to rape and is not a virgin. The word does not exist in any statute but has been introduced into the realm of law by medico-legal authors, and although the sexual history of a victim is now not supposed to be introduced at trial, any suggestion that the woman is a *habitué* virtually ensures that her rapist will be acquitted.

Rape itself is often not described as rape at all in judgments –it is described as everything from an 'unholy act' to an 'act of lust'. Rapists somehow simply manage to *lose control* of themselves when they see a woman. Their behaviour, by extension, is only nominally criminal–they are simply acting as men. Boys will be boys, after all.

Similarly, when it comes to prostitutes and victims of trafficking, they are vulgar sluts, whores, harlots, wenches, hookers etc. while the men who (ab)use them are portrayed with far more gentility: they are clients, customers, johns, and even patrons as Victor Malarek has pointed out, and this is not without purpose–he says, "It makes it easier for men and society to objectify, commodify and then dismiss the victims. They are social pariahs unworthy of compassion or understanding. The men who use them, on the other hand, can even be viewed as valuable members of society who occasionally dabble in questionable sexual behaviour. And as long as they don a condom, who gets hurt?"

Or as a comment on AlterNet put it, "academics and politicos shouldn't waste their time on anything as frivolous as sex. Prostitution is just a bit of fun! It doesn't have any harmful effects, except on a bunch of sluts who don't matter anyway. Oh, and the wives who may get infected with HIV, but if they were better in bed their husbands wouldn't be tempted by whores so it's really their fault."[39]

One sees similar issues crop up with respect to domestic violence. In English, they say that it takes two to tango. In Hindi, that it takes two hands to clap. I first heard the latter from a friend years ago and proceeded to give him Hell for saying so; what's particularly exasperating about the application of these sayings to domestic violence is that both of them imply that a woman who has been abused is to blame for being abused.

Somehow, almost every time a man is violent, he claims that he was *provoked* beyond all human endurance, after which he naturally–and incidentally, completely understandably–lost control of his temper. Men, as a general rule, supposedly act abusively only in the heat of the moment.

The Indian Penal Code says that nothing is an offence which is done in the exercise of the right of private defence.[40] However, this right is subject to several restrictions and it does not extend to the inflicting of more harm than is necessary for the purpose of self-defence. However, the provocation, such as it is, when it comes to domestic violence is often simply nagging which I grant is annoying but verbal abuse is not, except in this context, a justification for physical violence–try walking into a Court and saying that your having committed assault (or worse) on a stranger is not criminal because your victim said something you didn't want to hear.

In one case–Idu Beg, 1881[41]–a husband who struck his wife on her left side while they were fighting (verbally) thereby causing her to vomit, bleed from the nose and die within an hour due to her spleen having been ruptured by him was not held to be guilty of murder–he was held to be guilty only of having caused grievous hurt.

And in a far more recent case–Venkatasen v/s State, 1997[42] –a husband who suspected the fidelity of his wife and who assaulted her with a stone because her insulting words made him 'lose control' and kill her was held guilty of culpable homicide and not of murder.

The unqualified acceptance of the concept that women provoke men to abuse them ensures that, as Ptacek has pointed out, "abusive men are neither abnormal enough to be considered to be psychopaths, nor are they responsible enough to be held criminally liable for their actions."

## LEGISLATION

### The Child Marriage Restraint Act

The Universal Declaration of Human Rights, 1948 recognises the right to marry and to found a family as do the International

Covenant on Civil and Political Rights and the International Covenant on Economic, Social and Cultural Rights which were adopted by the UN General Assembly on December 16, 1966. It might have made more sense in the Indian context to speak of the right not to marry though.

If there's one thing I seem to hear a little too much of these days, it's marriage. It seems crazy but almost all my friends, or at least the female ones, no matter how smart or talented they are, define themselves almost entirely by their marriages (or lack thereof) although, to be honest, among the people I know, few of them have the happy marriage they've always dreamt of (with their dreams usually being plagiarised directly from Mills and Boon Ltd.). Not that that ever stops any of them from wanting to get married if not actually be married.*

A prominent figure in India's women's movement spoke of her marriage saying that she was one of the daughters of a widow and the groom was earning a four figure salary at the time (in the late 1960s). He said, "No dowry," and everyone else said, "Perfect match." No one ever thought of anything else. She got married and the match wasn't quite as perfect as it was thought to have been, to say the least.*

That made me think that we haven't changed very much over the last forty years–we still get married without really knowing who we're getting married to, without knowing whether we're compatible with the person in any way whatsoever. And often, it's just because it's convenient to be married; in many circles, it's the only thing a woman is valued for.*

I have friends who are in their early twenties and are truly desperate to marry not because they have any desire whatsoever to be married but simply because once they get married, they won't have to worry about being labelled with a long string of derogatory terms in the (not so) modern society we live in. It doesn't matter if it's a stranger. It doesn't matter if they have tested the limits of their relationship or not (assuming that they know their intended spouse at all). And it certainly doesn't matter if they marry an annoying twerp. The only thing that matters is that the person can enable them legitimately say that they are *Mrs* So-and-So.*

And I can completely understand that. Goodness knows, I spend a lot of time listening to people ask me about my non-existent marriage and children. However, the questions (not to mention the sniggers), far from tempting me to marry, usually leave me with a very strong urge to throw things at the people who bring up the subject. But what I find exceptionally annoying and sad is that, in many cases, if you do marry and your marriage happens not to work out well, you wind up being almost completely isolated. The neighbourhood Aunties & Co. who had earlier gone out of their way to make life miserable for you because of not being married tend to suddenly lose their inherent desire to meddle. After all, how can they 'interfere in a family matter'?*

And when a marriage does end, some men try to defeat the rights/claims of their wives by denying that they had ever married them.

On February 14, 2006, a bench of the Supreme Court comprising Justice Arijit Pasayat and Justice S H Kapadia directed that the registration of marriage be made compulsory for all citizens. In a fourteen page judgment, the Court observed:

> "If the record of marriage is kept, to a large extent, the dispute concerning solemnisation of marriage between the two persons is avoided. As rightly contended by the National Commission, in most cases, the non-registration of marriages affects women to a great measure.
>
> If their marriage is registered it also provides evidence of the marriage having taken place and would provide a rebuttable presumption of the marriage having taken place.
>
> It has been pointed out that compulsory registration of marriage would be a step in the right direction for the prevention of child marriage still prevalent in many parts of the country.
>
> Though, the registration itself cannot be the determinative factor regarding the validity of a marriage, yet it has a great evidentiary value in the matters of custody of children, rights of children born

> from the wedlock of the two persons whose marriage is registered and the age of parties to the marriage. That being so it would be in the interest of the society if marriages are made compulsorily registerable. The legislative intent in enacting Section 8 of the Hindu Act is apparent from the use of expression-for the purpose of facilitating the proof of Hindu Marriages."

The National Commission for Women supported such compulsory registration since it believed that it would help to:

- prevent of child marriages
- check illegal bigamy and polygamy
- prevent forced marriages
- enable married women to claim their right to live in their matrimonial home, to receive maintenance etc.
- enable widows to claim their inheritance rights and other benefits and privileges which they are entitled to after the death of their husband
- deter men from deserting their wives
- deter parents/guardians from selling their daughters/wards under the garb of marriage.

Hindu scriptures say that a wife should be one-third the age of her husband. The social reform movements of the 19th Century and the widely publicised death of an eleven-year-old girl - Phulmani Bai - as a result of sexual intercourse with her husband in 1891 led the British to raise the age of consent in the Native Marriage Act.

Also, after the 1921 census revealed that there were a large number of minor widows, Mahatma Gandhi launched the 'Vidhwa Kumari Movement' to create awareness against the practice of child marriage and his friend, Harbilas Sarda introduced the Child Marriage Restraint Bill in the Central Legislature. The Bill was finally passed as the Child Marriage Restraint Act in 1929.

Today, the Child Marriage Restraint Act says that the age of consent to marriage for women is eighteen years.

The Act, as the Supreme Court observed in Lila Gupta v/s Laxmi Narain, 1978, 'was enacted to carry forward the reformist movement of prohibiting child marriages and while it made marriage in contravention of the provisions of the Act punishable, simultaneously it did not render the marriage void'.

**The Child Marriage Restraint Act, 1929** extends to the whole of India except the State of Jammu and Kashmir and applies to all Indian citizens even when they are not in India. However, nothing in the Act applies to the Renoncants of Pondicherry.

In this Act, 'child' means a male who has not completed the age of twenty-one years or a female who has not completed the age of eighteen years, and a marriage to which either or the contracting parties (whose marriage is to be solemnised) is a child is a 'child marriage'. The word 'minor', however, applies to any person below the age of eighteen years.

A male above eighteen and below twenty-one years of age who contracts a child marriage is punishable with simple imprisonment which may extend to 15 days, or with a fine which may extend to one thousand INR, or with both imprisonment and a fine.[43]

A male above twenty-one years of age who contracts a child marriage is punishable with simple imprisonment which may extend to three months and is also liable to pay a fine.[44]

A person who performs, conducts or directs a child marriage is punishable with simple imprisonment which may extend to three months and is also liable to pay a fine unless he proves that he had reason to believe that the marriage was not a child marriage.[45]

Under Section 6 of the Act, where a minor contracts a child marriage, any person having charge of the minor, whether as a parent, guardian or in any other capacity, lawful or unlawful, who does any act to promote the marriage or permits it to be solemnised, or negligently fails to prevent it from being solemnised is punishable with simple imprisonment which may extend to three months and is also liable to pay a fine. However, no woman can be imprisoned under this Section. Also, for the purposes of this Section, there exists a rebuttable presumption that where a minor has contracted a child marriage, the person having charge of the minor, has negligently failed to prevent the marriage from being solemnised.[46]

The Code of Criminal Procedure applies to offences under this Act as if they are cognisable offences for the purpose of their investigation and for purposes other than the arrest of a person either on refusal to give his name and residence,[47] or without a warrant or an order of a magistrate.[48]

No Court other than that of a Metropolitan Magistrate or a Judicial Magistrate First Class can take cognisance of or try any offence under this Act notwithstanding anything contained in Section 190 of the Code of Criminal Procedure (which deals with the cognizance of offences by Magistrates).[49] Further, the Act directs that no Court take cognisance of any offence under it after the expiry of one year from the date on which the offence is alleged to have been committed.[50]

Any Court in receipt of a complaint of an offence of which it is authorised to take cognisance is supposed to either itself make an enquiry in accordance with Section 202 of the Code of Criminal Procedure or direct that a magistrate subordinate to it make such enquiry unless it dismisses the complaint under Section 203 of the Code of Criminal Procedure.[51]

The Court may issue an injunction prohibiting a child marriage against:

- any male person above 18 years of age about to enter into the child marriage
- any person who is to perform, conduct or direct the child marriage or
- any person having charge of the minor (as specified earlier)

If it is satisfied from the information laid before it from a complaint or otherwise that a child marriage in contravention of this Act has been arranged or is about to be solemnised.[52] However, the person against whom the injunction is to be issued should be given notice and afforded an opportunity to show cause against the issuance of the injunction.[53]

*The Court may*

- issue such an injunction notwithstanding anything contrary contained in the Act[54]

- either suo moto or on the application of an aggrieved person rescind or alter such an injunction.[55]

Where such an application is received, the Court is supposed to afford the applicant an early opportunity of appearing before it either in person or by a pleader, and if the Court rejects the application wholly or in part, it is supposed to record its reasons for doing so in writing.[56]

Under Section 12 (5) of the Act, a person who knows that an injunction has been issued against him and disobeys it is punishable; a man is punishable with either simple or rigorous imprisonment for a term which may extend to three months, or with a fine which may extend to one thousand INR, or with both imprisonment and a fine. However, no woman can be imprisoned under this subsection.[57]

However, the Child Marriage Restraint Act has been amended by the **Prevention of Child Marriages Bill, 2006** which was passed by Parliament.

The amendment does not change the minimum age of eighteen years for girls and twenty-one years for boys but it makes underage marriages void at the option of the underaged party.

The amended Act makes provision for:

1. The provision of ancillary relief

   Courts are to provide ancillary relief by directing that parties restore all money, valuables, ornaments and other gifts received at the marriage to each other.

2. The imposition of enhanced punishments

   The punishment for the various offences under the Act has been increased to a prison sentence of two years and a fine of one lakh INR. All offences are also cognisable and non-blailable.

   Also, a marriage solemnised in contravention of a preventive injunction to stop it is to be void ab initio.

The Child Marriage Restraint Act applies to all marriages regardless of whether they are governed by civil or personal law. Article 25 of the Constitution deals with freedom of conscience and free profession, practice and propagation of religion but it does not make such freedom absolute. It says:

(1) Subject to public order, morality and health and to the other provisions of the Part in the Constitution which deals with fundamental rights, all persons are equally entitled to freedom of conscience and the right freely to profess, practise and propagate religion.

(2) Nothing in this article shall affect the operation of any existing law or prevent the State from making any law:

   (a) Regulating or restricting any economic, financial, political or other secular activity which may be associated with religious practice.

   (b) Providing for social welfare and reform or the throwing open of Hindu religious institutions of a public character to all classes and sections of Hindus.

*Explanation I:* The wearing and carrying of Kirpans shall be deemed to be included in the profession of the Sikh religion.

*Explanation II:* In sub-clause (b) of clause reference to Hindus shall be construed as including a reference to persons professing the Sikh, Jain or Buddhist religion, and the reference to Hindu religious institutions shall be construed accordingly.

> *A husband must be constantly worshipped as a god by a dutiful wife even if he is destitute of virtue, seeks pleasure elsewhere or is devoid of good qualities.*
>
> –*Manusmriti [V.154]*

Thus, laws may be made for the purpose of social welfare and reform. Nonetheless, nearly 35% of Indian 'women'/girls get married between the ages of fifteen and eighteen. And once they do get married, they are expected to place their husband's, in-laws' and virtually every other random person's needs, wants, desires and idiosyncrasies above their own.

Even today, the mythical Savitri is considered to be the ideal wife, and, to this day, all wives are compared to her.

Savitri married her husband, Satyavan knowing that he was to die within a year; her devotion to him was such that she said that she was prepared to be his wife for a single year and a widow for fifty. When her husband's time finally came, she brought him back from the edge of death by following the God of Death, Yama to the end of the world and by using the three boons He bestowed on her to ask for her blind father-in-law to be given his eyesight and his kingdom back and, because Yama had forbidden her to ask for her husband's life, she finally asked for a hundred sons. Since she could marry no other, the God had to restore her husband by default–the couple then lived together for four hundred years and had one hundred sons.

Writing sometime between 100 and 200 AD, Tiru-Valluvar said that 'the true wife thinks not of God when she rises in the morning; she offers her worship to her husband and that is enough. Even the clouds will obey and pour rain at her comment'.[58]

Coming back to contemporary India though, women are still quite literally expected to consider their husbands to be their gods and to virtually (if not actually) worship them. A number of studies have shown that getting married young does nothing to help them retain control over their bodies, the type of contraception they do/do not use (if any at all), their education and their finances. Not too surprisingly, they wind up being firmly under the kind male dominance from which they have almost no chance of escaping.

### The National Commission for Women

The National Commission for Women Act, 1990 was passed to constitute a National Commission for Women. The Chairperson, Members and staff of the Commission are public servants.[59]

The Central Government is supposed to consult the Commission on all major policy matters affecting women.[60]

The Commission was set up in January 1992 and is financed by grants by the Central Government. There are those who say that it has been a colossal failure although my own opinion is that although it hasn't done anywhere near as much as one would have liked, it hasn't been completely ineffective either. And considering that dealing with crime and discrimination against women requires systemic changes, I'm not entirely sure how fair it is to expect the Commission to do very much beyond a point.

The National Commission for Women consists of:

- a Chairperson committed to the cause of women nominated by the Central Government
- five Members nominated by the Central Government from amongst persons of ability, integrity and standing who have had experience in law or legislation, trade unionism, management of an industry or organisation committed to increasing the employment potential of women, women's voluntary organisations (including women activists), administration, economic development, health, education or social welfare. At least one Member each is from amongst persons belonging to the Scheduled Castes and Scheduled Tribes respectively
- a Member-Secretary nominated by the Central Government.[61]

The Commission interacts with social activists, NGOs, academics and the media in the pursuance of its aims and functions. It sponsors research, publishes books and has established a library comprising material on women's studies.

The Commission has attempted to alleviate the condition of women by:

- increasing legal awareness among women
- recommending amendments to existing laws
- conducting seminars
- trying to en expedite investigations by the police
- receiving complaints of women's grievances as well as taking suo moto action where required.

It analyses complaints to enable it to suggest amendments in the law and also uses complaints as case studies to sensitise the judiciary and the bureaucracy (among others).

Under the Act, the functions of the Commission are to:[62]

- investigate and examine all matters relating to the safeguards provided for women under the Constitution and other laws.

  The Commission, while investigating any matter, has all the powers of a Civil Court trying a suit.
- present to the Central Government, annually and at such other times as the Commission may deem fit, reports upon the working of those safeguards
- make in such reports recommendations for the effective implementation of those safeguards for improving the conditions of women by the Union or any State
- review, from time to time, the existing provisions of the Constitution and other laws affecting women and recommend amendments thereto so as to suggest remedial legislative measures to meet any lacunae, inadequacies or shortcomings in such legislations
- take up the cases of violation of the provisions of the Constitution and of other laws relating to women with the appropriate authorities
- look into complaints and take suo moto notice of matters relating to:
  - the deprivation of women's rights
  - the non-implementation of laws enacted to provide protection to women and also to achieve the objective of equality and development
  - the non-compliance of policy decisions, guidelines or instructions aimed at mitigating hardships and ensuring welfare and providing relief to women, and take up the issues arising out of such matters with appropriate authorities

- call for special studies or investigations into specific problems or situations arising out of discrimination and atrocities against women and identify the constraints so as to recommend strategies for their removal
- undertake promotional and educational research so as to suggest ways of ensuring due representation of women in all-spheres and identify factors responsible for impeding their advancement, such as, lack of access to housing and basic services, inadequate support services and technologies for reducing drudgery and occupational health hazards and for increasing their productivity
- participate and advise on the planning process for the socio-economic development of women
- evaluate the progress of the development of women under the Union and any State
- inspect or cause to be inspected a gaol, remand home, women's institution or other place of custody where women are kept as prisoners or otherwise, and take up with the concerned authorities for remedial action, if found necessary
- fund litigation involving issues affecting a large body of women
- make periodical reports to the Government on any matter pertaining to women
- deal with any other matter which may be referred to it by Central Government.

The Commission may appoint such committees as may be necessary for dealing with such special issues as may be taken up by the Commission from time to time.[63]

The Central Government may, by notification in the Official Gazette, make rules to carry out the provisions of the National Commission for Women Act.[64]

Recently,[65] the National Commission for Women has been actively lobbying to have adultery treated as a civil offence and to have Section 198 (2) of the Criminal Procedure Code amended so that it no longer disqualifies a wife from initiating prosecution against her adulterous husband.

The Commission has, inter alia, also dealt with the issues of sexual harassment, domestic violence, harassment, dowry, torture, desertion, bigamy, rape, the refusal to register FIRs, gender discrimination, women in detention, prostitution and the empowerment of women, the development of healthcare, access to education, the requirements of mentally-disabled women, the credit needs of women, social mobilisation, maintenance for divorced women, contract women labourers, the gender bias in judicial decisions, Family Courts and the plight of the widows of Vrindavan. It has also made proposals to amend the Child Marriage Restraint Act so that brides can have their marriages declared void without being treated as divorcees, and to decrease the minimum age for emigration clearance for women to work abroad as domestic help from thirty years to twenty-one years.

According to the Commission, women have been losing out on employment opportunities in foreign countries because of the age criterion which does not allow them to work as domestic servants abroad unless they are over thirty years of age. However, to protect women's interests - especially considering the high incidence of complaints of sexual abuse made by Indian women who have worked in the Gulf and other countries - it has also, inter alia, recommended that a mechanism to deal with their complaints of sexual exploitation and other ill treatment be established.[66]

### The National Human Rights Commission

The National Commission for Human Rights was established under the Protection of Human Rights Act, 1993. 'Human rights' are defined in the Act as those rights relating to life, liberty, equality and dignity of the individual guaranteed under the Constitution or embodied in the International Covenants- i.e. the International Covenant on Civil and Political Rights and the International Covenant on Economic, Social and Cultural Rights adopted by the General Assembly of the United Nations on December 16, 1966–and enforceable by Indian Courts.

The National Commission for Human Rights is supposed to perform the following functions under the Act:

- inquire, on its own initiative or on a petition presented to it by a victim or any person on his behalf, into complaint of:
    - the violation of human rights or abetment or
    - negligence by a public servant in the prevention of the commission of such a violation
- intervene in any proceeding involving any allegation of the violation of human rights pending before a Court with the approval of such Court
- visit, under intimation to the State Government, any gaol or any other institution under the control of the State Government, where persons are detained or lodged for the purpose of treatment, reformation or protection to study the living conditions of the inmates and make recommendations thereon
- review the safeguards by or under the Constitution or any law for the time being in force for the protection of human rights and recommend measures for their effective implementation
- review the factors, including acts of terrorism that inhibit the enjoyment of human rights and recommend appropriate remedial measures
- study treaties and other international instruments on human rights and make recommendations for their effective implementation
- undertake and promote research in human rights
- spread human rights literacy among various sections of society and promote awareness of the safeguards available for the protection of these rights through publications, the media, seminars and other available means

- encourage the efforts of non-Governmental organizations and institutions working in the field of human rights
- perform such other functions as it may consider necessary for the promotion of human rights.

While inquiring into complaints under the Act, the Commission has all the powers of a Civil Court trying a suit under the Code of Civil Procedure, and, in particular, for the following:

- summoning and enforcing the attendance of witnesses and examining them on oath
- the discovery and production of any document
- receiving evidence on affidavits
- requisitioning any public record or copy thereof from any Court or office
- issuing commissions for the examination of witnesses or documents
- any other matter which may be prescribed.

Complaints are usually not entertained by the Commission if they are:

- in regard to events which happened more than one year before the making of the complaint
- in regard to matters which are subjudice
- vague, anonymous or pseudonymous
- of a frivolous nature
- such that they pertain to service matters or are not within the purview of its functions.

However, this does not seem to be a hard and fast rule. For example, the Commission rescued a young girl had been kept in captivity in a house in Dholpur, Rajasthan for about five years on the basis of an anonymous complaint.[67]

A few Human Rights Courts have been established although the Act says nothing about what the jurisdiction of these Courts is supposed to be–it simply speaks of their establishment and the appointment of Special Public Prosecutors to work in them. Also, the Act does not compulsorily require states to constitute State Human Rights Commissions although quite a few have done so voluntarily. The State Human Rights Commissions have the same functions as the National Commission apart from a few differences in the complaints they deal with and the territory within which they function.

Apart from the fact that the Act defines Human Rights narrowly, one of the primary problems with the functioning of the National Human Rights Commission has been that it has very little power to enforce its 'decisions' - all it can do is approach a Court, recommend that the concerned Government initiate proceedings against whoever it thinks is at fault, and recommend that compensation be paid.

**THE ROLE OF THE MEDIA**

A friend of mine often used to remind me that fighting for women's rights isn't about obtaining results overnight but about changing the attitudes of people over a period of time and as true as that might be, whether one talks about the implementation of the Convention on the Elimination of All Forms of Discrimination against Women, rape, incest, the rights of commercial sex workers, the almost all-pervasive domestic violence, dowry problems or witch-hunting, in my own life, I don't see attitudes changing at all and if media reports are anything to go by, they certainly aren't changing in rural areas even if they are changing in tiny pockets of urban India.*

> *She died without CNN covering her war... The target was her precious flesh that was once composed like music in her mother's body and sung in the anthem of birth.*
>
> –Carol Geneya Kaplan (Another Woman)[68]

The Convention on the Elimination of All Forms of Discrimination against Women,[69] for example, which was adopted in 1979 by the UN General Assembly has still not been ratified by many countries (including the USA) and even in countries where it has been ratified (such as India), apart from in a few cases like the much-publicised 1997 Vishakha case,[70] the convention–which is often referred to as an international bill of rights for women–doesn't really seem to have very much of an impact in everyday life. The implementation of law, however, is a completely different story and it isn't my subject at the moment; it's the process of 'creating awareness' and the media's role in doing so which is.*

For a long time, it wasn't easy to talk about women's right in the press at all unless it was about women who were either dead or dying–live women rarely elicited much sympathy or interest from editors or from anyone else, for that matter. Women *in* the press were usually asked to cover fun fairs and fashion festivals. And those who did cover *hard* news had the almost impossible and unenviable task of having to convey what a (usually) male editor thought was the *soft* female perspective whilst being as *objective* as a man.

The one thing which women's magazines did not cover was politics–what they did cover, for the most part, was the discovery of two hundred different ways in which to cook potatoes. *Fluff,* as an editor I know used to describe it. And the presence of women who wrote in various publications didn't do a great deal to help. A few were anti-feminist on paper, possibly to try to gain the approval of the (primarily male) powers that were and most simply weren't inclined to fight to write about women's issues.

The few women who did write about women's rights often seemed to commit career suicide by default, or at the very least, reach a dead end. Out of all the articles I've ever written in newspapers, I can remember only one that was about women's rights. (The article was about men who exploit gender biases in society to abuse divorce laws.) I didn't have much of a problem getting it in–the editor I dealt with was a liberal and sensitive chap–I did nonetheless wind up being *accused* of being too much of a feminist for a long time after it came out. The strange thing was that at the time, you could write about the rights or the exploitation of virtually any group–children, bonded labourers, prisoners, refugees, minorities, you name it. But you couldn't easily write about women.

That has, however, changed in recently. But although it's certainly a relief that some sections of the media seem to be doing more than simply looking at women as personifications of Page 3, what often stuns me was the way in which topics are handled.*

I once saw two documentaries in one evening, one on foreign commercial sex workers in Hindi and the other on Witch Hunts in English.*

The programme on foreign prostitutes, apart from playing (and replaying) their earnings (which are much higher than that of average Indians), spoke of problems in terms of things like the spread of AIDS–reasonable enough, I suppose–and national security being compromised–Mata Hari, slightly confused, has been reincarnated, after all! The feeling the documentary gave me was that the producers just didn't like the idea of the existence of foreign prostitutes and were looking for legitimate (?) excuses with which to justify their condemnation.*

And in the programme about Witch Hunting, on the other hand, people who were unfamiliar with the topic would have been left thinking that the phenomenon was entirely due to illiteracy, ignorance and superstition although it has been seen often enough that while ignorance plays a part, the reason why women are branded as witches often has little to do with ignorance and everything to do with controlling women who try to assert their rights whether it is in regard to political rights or in relation to the right to inherit property.*

And then of course, there's also the question of what the media chooses to cover. For example, on August 23, 2006, a major national paper covered two stories on women's rights.

One was a wishy-washy article about a tribal woman from Tulsipura village about 245 km from Bhopal who had committed Sati–the article, however, spent a long time talking about how she may have actually committed *suicide* and not Sati, and thus, may not have been a victim of violence. It covered about 180 sq cm.

The second article in which the woman involved clearly was a victim of violence covered and area of 16 sq cm. It was about a landmark judgment in which the Karnataka High Court sentenced a man named Joseph Rodrigues to life imprisonment for attacking one Haseena Hussain with acid on April 20, 1999. The article was in tiny print and was two sentences long–it was all too easy to miss.

It's sad that that is how stories about violence against women are treated in newspapers particularly since newspapers do have tremendous potential to do good. As Shashi Tharoor once wrote, "The cold calmness of print can permit more serious reflection than the heat of television or the haste of the Internet. If breaking news is now the lifeblood of the television news channel, taking broken news and making it whole is something only a newspaper can do."[71]

Also, I can't help but think that journalists need to have a better idea of what they're doing when they talk about women's rights and issues relating to women. In the recent case, for example, where Maninder Pal Singh Kohli confessed to a TV journalist that he had raped and murdered seventeen-year-old Hannah Claire Foster near her home in Southampton, England,[72] initially, the journalists involved thought that the confession could be used to indict Kohli and by extension, they simply weren't aware of the legal ramifications of the confession which was made while Kohli was in police custody.[*]

If fighting for women's rights is, to a great extent, at this stage, about increasing awareness, the media as a whole, to my mind, has to do a better job although there are, of course, cases where the press has played a constructive role. In January 12, 1994, a newspaper reported that Amritsar Police personnel apparently had the words Jeb Katri–pickpocket–tattooed on the foreheads of four women. The victims filed a Writ Petition before the Punjab and Haryana High Court praying for the Government of Punjab, Superintendent of Police, Amritsar and others to be directed to arrange for plastic surgery for removal of the tattoos, to pay compensation and to punish the guilty police personnel. Taking cognisance of the newspaper report, the National Human Rights Commission intervened in the case under Section 12 (b) of the Protection of Human Rights Act and, with the Court's permission, filed an affidavit asking for the investigation to be handed over the CBI (since the accused belonged to the State Police and an investigation by a 'sister' wing did not inspire confidence), for the plastic surgery to be conducted at State cost, and for the victims to be given interim compensation. The High Court allowed all the prayers of the NHRC.[73]

And then of course, there is also the possibility of displeasing the judiciary even if not actually committing contempt of Court to be considered. A Bench of the Supreme Court comprising Justice Hegde and Justice S B Sinha cautioned the press against publishing one-sided stories while it was dealing with a case of alleged dowry death in Kolkata. The Bench said (with reference to an article which had been published in a Bangla magazine):

> "The facts narrated therein are all materials that may be used in the forthcoming trial in this case and we have no hesitation that this type of article appearing in the media would certainly interfere with the administration of justice. We deprecate this practice and caution the publisher, editor and the journalist who are responsible for the said articles against indulging in such trial by media when the issue is subjudice. Others concerned in journalism would take note of this displeasure expressed by us for interfering with the administration of justice."[74]

The main obstacle though is that 'news today is a product and those whom it's supposed to keep informed are consumers'.[75]

In *Lulling us into Submission – Advertising, Core Truths, and the Great Electronic Tranquilliser*, Media Lens pointed out, "The 'quality press' doesn't like to talk too openly about the fact that it depends for 75% of its revenue on corporate advertising. Corporations, after all, are strictly hierarchical, undemocratic institutions motivated by limitless greed – it's hard to reconcile their needs with democracy, human rights and the public's right to know."[76]

As the lady who wrote *Princess, Daughters of Arabia* and *Desert Royal* with Jean Sasson said, if I remember correctly, that there is little chance of international pressure helping to improve the lives of women since, not controlling oil or anything else, their lives are of no real interest to foreign Governments who have rarely, if ever, done anything substantial to advocate their cause. And that is where, and why, to my mind, the Fourth Estate should step in but it usually doesn't.*

And that, I suppose, is the bottom line. Nobody in the corporate world really wants to talk about human rights, let alone women's rights. A few sensational stories here and there keep life interesting... Remember the O.J. Simpson trial and how watching it turned into everybody's favourite way to waste time?*

And more recently, closer to home, the media spent endless amounts of air time, not to mention column space, talking about the Gudiya-Taufeeq-Arif triangle[77] completely forgetting that there were real people involved who weren't playing parts written by an imaginative scriptwriter in a soap opera. What precisely the need to sensationalise news was and to have a field day with what was so obviously a personal tragedy for those involved is something that completely escapes me.*

In 2006, the press spent a lot of time covering the murders of Priyadarshini Mattoo, Nitin Katara and Jessica Lall, and while I'm glad that those three individuals seem to be getting some form of justice, they are, ultimately, three individuals, from Delhi, who belong to the higher socio-economic class. Whether they would have got one-tenth the amount of attention if they'd been poor and from a village is doubtful. Attention to a few isolated cases doesn't do much to change the system itself.

'Human rights' today generally isn't news and isn't on any Government's agenda unless it involves sex and/or money.

Nina Shapiro pointed out in *The New Abolitionists*, "Freeing 'sex slaves' is now at the top of the human rights agenda, thanks to Christian evangelicals, the Bush administration, and two former Washington politicians, Linda Smith and John Miller." When John Miller was appointed Director on the Office to Monitor and Combat Trafficking in Persons, he said that the struggle to abolish 'modern day slavery' is tied to the United States' role in the world, that the issue that cries for national and international leadership, and that the country to provide that leadership is–no surprise here–the US of A.

The anti-trafficking crusade, however, tends to be used not only to engage in policies which have little to do with women's rights (such as the support of anti-migration policies, the furtherance of sexual conservatism and the reinforcement of patriarchy) but also to side-track almost every other women's issue and turn what is real suffering for many people into soft porn for almost everyone else.

Women's rights need to stop being trivialised and be looked at more compassionately and also, more comprehensively. It isn't all about prostitution and sex slavery.

It's about being able to live life with the same kind of respect which men take for granted.

## NOTES

1. Air India v Nargesh Meerza; AIR 1981 SC 1829.
2. Rajan, Rajeswari Sunder; Beyond the Hysterectomies Scandal; 2005.
3. Article 13; The Constitution of India.
4. Cheshire and North; Private International Law; Butterworths; 12th Edition; 1992.
5. AIR 1952 Bom 84. In fact, in this case–the Narasu Appa Mali case–the Court held that Personal Laws are not included in the term 'laws in force' in Article 13 of the Constitution and therefore cannot be declared void by reason of their being in conflict with Part III of the Constitution.
6. Article 44. Uniform Civil Code for the citizens: The State shall endeavour to secure for the citizens a Uniform Civil Code throughout the territory of India.
7. Jaisingh, Indira (ed.); Men's Laws, Women's Lives; Women Unlimited; 2005.
8. 1986 (1) SCR 371; the Mary Roy case.
9. Madhu Kishwar v State of Bihar; (1996) 5 SCC 125.
10. Githa Hariharan, 1999.
11. Rao and Sheffield (ed.); Alternative Dispute Resolution; Universal Law Publishing; 1997.
12. AIR 1974 SC 555.
13. AIR 1981 SC 1829.
14. AIR 1988 SC 835
15. **Article 19.** Protection of certain rights regarding freedom of speech etc.

(1) All citizens shall have the right:

  (a) To freedom of speech and expression
  (b) To assemble peaceably and without arms
  (c) To form associations or unions
  (d) To move freely throughout the territory of India
  (e) To reside and settle in any part of the territory of India and
  (f) (Repealed)
  (g) To practise any profession, or to carry on any occupation, trade or business.

(2) Nothing in sub-clause (a) of clause (1) shall affect the operation of any existing law, or prevent the State from making any law, in so far as such law imposes reasonable restrictions on the exercise of the right conferred by the said sub-clause in the interests of the sovereignty and integrity of India, the security of the State, friendly relations with foreign States, public order, decency or morality or in relation to contempt of Court, defamation or incitement to an offence.

(3) Nothing in sub-clause (b) of the said clause shall affect the operation of any existing law in so far as it imposes, or prevent the State from making any law imposing, in the interests of the sovereignty and integrity of India or public order, reasonable restrictions on the exercise of the right conferred by the said sub-clause.

(4) Nothing in sub-clause (c) of the said clause shall affect the operation of any existing law in so far as it imposes, or prevent the State from making any law imposing, in the interests of the sovereignty and integrity of India or public order or morality, reasonable restrictions on the exercise of the right conferred by the said sub-clause.

(5) Nothing in sub-clauses (d) and (e) of the said clause shall affect the operation of any existing law in so far as it imposes, or prevent the State from making any law imposing, reasonable restrictions on the exercise of any of the rights conferred by the said sub-clauses either in the interests of the general public or for the protection of the interests of any Scheduled Tribe.

(6) Nothing in sub-clause (g) of the said clause shall affect the operation of any existing law in so far as it imposes, or prevent the State from making any law imposing, in the interests of

the general public, reasonable restrictions on the exercise of the right conferred by the said sub-clause, and, in particular, nothing in the said sub-clause shall affect the operation of any existing law in so far as it relates to, or prevent the State from making any law relating to:

(i) the professional or technical qualifications necessary for practising any profession or carrying on any occupation, trade or business, or

(ii) the carrying on by the State or by a corporation owned or controlled by the State, of any trade, business, industry or service, whether to the exclusion, complete or partial, of citizens or otherwise.

**Article 20.** Protection in respect of conviction for offences:

(1) No person shall be convicted of any offence except for violation of the law in force at the time of the commission of the act charged as an offence, nor be subjected to a penalty greater than that which might have been inflicted under the law in force at the time of the commission of the offence.

(2) No person shall be prosecuted and punished for the same offence more than once.

(3) No person accused of any offence shall be compelled to be a witness against himself.

**Article 21.** Protection of life and personal liberty:

No person shall be deprived of his life or personal liberty except according to procedure established by law.

**Article 22.** Protection against arrest and detention in certain cases:

(1) No person who is arrested shall be detained in custody without being informed, as soon as may be, of the grounds for such arrest nor shall he be denied the right to consult, and to be defended by, a legal practitioner of his choice.

(2) Every person who is arrested and detained in custody shall be produced before the nearest magistrate within a period of twenty-four hours of such arrest excluding the time necessary for the journey from the place of arrest to the Court of the magistrate and no such person shall be detained in custody beyond the said period without the authority of a magistrate.

(3) Nothing in clauses (1) and (2) shall apply (a) to any person who for the time being is an enemy alien or (b) to any person

who is arrested or detained under any law providing for preventive detention.

(4) No law providing for preventive detention shall authorise the detention of a person for a longer period than three months unless- (a) an Advisory Board consisting of persons who are, or have been, or are qualified to be appointed as, Judges of a High Court has reported before the expiration of the said period of three months that there is in its opinion sufficient cause for such detention.

(5) When any person is detained in pursuance of an order made under any law providing for preventive detention, the authority making the order shall, as soon as may be, communicate to such person the grounds on which the order has been made and shall afford him the earliest opportunity of making a representation against the order.

(6) Nothing in clause (5) shall require the authority making any such order as is referred to in that clause to disclose facts which such authority considers to be against the public interest to disclose.

(7) Parliament may by law prescribe (a) The circumstances under which, and the class or classes of cases in which, a person may be detained for a period longer than three months under any law providing foı preventive detention without obtaining the opinion of an Advisory Board in accordance with the provisions of sub-clause (a) of clause (4) (b) The maximum period for which any person may in any class or classes of cases be detained under any law providing for preventive detention and (c) The procedure to be followed by an Advisory Board in an inquiry under sub-clause (a) of clause (4).

16. AIR 1964 SC 416.
17. AIR 1997 SC 3014.
18. Saikia, Nandita; 'Domestic Violence against Women and Children in the European Union'; POROS Project; 2006.
19. AIR 1978 SC 597.
20. AIR 1991 SC 207.
21. AIR 2002 Del 217.
22. AIR 2003 P&H 353.
23. (1994) 3 SCC 394.
24. (1996) 2 SCC 648.

25. AIR 1997 SC 3021.
26. Also see AIR 1987 SC 191.
27. Manu VIII: 356.
28. Manu VIII: 371.
29. Shalishi in West Bengal by Shramajibee Mahila Samiti (EPW, April 26, 2003).
30. Article 37; The Constitution of India.
31. Making rights a reality: The duty of states to address violence against women; http://web.amnesty.org/library/index ENGACT770492004.
32. AIR 1976 SC 1207.
33. AIR 1980 SC 470.
34. AIR 1997 SC 3014.
35. 1993(2) SCC 746; this case involved the death of a young man in police custody.
36. Bakshi, P M; The Constitution of India; Universal Law Publishing; 2003.
37. 2002 (2) MhLJ 951 It was by this notification that the Government remitted the fees payable by women litigants on any of the plaints, applications, petitions, memorandum of appeals on any other documents specified in the first and second schedules to the Bombay Court Fees Act, 1959 to be filed in any Civil, Family or Criminal Court in respect of cases relating to violence, property, maintenance and divorce.
38. This article was published as the article of the month in TIG's Panorama in September, 2003.
39. This was in response to 'Sex Workers' Lit Ruined My Sex Life' by Anneli Rufus posted December 16, 2006.
40. Section 96; Indian Penal Code.
41. (1881) 3 All 776; also see 1986 CrLJ 438 (Ori).
42. 1997 CrLJ 3854 (Mad)
43. Section 3; The Child Marriage Restraint Act.
44. Section 4; The Child Marriage Restraint Act.
45. Section 5; The Child Marriage Restraint Act.
46. Section 6; The Child Marriage Restraint Act.
47. Section 42; The Code of Criminal Procedure.

48. Section 7; The Child Marriage Restraint Act.
49. Section 8; The Child Marriage Restraint Act.
50. Section 9; The Child Marriage Restraint Act.
51. Section 10; The Child Marriage Restraint Act.
52. Section 12 (1); The Child Marriage Restraint Act.
53. Section 12 (2); The Child Marriage Restraint Act.
54. Section 12 (1); The Child Marriage Restraint Act.
55. Section 12 (3); The Child Marriage Restraint Act.
56. Section 12 (4); The Child Marriage Restraint Act.
57. Section 12 (5); The Child Marriage Restraint Act.
58. Rajagopalachari C. (trans.); Tirukkural c. 100 AD; Bharatiya Vidya Bhawan; 2002.
59. Section 15; The National Commission for Women Act, 1990.
60. Section 16; The National Commission for Women Act, 1990.
61. Section 3; The National Commission for Women Act, 1990.
62. Section 10; The National Commission for Women Act, 1990.
63. Section 8; The National Commission for Women Act, 1990.
64. Section 17; The National Commission for Women Act, 1990.
65. Towards the end of 2006.
66. PTI Report published in the Times of India; 15.1.2007.
67. NHRC Case No. 496/20/97-98.
68. http://shout-out.org/anotherwoman.htm.
69. The Convention on the Elimination of All Forms of Discrimination against Women; www.un.org/womenwatch/daw/cedaw/econvention.htm.
70. AIR 1997 SC 3014.
71. Tharoor, Shashi; A Good Paper is Society Talking to Itself; The Times of India; 19.11.2006.
72. www.hindustantimes.com/news/7242_916472,00180008.htm.
73. http://nhrc.nic.in/ChildCases.htm.
74. SC Cautions Media on 'One Sided Reporting' of Criminal Trials; Indlaw; 5.2.2005.
75. Marshall, Lucinda; (Not) In the News: Media Culpability in the Continuum of Violence against Women.
76. www.medialens.org/alerts/2003/031010_Lulling_Submission.HTM
77. www.indianexpress.com/full_story.php?content_id=55607

# APPENDIX

The appendix contains details of the relevant provisions of various Indian laws which have been mentioned in the main text. Of those provisions which are mentioned in the appendix, the table below shows how some of them are related to each other.

| | *The Code of Criminal Procedure* | *The Indian Evidence Act* | *The Indian Penal Code* |
|---|---|---|---|
| | | *Section Numbers* | |
| Adultery | 198 (2) | 122 | 497 |
| Assault | | | 354, 355 |
| Criminal Intimidation | | | 506 |
| Cruelty | | 113 A | 498 A |
| Dowry Death | | 113 B | 304 B |
| Force | | | 350 |
| Miscarriage | | | 91, 312 to 316 |
| Offences in Relation to Marriage | 198 | 122 | 493 to 498 A |
| Prostitution, trafficking etc. | 98 | | 366 to 373 |
| Rape | 198 (6) | 114 A | 375, 376 |

## THE CODE OF CRIMINAL PROCEDURE

### Public Prosecutors

**2 (u).** 'Public Prosecutor' means any person appointed under Section 24, and includes any person acting under the directions of a Public Prosecutor.

24. *Public Prosecutors*

(1) For every High Court, the Central Government or the State Government shall, after consultation with the High Court, appoint a Public Prosecutor for conducting, in such Court, any prosecution, appeal or other proceeding on behalf of the Central or State Government, as the case may be.

(2) For every district the State Government shall appoint a Public Prosecutor and may also appoint one or more Additional Public Prosecutors for the district.

(3) The District Magistrate shall, in consultation with the Sessions Judge, prepare a panel of names of persons who are, in his opinion, fit to be appointed as the Public Prosecutor or Additional Public Prosecutor for the district.

(4) No person shall be appointed by the State Government as the Public Prosecutor or Additional Public Prosecutor for the district unless his name appears on the panel of names prepared by the District Magistrate under subsection (3).

(5) A person shall only be eligible to be appointed as a Public Prosecutor or an Additional Public Prosecutor under subsection (1) or subsection (2), if he has been in practice as an advocate for not less than seven years.

(6) The Central Government or the State Government may appoint, for the purposes of any case or class of cases, an advocate who has been in practice for not less than ten years, as a Special Public Prosecutor.

### Abducted Females

98. *Power to compel restoration of abducted females*

Upon complaint made on oath of the abduction or unlawful detention of a woman, or a female child under the age of eighteen years, for any unlawful purpose, a District Magistrate, Sub-Divisional Magistrate or Magistrate of the First Class may make an order for the immediate restoration of such woman to her liberty, or of such female child to her husband, present, guardian or other person having the lawful charge of such child, and may compel compliance with such order, using such force as may be necessary.

**Confessions and Statements**

*164. The recording of confessions and statements*

(1) Any Metropolitan Magistrate or Judicial Magistrate may, whether or not he has jurisdiction in the case, record any confession or statement made to him in the course of an investigation or at any time afterwards before the commencement of the inquiry or trial provided that no confession shall be recorded by a police officer on whom any power of a Magistrate has been conferred under any law for the time being in force.

(2) The Magistrate shall, before recording any such confession, explain to the person making it that he is not bound to make a confession and that, if he does so, it may be used as evidence against him; and the Magistrate shall not record any such confession unless, upon questioning the person making it, he has reason to believe that it is being made voluntarily.

(3) If at any time before the confession is recorded, the person appearing before the Magistrate states that he is not willing to make the confession, the Magistrate shall not authorise the detention of such person in police custody.

(4) Any such confession shall be recorded in the manner provided in Section 281 for recording the examination of an accused person and shall be signed by the person making the confession; and the Magistrate shall make a memorandum at the foot of such record to the following effect:

*"I have explained to (name) that he is not bound to make a confession and that, if he does so, any confession he may make may be used as evidence against him and I believe that this confession was voluntarily made. It was taken in my presence and hearing, and was read over to the person making it and admitted by him to be correct, and it contains a full and true account of the statement made by him.*

*(Signed) A.B.*

*Magistrate"*

(5) Any statement (other than a confession) made under subsection (1) shall be recorded in such manner hereinafter provided for

the recording of evidence as is, in the opinion of the Magistrate, best fitted to the circumstances of the case; and the Magistrate shall have power to administer oath to the person whose statement is so recorded.

(6) The Magistrate recording a confession or statement under this Section shall forward it to the Magistrate by whom the case is to be inquired into or tried.

**Offences against Marriage**

*198. Prosecution for offences against marriage*

(1) No Court shall take cognizance of an offence punishable under Chapter XX of the Indian Penal Code [which deals with offences against marriage] except upon a complaint made by some person aggrieved by the offence provided that:

  (a) where such person is under the age of eighteen years, or is an idiot or a lunatic, or is from sickness or infirmity unable to make a complaint, or is a woman who, according to the local customs and manners, ought not to be compelled to appear in public, some other person may, with the leave of the Court, make a complaint on his or her behalf,

  (b) where such person is the husband and he is serving in any of the Armed Forces of the Union under conditions which are certified by his Commanding Officer as precluding him from obtaining leave of absence to enable him to make a complaint in person, some other person authorised by the husband in accordance with the provisions of subsection (4) may make a complaint on his behalf,

  (c) where the person aggrieved by an offence punishable under Section 494 of the Indian Penal Code(45 of 1860) is the wife, complaint may be made on her behalf by her father, mother, brother, sister, son or daughter or by her father's or mother's brother or sister.

(2) For the purposes of subsection (1), no person other than the husband of the woman shall be deemed to be aggrieved by any offence punishable under Section 497 or Section 498 of the said Code provided that in the absence of the husband, some person who had care of the woman on his behalf at the time when such offence was committed may, with the leave of the Court, make a complaint on his behalf.

(3) When in any case falling under clause (a) of the proviso to subsection (1), the complaint is sought to be made on behalf of a person under the age of eighteen years or of a lunatic by a person who has not been appointed or declared by a competent authority to be the guardian of the person of the minor or lunatic, and the Court is satisfied that there is a guardian so appointed or declared, the Court shall, before granting the application for leave, cause notice to be given to such guardian and give him a reasonable opportunity of being heard.

(4) The authorisation referred to in clause (b) of the proviso to subsection (1), shall be in writing, shall be signed or otherwise attested by the husband, shall contain a statement to the effect that he has been informed of the allegations upon which the complaint is to be founded, shall be countersigned by his Commanding Officer, and shall be accompanied by a certificate signed by that Officer to the effect that leave of absence for the purpose of making a complaint in person cannot for the time being be granted to the husband.

(5) Any document purporting to be such an authorisation and complying with the provisions of subsection (4), and any document purporting to be a certificate required by that subsection shall, unless the contrary is proved, be presumed to be genuine and shall be received in evidence.

(6) No Court shall take cognizance of an offence under Section 376 of the Indian Penal Code where such offence consists of sexual intercourse by a man with his own wife, the wife being under fifteen years of age, if more than one year has elapsed from the date of the commission of the offence.

(7) The provisions of this Section apply to the abetment of, or attempt to commit, an offence as they apply to the offence.

## THE COMMISSION OF SATI (PREVENTION) ACT

The Commission of Sati (Prevention) Act, 1987 was passed to provide for the more effective prevention of the commission of Sati and its glorification and for matters connected herewith or incidental thereto. It extends to the whole of India except the State of Jammu and Kashmir. The preamble says that Sati or the burning or burying alive of widows or women is revolting to the feelings of human nature and is nowhere enjoined by any of the religions of India as an imperative duty and that it is necessary to take more effective measures to prevent the commission of Sati and its glorification.

All laws in force in any State immediately before the commencement of this Act in that State which provided for the prevention of the glorification of Sati stood repealed on the commencement of this Act. Notwithstanding such repeal, anything done or any action taken under any law so repealed were deemed to have been done or taken under the corresponding provisions of this Act, and, in particular, any case taken cognizance of by a Special Court under the provisions of any such repealed law and pending before it immediately before the commencement of this Act in that State were continued to be dealt with by that Special Court after the commencement of this Act as if such Special Court had been constituted by this Act.[1]

The provisions of this Act or any rule or order made under it shall have effect notwithstanding anything inconsistent therewith contained in any enactment other than this Act or in any instrument having effect by virtue of any enactment other than this Act.[2]

**Definitions**[3]

'Glorification', in relation to Sati, whether such Sati was committed before or after the commencement of this Act, includes:

(a) the observance of any ceremony or the taking out of a procession in connection with the commission of Sati

(b) the supporting, justifying or propagating the practice of Sati in any manner

(c) the arranging of any function to eulogise the person who has committed Sati

(d) the creation of a trust or the collection of funds or the construction of a temple or other structure or the carrying on of any form of worship or the performance of any ceremony there with a view to perpetuate the honour of or to preserve the memory of a person who has committed Sati.

*'Sati' means the burning or burying alive of*

(a) any widow along with the body of her deceased husband or any other relative or with any article, object or thing associated with the husband or such relative

(b) any woman along with the body of any of her relatives, irrespective of whether such burning or burying is claimed to be voluntary on the part of the widow or the woman or otherwise.

'Special Court' means a Special Court constituted under Section 9 which says:

> Notwithstanding anything contained in the Code of Criminal Procedure, all offences under this Act shall be triable only by a Special Court constituted under this Section. The State Government shall, by notification in the official Gazette, constitute one or more Special Courts for the trial of offences under this Act and every Special Court shall exercise jurisdiction in respect of the whole or such part of the State as may be specified in the notification.

A Special Court shall be presided over by a Judge to be appointed by the State Government with the concurrence of the Chief Justice of the High Court. A person shall not be qualified for appointment as a Judge of a Special Court unless he is, immediately before such appointment, a Sessions Judge or an Additional Sessions Judge in the State.

'Temple' includes any building or other structure, whether roofed or not, constructed or made to preserve the memory of a person of whom Sati has been committed or used or intended to be used for the carrying on of any form of worship or for the observance of any ceremony in connection with such commission.

Words and expressions used but not defined in this Act and defined in the Indian Penal Code or in the Code of Criminal Procedure shall have the same meanings as are respectively assigned to them in the Indian Penal Code or the Code of Criminal Procedure.

**An attempt to commit Sati**[4]

Notwithstanding anything contained in the Indian Penal Code, whoever attempts to commit Sati and does any act towards such commission shall be punishable with imprisonment for a term which may extend to one year or with fine or with both provided that the Special Court trying an offence under this Section shall, before convicting any person take into consideration the circumstances leading to the commission of the offence, the act committed, the state of mind of the person charged of the offence at the time of the commission of the act and all other relevant factors.

**The Abetment of Sati**[5]

Notwithstanding anything contained in the Indian Penal Code, if any person commits Sati, whoever, abets the commission of such Sati, either directly or indirectly, he shall be punishable with death or imprisonment for life and shall also be liable to fine.

If any person attempts to commit Sati, whoever abets such attempt, either directly or indirectly, shall be punishable with imprisonment for life and shall also be liable to fine.

Any of the following acts or the like shall also be deemed to be an abetment:

- any inducement to a widow or woman to get her burnt or buried alive along with the body of her deceased husband or with any other relative irrespective of whether she is in a fit state of mind or is labouring under a state of intoxication or stupefaction or other case impeding the exercise of her free will
- making a widow or woman believe that the commission of Sati would result in some spiritual benefit to her or her deceased husband or relative or the general well being of the family
- encouraging a widow or woman to remain fixed in her resolve to commit Sati and thus instigating her to commit Sati
- participating in the procession in connection with the commission of Sati or aiding the widow or woman in her decision to commit Sati by taking her along with the body of her deceased husband or relative to the cremation or burial ground
- being present at the place where Sati is committed as an active participant to such commission or to any ceremony connected with it
- preventing or obstructing the widow or woman from saving herself from being burnt or buried alive
- obstructing or interfering with the police in the discharge of its duties of taking any steps to prevent the commission of Sati.

Where any person is prosecuted for such an offence, the burden of proving that he had not committed the offence under the said Section shall be on him.[6]

### Punishments, Duties and Disqualifications

Whoever does any act for the glorification of Sati shall be punishable with imprisonment for a term which shall not be less than one year but which may extend to seven years and with fine which shall not be less than five thousand rupees but which may extend to thirty thousand rupees.[7]

A person convicted of an offence in relation to the commission of Sati shall be disqualified from inheriting the property of the person in respect of whom such Sati has been committed or the property of any other person such which he would have been entitled to inherit on the death of the person in respect of whom such Sati has been committed.[8]

All officers of Government are required and empowered to assist the police in the execution of the provisions of this Act or any rule or order made under it. All village officers and such other officers as may be specified by the Collector or the District Magistrate in relation to any area and the inhabitants of such area shall, if they have reason to believe or have the knowledge that Sati is about to be or has been committed in the area, forthwith report it to the nearest police station. Whoever does not do so shall be punishable with imprisonment of either description for a term which may extend to two years and shall also be liable to fine.[9]

No suit, prosecution or other legal proceeding shall lie against the State Government or any officer or authority of the State Government for anything which is in good faith done or intended to be done in pursuance of this Act or any rules or orders made under this Act.[10]

The Commission of Sati (Prevention) Act, 1987 also amended the Representation of the People Act, 1951 by providing that a person convicted by a Special Court for the contravention of any of the provisions under it would be disqualified from the date of such conviction and would continue to be disqualified to stand for election for a period of five years from his release. Also, the propagation of the practice or the commission of Sati or its glorification by a candidate or his agent or any other person with the consent of the candidate or his election agent for the furtherance of prospects of the election of that candidate or for prejudicially affecting the election of any candidate is illegal.[11]

### The Powers of the Collector or District Magistrate to Prevent Offences Relating to Sati

Where the Collector or the District Magistrate is of the opinion that Sati or any abetment thereof is being or is about to be committed, he may, by order, prohibit the doing of any act towards the commission of Sati by any person in any area or areas specified in the order. He may also, by order, prohibit the glorification in any manner of Sati by any person in any area or areas specified in the order. Whoever contravenes any such order made shall, if such contravention is not punishable under any other provision of this Act, be punishable with imprisonment for a term which shall not be less than one year but which may extend to seven years and with fine which shall not be less than five thousand rupees but which may extend to thirty thousand rupees.[12]

The State Government may, if it is satisfied that in any temple or other structure which has been in existence for not less than twenty years, any form of worship or the performance of any ceremony is carried on with a view to perpetuate the honour of or to preserve the memory of, any person in respect of whom Sati has been committed, by order, direct the removal of such temple or other structure.

The Collector or the District Magistrate may, if he is satisfied that in any temple or other structure, other than that referred to earlier, any form of worship or the performance of any ceremony is carried on with a view to perpetuate the honour of or to preserve the memory of, any person in respect of whom Sati has been committed, by order, direct the removal of such temple or other structure. Where any such order is not complied with, the State Government or the Collector or the District Magistrate as the case may be, shall cause the temple or other structure to be removed through a police officer not below the rank of a Sub-Inspector at the cost of defaulter.[13]

Where the Collector or the District Magistrate has reason to believe that any funds or property have been collected or acquired for the purpose of glorification of the commission of any Sati or which may be found under circumstances which create suspicion of the commission of any offence under this Act, he may seize such funds or property. He shall report the seizure to the Special Court, if any, constituted to try any offence in relation to which such funds or property were collected or acquired and shall await the order of such Special Court as to the disposal of the same.[14]

No suit, prosecution or other legal proceeding shall lie against the State Government or any officer or authority of the State Government for anything which is in good faith done or intended to be done in pursuance of this Act or any rules or orders made under this Act.[15]

**Special Public Prosecutors**

For every Special Court, the State Government shall appoint a person to be a Special Public Prosecutor. A person shall be eligible to be appointed as a Special Public Prosecutor under this Section only if he had been in practice as an advocate for not less than seven years or has held any post for a period of not less than seven years under the State requiring special knowledge of law.

Every person appointed as a Special Public Prosecutor under this Section shall be deemed to be a Public Prosecutor within the meaning of Section 2 (u) of the Code of Criminal Procedure and the provisions of the Code of Criminal Procedure shall have effect accordingly.[16]

**The Procedure and Powers of Special Courts**

A Special Court may take cognizance of any offence, without the accused being committed to it for trial upon receiving a complaint of facts which constitute such offence or upon a police report of such facts.

Subject to the other provisions of this Act, a Special Court shall, for the purpose of the trial of any offence, have all the powers of a Court of Sessions and shall try such offence as if it were a Court of Session, so far as may be, in accordance with the procedure prescribed in the Code of Criminal Procedure for trial before a Court of Session.[17]

When trying any offence under this Act, a Special Court may also try any other offence with which the accused may, under the Code of Criminal Procedure, be charged at the same trial if the offence is connected with such other offence. If, in the course of any trial of any offence under this Act it is found that the accused person has committed any other offence under this Act or under any other law, a Special Court may convict such person also of such other offence and pass any sentence authorised by this Act or such other law for punishment thereof.

In every inquiry or trial, the proceedings shall be held as expeditiously as possible, and, in particular, where the examination of witnesses has begun, the same shall be continued from day to day until all the witnesses in attendance have been examined and if any Special Court finds the adjournment of the same beyond the following date to be necessary, it shall record its reasons for doing so.[18]

Where a person has been convicted of an offence under this Act, the Special Court trying such offence may, if it is considered necessary so to do, declare that any funds or property seized under Section 8 shall stand forfeited to the State.[19]

(Section 8, inter alia, says that where the Collector or the District Magistrate has reason to believe that any funds or property have been collected or acquired for the purpose of glorification of the commission of any Sati or which may be found under circumstances which create suspicion of the commission of any offence under this Act, he may seize such funds or property.)

**Appeals**

Notwithstanding anything contained in the Code of Criminal Procedure, an appeal shall lie as a matter of right from any judgment, sentence or order, not being an interlocutory order, of a Special Court to the High Court both on facts and on law. Every appeal under this Section shall be preferred within a period of thirty days from the date of the judgment, sentence or order appealed from provided that the High Court may entertain an appeal after the expiry of the said period of thirty days if it is satisfied that the appellant had sufficient cause for not preferring the appeal within the period of thirty days.[20]

**Rules**

The Central Government may, by notification in the official Gazette, make rules for carrying out the provisions of this Act. Every such rule made under this Section shall be laid, as soon as may be after it is made, before each House of Parliament, while it is in session, for a total period of thirty days which may be comprised in one session or in two or more successive sessions, and if, before the expiry of the session immediately following the session or the successive sessions aforesaid, both Houses agree in making any modification in the rule or both Houses agree that the rule should not be made, the rule shall thereafter have effect only in such modified form or be of no effect, as the case may be; so, however, that any such modification or annulment shall be without prejudice to the validity of anything previously done under that rule.[21]

In pursuance of this power, the Commission of Sati (Prevention) Rules, 1988 were framed as follows:

> The State Government may, by order and subject to such conditions as it may deem fit to impose, direct that the powers of the Collector or the District Magistrate (under Section 6 of the Act) to prevent the commission of offences relating to Sati may also be exercised by such other officers, not below the rank of the village officers.[22]

Every prohibitory order (under Section 6 of the Act) to prevent the commission of offences relating to Sati shall be made by beat of drum or other customary mode, in the concerned village or in case of town or city, in the locality in which the act prohibited is likely to occur or has taken place. The prohibitory order shall be displayed at some conspicuous place in the area or areas to which such acts relates and a copy thereof shall also be displayed in the office of the officer issuing the prohibitory order and such display shall be taken as a sufficient notice to all persons concerned in the area or areas to which such order relates.[23]

Before making any order under Section 7 (1) for the removal of any temple or structure, the State Government or any other officer authorised by the State Government in this behalf, shall give at least 90 days notice to the person or persons involved in the acts complained of, and also to the owners and occupiers of the temple or structure proposed to be removed. The notice shall specify:

- the temple/structure proposed to be removed, its location and other particulars
- the owners/occupiers of the temple/structure
- the specific instance or instances of worship or ceremony contravening the provisions of Section 7.

The State Government or the officer authorised by the State Government in this behalf shall, after giving reasonable opportunity of being heard to persons specified in the notice order the removal of the temple or structure through a police officer not below the rank of the Sub-Inspector.[24]

After the issue of a prohibitory order (under Section 6 of the Act) to prevent the commission of offences relating to Sati, the Collector or the District Magistrate or such other officer as directed by the State Government by order under these rules, shall, before making any order for removal of any temple or structure, give at least 90 days notice to the person or persons involved in the acts complained of, and also to the owners and occupiers of the temple or structure proposed to be removed. The Collector or the District Magistrate or such other officer as directed by the State Government by order, shall follow the provisions of these rules.[25]

As soon as the order of removal of the temple or structure is executed, the State Government or the Collector or the District Magistrate or as the case may be, the officer as directed by the State Government, shall prepare an inventory of all the material and other property obtained after removal of such temple or structure specifying in it the place where it is lodged or kept, and shall forward the intimation thereof to the Special Court for declaration of forfeiture of the said material or property to the State under Section 13, if the Special Court considers it necessary so to do, and shall also give a copy of the inventory to the owners/occupiers of the temple/structure removed.[26] These Sections, inter alia, say:

**Section 8**

Where the Collector or the District Magistrate has reason to believe that any funds or property have been collected or acquired for the purpose of glorification of the commission of any Sati or which may be found under circumstances which create suspicion of the commission of any offence under this Act, he may seize such funds or property.

**Section 13**

Where a person has been convicted of an offence under this Act, the Special Court trying such offence may, if it is considered necessary so to do, declare that any funds or property seized under Section 8 shall stand forfeited to the State.

## THE IMMORAL TRAFFIC PREVENTION ACT

**Definitions**[27]

- 'brothel' includes any house room, conveyance or place or any portion of any house, room, conveyance or place, which is used for purposes of sexual exploitation or abuse] for the gain of another person or for the mutual gain of two or more prostitutes
- 'child' means a person who has not completed the age of sixteen years
- 'corrective institution' means an institution, by whatever name called (being an institution established or licensed as such under the provisions of Section 21 which deal with protective homes), in which persons, who are in need of correction, may be detained under this Act, and includes a shelter where under-trials may be kept in pursuance of this Act
- 'major' means a person who has completed the age of eighteen years
- 'minor' means a person who has completed the age of sixteen years but has not completed the age of eighteen years
- 'prostitution' means the sexual exploitation or abuse of persons for commercial purposes, and the expression 'prostitute' shall be construed accordingly
- 'protective home' means an institution by whatever name called (being an institution established or licensed as such

under the provisions of Section 21 which deal with protective homes), in which persons, who are in need of care and protection, may be kept under this Act and where appropriate technically qualified persons, equipment and other facilities have been provided, but does not include

- a shelter where undertrials may be kept in pursuance of this Act
- a corrective institution

- 'public place' means any place intended for use by or accessible to, the public and includes any public conveyance
- 'special police officer' means a police officer appointed by or on behalf of the State Government to be in charge of police duties within a specified area for the purpose of this Act
- 'trafficking police officer' means a police officer appointed by the Central Government under Section 13 (4).

**Provisions**

Any person who keeps or manages or acts or assists in the keeping or management of, a brothel shall be punishable on first conviction with rigorous imprisonment for a term of not less than one year and not more than three years and also with fine which may extend to two thousand rupees and in the event of a second or subsequent conviction, with rigorous imprisonment for a term of not less than two years and not more than five years and also with fine which may extend to two thousand rupees.

Any person who:

(a) being the tenant, lessee, occupier or person-in-charge of any premises, uses or knowingly allows any other person to use, such premises or any part thereof as a brothel

(b) being the owner, lessor or landlord of any premises or the agent of such owner, lessor or landlord, lets the same or any part thereof with the knowledge that the same or any part thereof is intended to be used as a brothel or is wilfully a party to the use of such premises or any part thereof as a brothel.

Shall be punishable on first conviction with imprisonment for a term which may extend to two years and with fine which may extend to two thousand rupees and in the event of a second or subsequent conviction, with rigorous imprisonment for a term which may extend to five years and also with fine. [28]

It shall be presumed until the contrary is proved, that any such person is knowingly allowing the premises or any part thereof to be used as a brothel or, as the case maybe, has knowledge that the premises or any part thereof are being used as a brothel, if:

(a) a report is published in a newspaper having circulation in the area in which such person resides to the effect that the premises or any part thereof have been found to be used for prostitution as a result of a search made under this Act

(b) a copy of the list of all things found during the search referred to earlier is given to such person.

Notwithstanding anything contained in any other law for the time being in force, on conviction of any such person of any offence mentioned earlier, any lease or agreement under which such premises have been leased out or are held or occupied at the time of the commission of the offence, shall become void and inoperative with effect from the date of the said conviction.

Any person over the age of eighteen years who knowingly lives, wholly or in part, on the earnings of the prostitution of any other person shall be punishable with imprisonment for a term which may extend to two years or with fine which may extend to one thousand rupees or with both and where such earnings relate to the prostitution of a child or a minor, shall be punishable with imprisonment for a term of not less than seven years and not more than ten years.

Where any person over the age of eighteen years is proved:

(a) to be living with or to be habitually in the company of, a prostitute

(b) to have exercised control, direction or influence over the movements of a prostitute in such a manner as to show that such person is aiding, abetting or compelling her prostitution

(c) to be acting as a tout or pimp on behalf of a prostitute it shall be presumed, until the contrary is proved, that such person is knowingly living on the earnings of prostitution of another person.[29]

Any person who:

- procures or attempts to procure a person, whether with or without his consent, for the purpose of prostitution
- induces a person to go from any place with the intent that he may for the purpose of prostitution become the inmate of or frequent a brothel

- takes or attempts to take a person or causes a person to be taken from one place to another with a view to his carrying on or being brought up to carry on prostitution
- causes or induces a person to carry on prostitution.

Shall be punishable on conviction with rigorous imprisonment for a term of not less than three years and not more than seven years and also with fine which may extend to two thousand rupees, and if any offence mentioned earlier is committed against the will of any person, the punishment of imprisonment for a term of seven years shall extend to imprisonment for a term of fourteen years provided that if the person against whom an offence committed:

- is a child, the punishment shall extend to rigorous imprisonment for a term of not less than seven years but may extend to life
- is a minor, the punishment shall extend to rigorous imprisonment for a term of not less than seven years and not more than fourteen years.

An offence under this Section shall be triable:

- in the place from which a person is procured, induced to go, taken or caused to be taken or from which an attempt to procure or take such person is made
- in the place to which he may have gone as a result of the inducement or to which he is taken or caused to be taken or an attempt to take him is made.[30]

Any person who detains any other person whether with or without his consent:

(a) in any brothel or

(b) in or upon any premises with intent that such person may have sexual intercourse with a person who is not the spouse of such person

Shall be punishable on conviction, with imprisonment of either description for a term which shall not be less than seven years but which may be for life or for a term which may extend to ten years and shall also be liable to fine provided that the Court may, for adequate and special reasons to be mentioned in the judgement, impose a sentence of imprisonment for a term of less than seven years.

Where any person is found with a child in a brothel, it shall be presumed, unless the contrary is proved, that he has committed an offence. Where a child or minor found in a brothel, is on medical examination, detected to have been sexually abused, it shall be presumed unless the contrary is proved, that the child or minor has been detained for purposes of prostitution or, as the case may be, has been sexually exploited for commercial purposes.

A person shall be presumed to detain a woman or girl in a brothel or in or upon any premises for the purpose of sexual intercourse with a man other than her lawful husband, if such person, with intent to compel or induce her to remain there:

- withholds from her any jewellery, wearing apparel, money or other property belonging to her or
- threatens her with legal proceedings if she takes away with her any jewellery, wearing apparel, money or other property lent or supplied to her by or by the direction of such person.

Notwithstanding any law to the contrary, no suit, prosecution or other legal proceeding shall lie against such woman or girl at the instance of the person by whom she has been detained, for the recovery of any jewellery, wearing apparel or other property alleged to have been lent or supplied to or for such woman or girl or to have been pledged by such woman or girl or the recovery of any money alleged to be payable by such woman or girl.[31]

Any person, who carries on prostitution and the person with whom such prostitution is carried on, in any premises:

(a) which are within notified areas (The State Government may, having regard to the kinds of persons frequenting any area or areas in the State, the nature and the density of population therein and other relevant considerations, by notification in the Official Gazette, direct that prostitution shall not be carried on in such area or areas as may be specified in the notification.)

(b) which are within a distance of two hundred metres of any place of public religious worship, educational institution, hostel, hospital, nursing home or such other public place of any kind as may be notified in this behalf by the Commissioner of Police or Magistrate in the manner prescribed.

Shall be punishable with imprisonment for a term which may extend to three months. Where an offence committed is in respect of a child or minor, the person committing the offence shall be punishable with imprisonment of either description for a term which shall not be less than seven years but which may be for life or for a term which may extend to ten years and shall also be liable to fine provided that the Court may, for adequate and special reasons to be mentioned in the judgement impose a sentence of imprisonment for a term of less than seven years.

Any person who:

- being the keeper of any public place knowingly permits prostitution for purposes of their trade to resort to or remain in such place
- being the tenant, lessee, occupier or person-in-charge of any such premises knowingly permits the same or any part thereof to be used for prostitution
- being the owner, lessor or landlord, of any such premises, or the agent of such owner, lessor or landlord, lets the same or any part thereof may be used for prostitution or is wilfully a party to such use.

Shall be punishable on first conviction with imprisonment for a term which may extend to three months or with fine which may extend to two hundred rupees or with both, and in the event of a second or subsequent conviction with imprisonment for a term which may extend to six months and also with fine which may extend to two hundred rupees, and if the public place or premises happen to be a hotel, the license for carrying on the business of such hotel under any law for the time being in force shall also be liable to be suspended for a period of not less than three months but which may extend to one year provided that if an offence committed is in respect of a child or minor in a hotel, such license shall also be liable to be cancelled.[32]

Whoever, in any public place or within sight of, and in such manner as to be seen or heard from any public place, whether from within any building or house or not:

(a) by words, gestures, wilful exposure of her person (whether by sitting by a window or on the balcony of a building or house or in any other way) or otherwise tempts or endeavours to tempt or attracts or endeavours to attract the attention of, any person for the purpose of prostitution

(b) solicits or molests any person or loiters or acts in such manner as to cause obstruction or annoyance to persons residing nearby or passing by such public place or to offend against public decency, for the purpose of prostitution.

Shall be punishable on first conviction, with imprisonment for a term which may extend to six months or with fine which may extend to five hundred rupees or with both, and in the event of a second or subsequent conviction, with imprisonment for a term which may extend to five hundred rupees, and also with fine which may extend to five hundred rupees provided that where an offence under this Section is committed by a man he shall be punishable with imprisonment for a period of not less than seven days but which may extend to three months.[33]

Any person who having the custody, charge or care of or a position of authority over any person, causes or aids or abets the seduction for prostitution of that person shall be punishable on conviction with imprisonment of either description for a term which shall not be less than seven years but which may be for life or for a term which may extend to ten years and shall also be liable to fine provided that the Court may, for adequate and special reasons to be mentioned in the judgement, impose a sentence of imprisonment for a term of less than seven years.[34]

Where:

(a) a female offender is found guilty of an offence under Section 7 or Section 8–which deal with prostitution in or in the vicinity of public places, and seducing or soliciting for the purpose of prostitution–and

(b) the character, state of health and mental condition of the offender and the other circumstances of the case are such that it is expedient that she should be subjected to detention for such term and such instruction and discipline as are conducive to her correction.

It shall be lawful for the Court to pass, in lieu of a sentence of imprisonment, an order for detention in a corrective institution for such term, not being less than two years and not being more than five years, as the Court thinks fit provided that before passing such an order:

(i) the Court shall give an opportunity to the offender to be heard and shall also consider any representation which the offender may make to the Court as to the suitability of the case for treatment in such an institution, as also the report of the probation officer appointed under the Probation of Offenders Act, 1958 and

(ii) the Court shall record that it is satisfied that the character, state of health and mental condition of the offender and the other circumstances of the case are such that the offender is likely to benefit by such instruction and discipline as aforesaid.

The provisions of the Code of Criminal Procedure, 1973 relating to appeal, reference and revision and of the Limitation Act, 1963 as to the period within which an appeal shall be filed, shall apply in relation to an order of detention as if the order had been a sentence of imprisonment for the same period as the period for which the detention was ordered.

Subject to such rules as may be made in this behalf, the State Government or authority authorised in this behalf may, at any time after the expiration of six months from the date of an order for detention in a corrective institution if it is satisfied that there is a reasonable probability that the offender will lead a useful and industrious life, discharge her from such an institution, without condition or with such conditions as may be considered fit, and grant her a written license in such form as may be prescribed.

The conditions on which an offender is discharged may include requirements relating to residence of the offender and supervision over the offender's activities and movements.

When any person having been convicted:

(a) by a Court in India of an offence punishable under this Act or punishable under Section 363, Section 365, Section 366, Section 366A, Section 366B, Section 367, Section 368, Section 370, Section 371, Section 372 or Section 373 of the Indian Penal Code with imprisonment for a term of two years or upwards

(b) by a Court or tribunal in any other country of an offence which would, if committed in India, have been punishable under this Act or under any of the aforesaid Sections with imprisonment for a life term.

Is within a period of five years after release from prison, again convicted of any offence punishable under this Act or under any of those Sections with imprisonment for a term of two years or upwards by a Court, such Court may, if it thinks fit, at the time of passing the sentence of imprisonment on such person, also order that his residence, and any change of or absence from such residence after release be notified for a period not exceeding five years from the date of expiration of that sentence.

If such a conviction is set aside on appeal or otherwise such order shall become void. An order under this Section may also be made by an Appellate Court or by the High Court when exercising its powers or revision.

There shall be for each area to be specified by the State Government in this behalf a special police officer appointed by or on behalf of that

Government for dealing with offences under this Act in that area. The special police officer shall not be below the rank of an Inspector of Police.

The District Magistrate may if he considers it necessary or expedient so to do, confer upon any retired police or military officer all or any of the powers conferred by or under this Act on a special police officer, with respect to particular cases or classes of cases or to cases generally provided that no such power shall be conferred on:

(a) a retired police officer unless such officer, at the time of his retirement, was holding a post not below the rank of an inspector

(b) a retired military officer unless such officer, at the time if his retirement, was holding a post not below the rank of a commissioned officer.

For the efficient discharge of his functions in relation to offences under this Act:

- the special police officer of an area shall be assisted by such number of subordinate police officers (including women police officers wherever practicable) as the State Government may think fit; and
- the State Government may associate with the special police officer a non-official advisory body consisting of not more than five leading social welfare workers of that area (including women social welfare workers wherever practicable) to advise him on questions of general importance regarding the working of this Act.
- the Central Government may, for the purpose of investigating any offence under this Act or under any other law for the time being in force dealing with sexual exploitation of persons and committed in more than one State, appoint such number of police officers as trafficking police officers and they shall exercise all the powers and discharge all the functions as are exercisable by special police officers under this Act with the modification that they shall exercise such powers and discharge such functions in relation to the whole of India.[35]

Notwithstanding anything contained in the Code of Criminal Procedure, 1973 any offence punishable under this Act shall be deemed to be a cognizable offence within the meaning of that Code provided that, notwithstanding anything contained in that Code:

(i) arrest without warrant may be made only by special police officer or under his direction or guidance or s ıbject to his prior approval

(ii) when the special police officer requires any officer subordinate to him to arrest without warrant otherwise than in his presence any person for an offence under this Act, he shall give that subordinate officer an order in writing, specifying the person to be arrested and the offence for which the arrest is being made; and the latter officer before arresting the person shall inform him of the substance of the order and, on being required by such person, show him the order

(iii) any police officer not below the rank of sub-inspector specially authorised by the special police officer may, if he has reason to believe that on account of delay involved in obtaining the order of the special police officer, any valuable evidence relating to any offence under this Act is likely to be destroyed or concealed or the person who has committed or is suspected to have committed the offence is likely to escape or if the name and address of such a person is unknown or there is reason to suspect that a false name or address has been given, arrest the person concerned without such order, but in such a case he shall report, as soon as may be, to the special police officer the arrest and the circumstances in which the arrest was made.[36]

Notwithstanding anything contained in any other law for the time being in force, whenever the special police officer or the trafficking police officer, as the case may be,] has reasonable grounds for believing that an offence punishable under this Act has been or is being committed in respect of a person living in any premises, and that search of the premises with warrant cannot be made without undue delay, such officer may, after recording the grounds of his belief, enter and search such premises without a warrant.

The special police officer or the trafficking police officer, as the case may be, shall call upon two or more respectable inhabitants (at least one of whom shall be a woman) of the locality in which the place to be searched is situated, to attend and witness the search, and may issue an order in writing to them or any of them so to do provided that the requirement as to the respectable inhabitants being from the locality in which place to be searched is situate shall not apply to a woman required to attend and witness the search.

Any person who, without reasonable cause, refuses or neglects, to attend and witness a search under this Section, when called upon to do so by an order in writing delivered or tendered to him, shall be deemed to have committed an offence under Section 187 of the Indian Penal Code.

The special police officer or the trafficking police officer, as the case may be, entering any premises shall be entitled to remove from there all the persons found therein.

The special police officer or the trafficking police officer, as the case may be, after removing the person shall forthwith produce him before the appropriate Magistrate. Any person who is produced before a Magistrate shall be examined by a registered medical practitioner for the purposes of determination of the age of such person or for the detection of any injuries as a result of sexual abuse or for the presence of any sexually transmitted diseases.

The special police officer or the trafficking police officer, as the case may be, and other persons taking part in or attending, and witnessing a search shall not be liable to any civil or criminal proceedings against them in respect of anything lawfully done in connection with or for the purpose of the search.

The special police officer or the trafficking police officer, as the case may be, making a search under this Section shall be accompanied by at least two women police officers, and where any women or girl removed is required to be interrogated, it shall be done by a woman police officer and if no woman police officer is available, the interrogation shall be done only in the presence of a lady member of a recognised welfare institution or organisation.[37]

Where a magistrate has reason to believe from information received from the police or from any other person authorised by the State Government in this behalf or otherwise, that any person is living or is carrying on or is being made to carry on, prostitution in a brothel, he may direct a police officer not below the rank of a sub-inspector to enter such brothel, and to remove from there such person and produce him before him. The police officer, after removing the person, shall forthwith produce him before the magistrate issuing the order.[38]

When the special police officer removing a person or a police officer rescuing a person is for any reason unable to produce him before the appropriate magistrate, he shall forthwith produce him before the nearest magistrate of any class, who shall pass such orders as he deems proper for his safe custody until he is produced before the appropriate magistrate or, as the case may be, the magistrate issuing the order provided that no person shall be:

(i) detained in custody for a period exceeding ten days from the date of the order

(ii) restored to or placed in the custody of a person who may exercise a harmful influence over him.

When the person is produced before the appropriate magistrate, he shall, after giving him an opportunity of being heard, cause an inquiry to be made as to the correctness of the information received, the age, character and antecedents of the person and the suitability of his parents, guardian or husband for taking charge of him and the nature of the influence which the conditions in his home are likely to have on him if he is sent home, and, for this purpose, he may direct a probation officer appointed under the Probation of Offenders Act, 1958, to inquire into the circumstances mentioned earlier and into the personality of the person and the prospects of his rehabilitation.

The magistrate may, while an inquiry is made, pass such orders as he deems proper for the safe custody of the person provided that where a person rescued (under Section 16) is a child or minor, it shall be open to the magistrate to place such child or minor in any institution established or recognised under any Children Act for the time being in force in any State for the safe custody of children provided further that, no person shall be kept in custody for this purpose for a period exceeding three weeks from the date of such an order, and no person shall be kept in the custody of a person likely to have a harmful influence over him.

Where the magistrate is satisfied, after making an inquiry:

- that the information received is correct and
- that he is in need of care and protection.

He may make an order that such person be detained for such period, being not less than one year and not more than three years, as may be specified in the order, in a protective home or in such other custody as he shall, for reasons to be recorded in writing, consider suitable provided that such custody shall not be that of the person or body of persons of a religious persuasion different from that of the person and that those entrusted with the custody of the person including the persons-in-charge of a protective home, may be required to enter into a bond which may, where necessary and feasible, contain undertakings based on directions relating to the proper care, guardianship, education, training and medical and psychiatric treatment of the person as well as supervision by a person appointed by the Court, which will be in force for a period not exceeding three years.

In discharging his functions, a magistrate may summon a panel of five respectable persons, three of whom shall, wherever practicable, be women to assist him; and may, for this purpose, keep a list of experienced social welfare workers, particularly women social welfare workers, in the field of suppression of immoral traffic in persons. An appeal against an order shall lie to the Court of Session whose decision on such appeal shall be final.[39]

The magistrate may before passing an order for handing over any persons rescued to their parents, guardian or husband, satisfy himself about the capacity or genuineness of the parents, guardian or husband to keep such person by causing an investigation to be made by a recognised welfare institution or organisation.[40]

A magistrate may, on receipt of information from the police or otherwise, that any house, room, place or any portion thereof within a distance of two hundred meters of any public place referred to is being run or used as a brothel by any person or is being used by prostitutes for carrying on their trade, issue notice on the owner, lessor or landlord of such house, room, place, portion or the agent of the owner, lessor or landlord or on tenant, lessee, occupier of or any other person-in-charge of such house, room, place or portion, to show cause within seven days of the receipt of the notice why the same should not be attached for improper uses thereof; and if, after hearing the person concerned, the magistrate is satisfied that the house, room, place or portion is being used as a brothel or for carrying on prostitution, then the magistrate may pass orders:

- directing eviction of the occupier within seven days of the passing of the order from the house, room, place or portion
- directing that before letting it out during the period of one year or in a case where a child or minor has been found in such house, room, place or portion during a search during the period of three years immediately after the passing of the order, the owner, lessor or landlord or the agent of the owner, lessor or landlord shall obtain the previous approval of the magistrate provided that, if the magistrate finds that the owner, lessor or landlord as well as the agent of the owner, lessor or landlord, was innocent of the improper user of the house, room, place or portion, he may cause the same, to be restored to the owner, lessor or landlord or the agent of the owner, lessor or landlord, with a direction that the house, room, place or portion shall not be leased out or otherwise given possession of, to or for the benefit of the person who was allowing the improper user therein.

A Court convicting a person of any offence involving knowingly allowing any place to be used for prostitution may pass orders without further notice to such person to show cause. Orders passed by the magistrate or Court shall not be subject to appeal and shall not be stayed or set aside by the order of any Court, civil or criminal and the said orders shall cease to have validity after the expiry of one year or three years, as the case may be provided that where a conviction is set aside on appeal on the ground that such house, room, place or any portion thereof is not being run or used as a brothel or is not being used by prostitutes for carrying on their trade, any order passed by the Trial Court shall also be set aside.

Notwithstanding anything contained in any other law for the time being in force, when a magistrate passes an order, any lease or agreement under which the house, room, place or portion is occupied at the time shall become void and inoperative.

When an owner, lessor or landlord or the agent of such owner, lessor or landlord fails to comply with a direction given, he shall be punishable with fine which may extend to five hundred rupees or when he fails to comply with a direction under the proviso to that subsection, he shall be deemed to have committed the offence of carrying on prostitution in or in the vicinity of public places and be punished accordingly.[41]

A person, who is carrying on or is being made to carry on prostitution, may make an application to the magistrate within the local limits of whose jurisdiction he is carrying on or is being made to carry on prostitution, for an order that he may be kept in a protective home or provided care and protection by the Court.

The Magistrate may, pending inquiry, direct that the person be kept in such custody as he may consider proper, having regard to the circumstances of the case.

If the magistrate, after hearing the applicant and making such inquiry as he may consider necessary, including an inquiry by a probation officer appointed under the Probation of Offenders Act, 1958 into the personality, conditions of home and prospects of rehabilitation of the applicant, is satisfied that an order should be made under this Section, he shall, for reasons to be recorded, make an order that the applicant be kept:

(a) in a protective home or

(b) in a corrective institution or

Under the supervision of a person appointed by the magistrate, for such period as may be specified in the order.[42]

A magistrate on receiving information that any person residing in or frequenting any place within the local limits of his jurisdiction is a prostitute, may record the substance of the information received and issue a notice to such person requiring him to appear before the magistrate and show cause why he should not be required to remove himself from the place and be prohibited from re-entering it.

Every notice issued shall be accompanied by a copy of the record aforesaid, and the copy shall be served along with the notice on the person against whom the notice is issued.

The magistrate shall after the service of the notice referred to, proceed to inquire into the truth of the information received, and after giving the person an opportunity of adducing evidence, take such further evidence as he thinks fit, and if upon such inquiry it appears to him that such person is a prostitute and that it is necessary in the interests of the general public that such person should be required to remove himself from there and be prohibited from re-entering the same, the magistrate shall, by order in writing communicated to the person in the manner specified therein, require him after a date (to be specified in the order) which shall not be less than seven days from the date of the order, to remove himself from the place to such place whether within or without the local limits of his jurisdiction, by such route or routes and within such time as may be specified in the order and also prohibit from re-entering the place without the permission in writing of the magistrate having jurisdiction over such place.

Whoever:

- fails to comply with an order issued under this Section, within the period specified therein or whilst an order prohibiting him from re-entering a place without permission is in force, re-enters the place without such permission or
- knowing that any person has, under this Section, been required to remove himself from the place and has not obtained the requisite permission to re-enter it, harbours or conceals such person in the place shall be punishable with fine which may extend to two hundred rupees and in the case of continuing offence with an additional fine which may extend to twenty rupees for every day after the first during which he has persisted in the offence.[43]

### Protective Homes[44]

The State Government may in its discretion establish as many protective homes and corrective institutions under this Act as it thinks fit and such homes and institutions, when established, shall be maintained in such manner as may be prescribed.

No person or authority other than the State Government shall after the commencement of this Act, establish or maintain any protective home or corrective institution except under and in accordance with the conditions of, a license issued under this Section by the State Government.

The State Government may, on application made to it in this behalf by a person or authority, issue to such person or authority a license in the prescribed form for establishing and maintaining or, as the case may be, for maintaining a protective home or corrective institution and a license so issued may contain such conditions as the State Government may think fit to impose in accordance with the rules made under this Act. Any such condition may require that the management of the protective home or corrective institution shall, wherever practicable, be entrusted to women.

Before issuing a license the State Government may require such officer or authority as it may appoint for this purpose, to make a full and complete investigation in respect of the application received in this behalf and report to it the result of such investigation and in making any such investigation the officer or authority shall follow such procedure as may be prescribed.

A license, unless sooner revoked, shall remain in force for such period as may be specified in the license and may, on application made in this behalf at least thirty days before the date of its expiration, be renewed for a like period.

No license issued or renewed under this Act shall be transferable.

Where any person or authority to whom a license has been granted under this Act or any agent or servant of such person or authority commits a breach of any of the conditions thereof or any of the provisions of this Act or of any of the rules made under this Act or where the State Government is not satisfied with the condition, management or superintendence of any protective home or corrective institution , the State Government may, without prejudice to any other penalty which may have been incurred under this Act, for reasons to be recorded, revoke the license by order in writing provided that no such order shall be made until an opportunity is given to the holder of the license to show cause why the license shall not be revoked.

Where a license in respect of a protective home or corrective institution has been revoked under the foregoing subsection such protective home shall cease to function from the date of such revocation.

Subject to any rules that may be made in this behalf, the State Government may also vary or amend any license issued or renewed under this Act.

The State Government or an authority authorised by it in this behalf may, subject to any rules that may be made in this behalf, transfer an inmate of a protective home to another protective home or to a corrective institution or an inmate of a corrective institution to another corrective institution or to a protective home, where such transfer is considered desirable having regard to the conduct of the person to be transferred, the kind of training to be imparted and other circumstances of the case provided that:

(a) no person who is transferred under this subsection shall be required to stay in the home or institution to which he is transferred for a period longer than he was required to stay in the home or institution from which he was transferred

(b) reasons shall be recorded for every order of transfer.

Whoever establishes or maintains a protective home or corrective institution except in accordance with the provisions of this Section, shall be punishable in the case of a first offence with fine which may extend to one thousand rupees and in the case of second or subsequent offence with imprisonment for a term which may extend to one year or with fine which may extend to two thousand rupees or with both.[45]

Every person or authority who is licensed to establish or maintain or as the case may be, for maintaining, a protective home or corrective institution shall, whenever required by a Court, produce the records and other documents maintained by such home or institution before such Court.[46]

**Special Courts**

If the State Government is satisfied that it is necessary for the purpose of providing for speedy trial of offences under this Act in any district or metropolitan area, it may, by notification in the Official Gazette and after consultation with the High Court, establish one or more Courts of Judicial Magistrates of the first class or as the case may be, Metropolitan Magistrates, in such district or metropolitan area.

Unless otherwise directed by the High Court, a Court established shall exercise jurisdiction only in respect of cases under this Act.[47]

The Central Government is satisfied that it is necessary for the purpose of providing for speedy trial of offences under this Act and committed in more than one state, it may, by notification in the Official Gazette and after consultation with the High Court concerned, establish one or more Courts of Judicial Magistrates of the first class or Metropolitan Magistrates for the trial of such offences.[48]

Notwithstanding anything contained in the Code of Criminal Procedure, 1973 the State Government may, if it considers it necessary so to do, direct that offences under this Act shall be tried in a summary way by a magistrate provided that in the case of any conviction in a summary trial under this Section it shall be lawful for the magistrate to pass a sentence of imprisonment for a term not exceeding one year although if at the commencement of or in the course of a summary trial under this Section, it appears to the magistrate that the nature of the case is such that a sentence of imprisonment for a term exceeding one year may have to be passed or that it is, for any other reason, undesirable to try the case summarily, the magistrate shall, after hearing the parties, record an order to that effect and, thereafter, recall any witness, who may have been examined and proceed to hear or re-hear the case in the manner provided by the said Code.[49]

**Rules[50]**

The State Government may, by notification in the Official Gazette, make rules for carrying out the purposes of this Act. In particular, and without prejudice to the generality of the foregoing powers, such rules may provide for:

- the notification of any place as a public place
- the placing in custody of persons for whose safe custody orders have been passed and their maintenance
- the discharge of an offender under Section 10 A (3) - which deals with detention in a corrective institution - from a corrective institution and the form of license to be granted to such offender
- the detention and keeping in protective homes or, as the case may be, in corrective institutions of persons under this Act and their maintenance
- the carrying out of the provisions of Section 11 regarding notification of residence or change of or absence from residence by released convicts
- the delegation of authority to appoint the special police officer under Section 13 (1)
- the establishment, maintenance, management and superintendence of protective homes and corrective institutions under Section 21 and the appointment, powers

and duties of persons employed in such homes or institutions

- the form in which an application for a license may be made and the particulars to be contained in such application
- the procedure for the issue or renewal of a license, the time within which such license shall be issued or renewed and the procedure to be followed in making a full and complete investigation in respect of an application for a license
- the form of license and the conditions to be specified therein
- the manner in which the accounts of a protective home and a corrective institution shall be maintained and audited
- the maintenance of registers and statements by a licensee and the form and such registers and statements
- the care, treatment, maintenance, training, instruction, control and discipline of the inmates of protective homes and corrective institutions
- the visits to and communication with such inmates
- the temporary detention of persons sentenced to detention in protective homes or in corrective institutions until arrangements are made for sending them to such homes or institutions
- the transfer of an inmate from one protective home to another or to a corrective institution or from one corrective institution to another one or to a protective home
- the transfer in pursuance of an order of the Court from a protective home or a corrective institution to a prison of a person found to be incorrigible or exercising bad influence upon other inmates of the protective home or the corrective institution and the period of his detention in such prison
- the transfer to a protective home or corrective institution of persons sentenced under Section 7 or Section 8–which deal with prostitution in or in the vicinity of public places, and seducing or soliciting for the purpose of prostitution– and the period of their detention in such home or institution
- the discharge of inmates from a protective home or corrective institution either absolutely or subject to conditions, and their arrest in the event of breach of such conditions

- the grant of permission to inmates to absent themselves for short periods
- the inspection of protective homes and corrective institutions and other institutions in which persons may be kept, detained and maintained
- any other matter which has to be or may be prescribed.

All rules made under this Act shall as soon as may be, after they are made, be laid before the State Legislature.

Nothing in this Act is in derogation of the provisions of the Reformatory Schools Act, 1897 or any State Act enacted in modification of the said Act or otherwise, relating to juvenile offenders.[51]

As from the date of the coming into force in any State of the provisions of this Act, all State Acts relating to suppression of immoral traffic in persons or to the prevention of prostitution, in force in that State immediately before such date stood repealed.

Notwithstanding the repeal by this Act of any State Act, anything done or any action taken (including any direction given, any register, rule or order made, any restriction imposed) under the provisions of such State Act shall in so far such thing or action is not consistent with the provisions of this Act be deemed to have been done or taken under the provisions of this Act as if the said provisions were in force when such thing was done or such action was taken and shall continue in force accordingly until superseded by anything done or any action taken under this Act.[52]

## THE INDECENT REPRESENTATION OF WOMEN ACT

Parliament passed the Indecent Representation of Women (Prohibition) Act in 1986. It extends to the whole of India except the State of Jammu and Kashmir and is to 'prohibit indecent representation of women through advertisements or in publications, writings, paintings, figures'.

*Indecent representation of women* means the depiction in any manner of the figure of a woman; her form or body or any part thereof in such way as to have the effect of being indecent or derogatory to or denigrating women or is likely to deprave, corrupt or injure public morality or morals.[53]

### Definitions

- 'advertisement' includes any notice, circular, label, wrapper or other document and also includes any visible representation made by means of any light, sound, smoke or gas

- 'distribution' includes distribution by way of samples whether free or otherwise
- 'label' means any written, marked, stamped, printed or graphic matter, affixed to or appearing upon, any package
- 'package' includes a box, a carton, tin or other container

**Provisions**

No person shall publish or cause to be published or arrange or take part in the publication or exhibition of, any advertisement which contains indecent representation of women in any form.[54]

No person shall produce or cause to be produced, sell, let to hire, distribute, circulate or send by post any book, pamphlet, paper, slide, film, writing, drawing, painting, photograph, representation or figure which contains indecent representation of women in any form.

However, this does not include:

(a) any book, pamphlet, paper, slide, film, writing, drawing, painting, photograph, representation or figure:
   (i) the publication of which is proved to be justified as being for the public good on the ground that such book, pamphlet, paper, slide, film, writing, drawing, painting, photography, representation or figure is in the interest of science, literature, art or learning, or other objects of general concern or
   (ii) which is kept or used bonafide for religious purposes

(b) any representation sculptured, engraved, painted or otherwise represented on or in:
   (i) any ancient monument within the meaning of the Ancient Monument and Archaeological Sites and Remains Act, 1958 or
   (ii) any temple or on any car used or the conveyance of idols or kept or used for any religious purpose
   (iii) any film in respect of which the provisions of Part II of the Cinematograph Act, 1952 are applicable.[55]

Any Gazetted Officer authorized by the State Government may, within the local limits of the area for which he is so authorized enter and search at all reasonable times, with such assistance, if any, as he considers necessary, any place in which he has reason to believe that an offence under this Act has been or is being committed. He may:

- seize any advertisement or any book, pamphlet, paper, slide, film, writing, drawing, painting, photograph, representation or figure which he has reason to believe contravenes any of the provisions of this Act
- examine any record, register, document or any other material object found in any place mentioned earlier and seize the same if he has reason to believe that it may furnish evidence of the commission of an offence punishable under this Act.

Although no such entry can be made into a private dwelling-house without a warrant and the power of seizure may be exercised in respect of any document, article or thing which contains any such advertisement, including the contents, if any, of such document, article or thing if the advertisement cannot be separated by reason of its being embossed or otherwise from such document, article or thing without affecting the integrity, utility or saleable value thereof. The provisions of the Code of Criminal Procedure apply to any search or seizure made under the authority of a warrant issued under Section 94 of the Criminal Procedure Code. The nearest Magistrate is to be informed of any such seizure as soon as possible and such magistrate is to give orders as to the custody whatever has been seized.[56]

Any person who is involved in the indecent representation of women contrary to the provisions of this Act is punishable on the first conviction with imprisonment of either description for a term which may extend to two years, and with fine which may extend to two thousand rupees, and in the event of a second or subsequent conviction with imprisonment for term of not less than six months but which may extend to five years and also with a fine not less than ten thousand rupees but which may extend to one lakh rupees.[57]

Where an offence under this Act has been committed by a company, every person, who, at the time the offence was committed, was in charge of and was responsible to the company for the conduct of the business of the company, as well as the company, is deemed to be guilty of the offence and is liable to be proceeded against and punished accordingly although no such person is liable to any punishment if he proves that the offence was committed without his knowledge or that he had exercised all due diligence to prevent the commission of the offence. However, where any offence under this Act has been committed by a company and it is proved that the offence has been committed with the consent or connivance of or is attributable to any neglect on the part of, any director, manager, secretary or other officer of the company, such director, manager, secretary or other officer will be proceeded against and punished accordingly.

A 'company' means any body corporate and includes a firm or other association of individuals; and a 'director', in relation to a firm, means a partner in the firm.[58]

Offences punishable under this Act are cognizable and bailable notwithstanding anything contained in the Code of Criminal Procedure, 1973.[59] No suit, prosecution or other legal proceeding shall lie against the Central Government or any State Government or any officer of the Central Government or any State Government for anything which is in good faith done or intended to be done under this Act.[60]

The Central Government may, by notification in the Official Gazette, make rules to carry out the provisions of this Act. Every rule made under this Act, shall be laid, as soon as may be after it is made, before each House of Parliament, while it is in session for a total period of thirty days, which may be comprised in one session or in two or more successive sessions, and if, before the expiry of the session immediately following the session or the successive session aforesaid, both Houses agree in making any modification in the rule or both Houses agree that the rule should not be made, the rule shall thereafter have effect only in such modified form or be of no effect, as the case may be; so, however, that any such modification or annulment shall be without prejudice to the validity of anything previously done under that rule.[61]

**In exercise of these powers the Central Government made the following rules which came into force on October 2, 1987**

### *The manner of seizure of articles*

The authorized officer seizing any advertisements or articles shall prepare a list of such advertisements or articles containing such details relating to the description, quality, quantity, mark, number and other particulars thereof as he may consider relevant to the identity of such advertisements or articles in any proceeding under the Act in the Form annexed to these rules.

The authorized officer shall pack and seal such advertisements or articles and shall deliver a copy of the list so prepared to the person from whom such advertisements or articles are seized.

The advertisements or articles so seized shall be marked with a distinguishing number and shall also be signed by the authorized officer, the person from whom such advertisements or articles have been seized and two respectable inhabitants of the locality. If it is not possible to mark any such advertisement or article, the marking may be done on the packaging or in any other manner which the authorised officer thinks proper.

**The manner of packing and dealing with advertisements or articles seized**

The advertisements or articles seized shall be packed in adequately strong paper, cloth or in any other packing material in such a way that the advertisements or articles may not be tampered with and the ends of the paper, cloth or other packing material shall be neatly folded and affixed by means of gum or other adhesive or stitched in or tied.

The package shall be further secured by means of strong twine or thread and the twine or thread shall be fastened on the package by means of sealing wax on which there shall be at least four distinct and clear impressions of the seal of the authorised officer of which one shall be on the top of the package, one at the bottom and the other two at the body of the package and knots of the twine or thread shall be covered by means of sealing wax bearing the impression of the seal of the authorized officer.

Where necessary, the authorized officer shall put the advertisements or articles in a box, a container of a suitable material and size and seal it.

However, if the authorized officer is of the opinion that it is not possible to seize and seal any advertisement or article in the manner prescribed earlier due to the size or the nature of such advertisement or article, he may take such steps as he thinks fit for the seizure and sealing of such advertisement or article without affecting the integrity, utility or saleable value thereof.

## THE INDIAN EVIDENCE ACT

### Statements by Persons who cannot be called as Witnesses

**32.** Cases in which the statement of relevant fact by person who is dead or cannot be found, etc. is relevant.

Statements, written or verbal, of relevant facts made by a person who is dead, or who cannot be found, or who has become incapable of giving evidence, or whose attendance cannot be procured without an amount of delay or expenses which, under the circumstances of the case, appears to the Court unreasonable, are themselves relevant facts in the following cases:

### (1) *When it relates to cause of death*

When the statement is made by a person as to the cause of his death, or as to any of the circumstances of the transaction which resulted in his death, in cases in which the cause of that person's death comes into question.

Such statements are relevant whether the person who made them was or was not, at the time when they were made, under expectation of death, and whatever may be the nature of the proceeding in which the cause of his death comes into question.

### (5) *Or relates to existence of relationship*

When the statement relates to the existence of any relationship by blood, marriage or, adoption between persons as to whose relationship by blood, marriage or adoption the person making the statement had special means of knowledge, and when the statement was made before the question in dispute was raised.

### (6) *Or is made in will or deed relating to family affairs*

When the statement relates to the existence of any relationship by blood, marriage or adoption between persons deceased, and is made in any will or deed relating to the affairs of the family to which any such deceased person belonged, or in any family pedigree, or upon any tombstone, family portrait or other thing on which such statements are usually made, and when such statement was made before the question in dispute was raised.

## Opinions

**50.** Opinion on relationship, when relevant

When the Court has to form an opinion as to the relationship of one person to another, the opinion expressed by conduct, as to the existence of such relationship, of any person who, as a member of the family or otherwise, has special means of knowledge on the subject, is a relevant fact provided that such opinion shall not be sufficient to prove a marriage in proceedings under the India Divorce Act, 1869 or in prosecutions under sections 494, 495, 497 or 498 of the Indian Penal Code.

## Cruelty

**113 A.** Presumption as to abetment of suicide by a married woman

When the question is whether the commission of suicide by a woman had been abetted by her husband or any relative of her husband and it is shown that she had committed suicide within a period of seven years from the date of her marriage and that her husband or such relative of her husband had subjected her to cruelty, the court may presume, having regard to all the other circumstance s of the case, that such suicide had been abetted by her husband or by such relative of her husband.

*Explanation:* For the purposes of this Section, 'cruelty' shall have the same meaning as in Section 498 A of the Indian Panel Code.

## Dowry Deaths

**113 B.** Presumption as to dowry death

When the question is whether a person has committed the dowry death of a woman and it is shown that soon before her death such woman had been subjected by such person to cruelty or harassment for, or in connection with, any demand for dowry, the Court shall presume that such person had caused the dowry death.

*Explanation:* For the purposes of this Section, 'dowry death' shall have the same meaning as in Section 304B of the Indian Penal Code.

## Rape

**114 A.** Presumption as to absence of consent in certain prosecutions for rape

In a prosecution for rape under Sections 376 (2) (a), (b), (c), (d), (e) or (g) of the Indian Penal Code, where sexual intercourse by the accused is proved and the question is whether it was without the consent of the woman alleged to have been raped and she states in her evidence before the Court that she did not consent, the Court shall presume that she did not consent.

## Communications during marriage

**122.** No person who is or has been married shall be compelled to disclose any communication made to him during marriage by any person to whom he is or has been married, nor shall he be permitted to disclose any such communication, unless the person who made it, or his representative in interest, consents, except in suits between married persons, or proceedings in which one married person is prosecuted for any crime committed against the other.

## THE INDIAN PENAL CODE

### Dowry Death

**304 B.** Dowry Deaths

(1) Where the death of a woman is caused by any burns or bodily injury or occurs otherwise than under normal circumstances within seven years of her marriage and it is shown that soon before her death she was subjected to cruelty or harassment by her husband or any relative of her husband for, or in connection with, any demand for dowry, such death shall be called 'dowry death', and such husband or relative shall be deemed to have caused her death.

*Explanation:* For the purpose of this subsection, 'dowry' shall have the same meaning as in Section 2 of the Dowry Prohibition Act, 1961.

(2) Whoever commits dowry death shall be punished with imprisonment for a term which shall not be less than seven years but which may extend to imprisonment for life.

### Miscarriage

**91.** Exclusion of acts which are offences independently of harm caused

The exceptions in Sections 87, 88 and 89 do not extend to acts which are offences independently of any harm which they may cause, or be intended to cause, or be known to be likely to cause, to the person giving the consent, or on whose behalf the consent is given.

*Illustration*

Causing miscarriage (unless caused in good faith for the purpose of saving the life of the woman) is an offence independently of any harm which it may cause or be intended to cause to the woman. Therefore, it is not an offence 'by reason of such harm'; and the consent of the woman or of her guardian to the causing of such miscarriage does not justify the act.

*The following acts are not offences under the Penal Code:*

87. Act not intended and not known to be likely to cause death or grievous hurt, done by consent.

88. Act not intended to cause death, done by consent in good faith for person's benefit.

89. Act done in good faith for benefit of child or insane person, by or by consent of guardian).

**312.** Causing miscarriage

Whoever voluntarily causes a woman with child to miscarry, shall, if such miscarriage be not caused in good faith for the purpose of saving the life of the woman, be punished with imprisonment of either description for a term which may extend to three years or with fine or with both; and, if the woman be quick with child, shall he punished with imprisonment of either description for a term which may extend to seven years and shall also be liable to fine. A woman who causes herself to miscarry is within the meaning of this Section.

**313.** Causing miscarriage without woman's consent

Whoever commits the offence defined in the last preceding Section without the consent of the woman, whether the woman is quick with child or not, shall be punished with imprisonment for life, or with imprisonment of either description for a term which may extend to ten years and shall also be liable to fine.

**314.** Death caused by act done with intent to cause miscarriage

Whoever, with intent to cause the miscarriage of a woman with child, does any act which causes the death of such woman, shall be punished with imprisonment of either description for a term may extend to ten years and shall also be liable to fine; and if the act is done without the consent of the woman, shall be punished either with imprisonment for life, or with the punishment mentioned earlier. It is not essential to this offence that the offender should know that the act is likely to cause death.

**315.** Act done with intent to prevent child being born alive or to cause it to die after birth

Whoever before the birth of any child does any act with the intention of thereby preventing that child from being born alive or causing it to die after its birth, and does by such act prevent that child from being born alive, or causes it to die after its birth, shall, if such act be not caused in good faith for the purpose of saving the life of the mother, be punished with imprisonment of either description for a term which may extend to ten years or with fine or with both.

**316.** Causing death of quick unborn child by act amounting to culpable homicide

Whoever does any act under such circumstances, that if he thereby caused death he would be guilty of culpable homicide, and does by such act cause the death of a quick unborn child, shall be punished with imprisonment of either description for a term which may extend to ten years, and shall also be liable to fine.

*Illustration:*

A, knowing that he is likely to cause the death of a pregnant woman does an act which, if it caused the death of the woman, would amount to culpable homicide. The woman is injured, but does not die but the death of an unborn quick child with which she is pregnant is thereby caused. A is guilty of the offence defined in this Section.

**Force**

**350.** Criminal force

Whoever intentionally uses force to any person, without that person's consent, in order to the committing of any offence, or intending by the use of such force to cause, or knowing it to be likely that by the use of such force he will cause injury, fear or annoyance to the person to whom the force is used, is said to use criminal force to that other.

*Illustration*

A intentionally pulls up a woman's veil. Here **A** intentionally uses force to her, and if he does so without her consent intending or knowing it to be likely that he may thereby injure, frighten or annoy her, he has used criminal force to her.

**Assault**

**354.** Assault or criminal force to woman with intent to outrage her modesty

Whoever assaults or uses criminal force to any woman, intending to outrage or knowing it to be likely that he will thereby outrage her modesty, shall be punished with imprisonment of either description for a term which may extend to two years or with fine or with both.

**355.** Assault or criminal force with intent to dishonour person otherwise than on grave provocation

Whoever assaults or uses criminal force to any person, intending thereby to dishonour that person, otherwise than on grave and sudden provocation given by that person, shall be punished with imprisonment of either description for a term which may extend to two years or with fine or with both.

**Prostitution, trafficking etc.**

**366.** Kidnapping, abducting or inducing woman to compel her marriage, etc.

Whoever kidnaps or abducts any woman with intent that she may be compelled or knowing it to be likely that she will be compelled, to marry any person against her will or in order that she may be forced or seduced to illicit intercourse or knowing it to be likely that she will be forced or seduced to illicit intercourse, shall be punished with imprisonment of either description for a term which may extend to ten years, and shall also be liable to fine; and whoever, by means of criminal intimidation as defined in this Code or of abuse of authority or any other method of compulsion, induces any woman to go from any place with intent that she may be or knowing that it is likely that she will be forced or seduced to illicit intercourse with another person shall be punishable as aforesaid.

**366A.** Procuration of minor girl

Whoever, by any means whatsoever, induces any minor girl under the age of eighteen years to go from any place or to do any act with intent that such girl may be or knowing that it is likely that she will be forced or seduced to illicit intercourse with another person shall be punishable with imprisonment which may extend to ten years, and shall also be liable to fine.

**366 B.** Importation of girl from foreign country

Whoever imports into India from any country outside India or from the State of Jammu and Kashmir any girl under the age of twenty-one years with intent that she may be or knowing it to be likely that she will be forced or seduced to illicit intercourse with another person shall be punishable with imprisonment which may extend to ten years and shall also be liable to fine.

**367.** Kidnapping or abducting in order to subject person to grievous hurt, slavery, etc.

Whoever kidnaps or abducts any person in order that such person may be subjected to or may be so disposed of as to be put in danger of being subject to grievous hurt or slavery or to the unnatural lust of any person or knowing it to be likely that such person will be so subjected or disposed of shall be punished with imprisonment of either description for a term which may extend to ten years, and shall also be liable to fine.

**372.** Selling minor for purposes of prostitution, etc.

Whoever sells, lets to hire or otherwise disposes of any person under the age of eighteen years with intent that such person shall at any age be employed or used for the purpose of prostitution or illicit intercourse with any person or for any unlawful and immoral purpose or knowing it to be likely that such person will at any age be employed or used for any such purpose shall be punished with imprisonment of either description for a term which may extend to ten years, and shall be liable to fine.

*Explanations*

- When a female under the age of eighteen years is sold, let for hire or otherwise disposed of to a prostitute or to any person who keeps or manages a brothel, the person so disposing of such female shall, until the contrary is proved, be presumed to have disposed of her with the intent that she shall be used for the purpose of prostitution.
- For the purposes of this Section 'illicit intercourse' means sexual intercourse between persons not united by marriage or by any union or tie which, though not amounting to a marriage, is recognised by the Personal Laws or custom of the community to which they belong or, where they belong to different communities, of both such communities, as constituting between them a quasi-marital relation.

**373.** Buying minor for purposes of prostitution, etc.

Whoever buys, hires or otherwise obtains possession of any person under the age of eighteen years with intent that such person shall at any age be employed or used for the purpose of prostitution or illicit intercourse with any person or for any unlawful and immoral purpose, of knowing it to be likely that such person will at any age be employed or used for any purpose, shall be punished with imprisonment of either description for a term which may extend to ten years, and shall also be liable to fine.

*Explanations*

- Any prostitute or any person keeping or managing a brothel who buys, hires or otherwise obtains possession of a female under the age of eighteen years shall, until the contrary is proved, be presumed to have obtained possession of such female with the intent that she shall be used for the purpose of prostitution.
- 'Illicit intercourse' has the same meaning as in Section 372.

**Sexual Offences**

**375.** Rape

A man is said to commit 'rape' who except in the case hereinafter excepted, has sexual intercourse with a woman under circumstances falling under any of the five following descriptions:

- Against her will.
- Without her consent.
- With her consent, when her consent has been obtained by putting her in fear of death or of hurt.
- With her consent, when the man knows that he is not her husband, and that her consent is given because she believes that he is another man to whom she is or believes herself to be lawfully married.
- With or without her consent, when she is under sixteen years of age.

*Explanation:* Penetration is sufficient to constitute the sexual intercourse necessary to the offence of rape.

*Exception:* Sexual intercourse by a man with his wife is not rape as long as she is not under fifteen years of age.

**376.** Punishment for Rape

(1) Whoever, except in the cases provided for by subsection (2), commits rape shall be punished with imprisonment of either description for a term which shall not be less than seven years but which may be for life or for a term which may extend to ten years and shall also be liable to fine, unless the women raped is his own wife and is not under twelve years of age, in which case, he shall be punished with imprisonment of either description for a term which may extend to two years or with fine or with both although the Court may, for adequate and special reasons to be mentioned in the judgement, impose a sentence of imprisonment for a term of less than seven years.

(2) Whoever:

- being a police officer commits rape:
  - (i) within the limits of the police station to which he is appointed or
  - (ii) in the premises of any station house whether or not situated in the police station to which he is appointed or
  - (iii) on a woman in his custody or in the custody of a police officer subordinate to him or
- being a public servant takes advantage of his official position and rapes a woman in his custody as such public servant or in the custody of a public servant subordinate to him or

- being on the management or on the staff of a gaol remand home or other place of custody established by or under any law for the time being in force or of a woman's or children's institution takes advantage of his official position and commits rape on any inmate of such gaol remand home place or institution
- being on the management or on the staff of a hospital takes advantage of his official position and commits rape on a woman in that hospital
- commits rape on a woman knowing her to be pregnant
- commits rape on a woman when she is under twelve years
- commits gang-rape shall be punished with rigorous imprisonment for a term which shall not be less than ten years but which may be for life and shall also be liable to fine although the Court may, for adequate and special reasons to be mentioned in the judgement, impose a sentence of imprisonment of either description for a term of less than ten years.

*Explanations*

- Where a woman is raped by one or more in a group of persons acting in furtherance of their common intention, each of the persons shall be deemed to have committed gang-rape within the meaning of this subsection.
- 'Women's or children's institution' means an institution, whether called an orphanage or a home for neglected women or children or a widows' home or any other name, which is established and maintained for the reception and care of women or children.
- 'Hospital' means the precincts of the hospital and includes the precincts of any institution for the reception and treatment of persons during convalescence or of persons requiring medical attention or rehabilitation.

**376 A.** Intercourse by a man with his wife during separation

Whoever has sexual intercourse with his own wife, who is living separately from him under a decree of separation or under any custom or usage, without her consent, shall be punished with imprisonment of either description for a term which may extend to two years and shall also be liable to fine.

**376 B.** Intercourse by public servant with woman in his custody

Whoever, being a public servant, takes advantage of his official position and induces or seduces, any woman, who is in his custody as such public servant or in the custody of a public servant subordinate to him, to have sexual intercourse with him, such sexual intercourse not amounting to the offence of rape, shall be punished with imprisonment of either description for a term which may extend to five years and shall also be liable to fine.

**376 C.** Intercourse by superintendent of gaol, remand home, etc.

Whoever, being the superintendent or manager of a gaol, remand home or other place of custody established by or under any law for the time being in force or of a woman's or children's institution takes advantage of his official position and induces or seduces any female inmate of such gaol, remand home, place or institution to have sexual intercourse with him, such sexual intercourse not amounting to the offence of rape, shall be punished with imprisonment of either description for a term which may extend to five years and shall also be liable to fine.

***Explanations***

- 'Superintendent' in relation to gaol, remand home or other place of custody or a woman's or- children's institution includes a person holding any other office in such gaol, remand home, place or institution by virtue of which he can exercise any authority or control over its inmates.
- The expression 'women's or children's institution' shall have the same meaning as in Explanation to Section 376 (2).

**376 D.** Intercourse by any member of the management or staff of a hospital with any woman in that hospital

Whoever, being on the management of a hospital or on the staff of a hospital takes advantage of his position and has sexual intercourse with any woman in that hospital, such sexual intercourse not amounting to the offence of rape, shall be punished with imprisonment of either description for a term which may extend to five years and shall also be liable to fine.

*Explanation:* The expression 'hospital' shall have the same meaning as in Explanation to Section 376 (2).

**Offences in Relation to Marriage**

**493.** Cohabitation deceitfully induced by a man

Every man who by deceit causes any woman who is not lawfully married to him to believe that she is lawfully married to him and to cohabit or have sexual intercourse with him in that belief shall be punished with imprisonment of either description for a term which may extend to ten years and shall also be liable to fine.

**494.** Marrying again during lifetime of husband or wife

Whoever, having a husband or wife living, marries in any case in which such marriage is void by reason of its taking place during the life of such husband or wife, shall be punished with imprisonment of either description for a term which may extend to seven years and shall also be liable to fine.

Exception: This Section does not extend to any person whose marriage with such husband or wife has been declared void by a Court of competent jurisdiction, nor to any person who contracts a marriage during the life of a former husband or wife, if such husband or wife, at the time of the subsequent marriage, shall have been continually absent from such person for the space of seven years, and shall not have been heard of by such person as being alive within that time provided the person contracting such subsequent marriage shall, before such marriage takes place, inform the person with whom such marriage is contracted of the real state of facts so far as the same are within his or her knowledge.

**495.** Same offence with concealment of former marriage from person with whom subsequent marriage is contracted

Whoever commits the offence defined in the last preceding Section having concealed from the person with whom the subsequent marriage is contracted the fact of the former marriage shall be punished with imprisonment of either description for a term which may extend to ten years, and shall also be liable to fine.

**496.** Fraudulent marriage ceremony without lawful marriage

Whoever, dishonestly or with a fraudulent intention, goes through the ceremony of being married, knowing that he is not thereby lawfully married shall be punished with imprisonment of either description for a term which may extend to seven years and shall also be liable to fine.

**498.** Enticing, taking away or detaining with criminal intent a married woman

Whoever takes or entices away any woman who is and whom he knows or has reason to believe to be the wife of any other man from that man or from any person having the care of her on behalf of that man, with intent that she may have illicit intercourse with any person, or conceals or detains with that intent any such woman, shall be punished with imprisonment of either description for a term which may extend to two years or with fine or with both.

**497.** Adultery

Whoever has sexual intercourse with a person who is and whom he knows or has reason to believe to be the wife of another man, without the consent or connivance of that man, such sexual intercourse not amounting to the offence of rape, is guilty of the offence of adultery, and shall be punished with imprisonment of either description for a term which may extend to five years or with fine or with both. In such case the wife shall not be punishable as an abettor.

**498 A.** Husband or his relative subjecting a woman to cruelty

Whoever, being the husband or the relative of the husband of a woman, subjects such woman to cruelty shall be punished with imprisonment for a term which may extend to three years and shall also be liable to fine.

*Explanation*

For the purpose of this Section, 'cruelty' means:

- any wilful conduct which is of such a nature as is likely to drive the woman to commit suicide or to cause grave injury or danger to life, limb or health (whether mental or physical) of the woman or
- harassment of the woman where such harassment is with a view to coercing her or any person related to her to meet any unlawful demand for any property or valuable security or is on account of failure by her or any person related to her to meet such demand.

**Criminal Intimidation**

**506.** Punishment for criminal intimidation

Whoever commits the offence of criminal intimidation shall be punished with imprisonment of either description for a term which may extend to two years, or with fine, or with both.

If threat be to cause death or grievous hurt, or to cause the destruction of any property by fire, or to cause an offence punishable with death or imprisonment for life, or with imprisonment for a term which may extend to seven years, or to impute unchastity to a woman, it shall be punished with imprisonment of either description for a term which may extend to seven years or with fine or with both.

## THE INFORMATION TECHNOLOGY ACT

This Act was passed by Parliament in 2000 primarily to provide legal recognition to eCommerce and is based on UNCITRAL's Model Law for Electronic Commerce which the UN General Assembly adopted on January 30, 1997.

### Obscene Information

**67.** Publishing of information which is obscene in electronic form

Whoever publishes or transmits or causes to be published in electronic form, any material which is lascivious or appeals to the prurient interest or if its effect is such as to tend to deprave and corrupt persons who are likely, having regard to all the relevant circumstances, to read, see or hear the matter contained or embodied in it, shall be punished on first conviction with imprisonment of either description for a term which may extend to five years and with fine which may extend to one lakh rupees and in the event of a second or subsequent conviction with imprisonment of either description for a term which may extend to ten years and with fine which may extend to two lakh rupees.

## THE NATIONAL COMMISSION FOR WOMEN ACT

This Act may be called the National Commission for Women Act, 1990. It extends to the whole of India except the State of Jammu and Kashmir.

### Definitions[62]

'Commission' means the National Commission for Women 'Member' means a Member of the Commission and includes the Member-Secretary.

### The National Commission for Women

The Central Government shall constitute a body to be known as the National Commission for Women to exercise the powers conferred on, and to perform the functions assigned to, it under this Act.

The Commission shall consist of:

1. A Chairperson, committed to the cause of women, to be nominated by the Central Government.
2. Five Members to be nominated by the Central Government from amongst persons of ability, integrity and standing who have had experience in law or legislation, trade unionism,

management of an industry or Organisation committed to increasing the employment potential of women, women's voluntary organisations (including women activists), administration, economic development, health, education or social welfare provided that at least one Member each shall be from amongst persons belonging to the Scheduled Castes and Scheduled Tribes respectively.

3. A Member-Secretary to be nominated by the Central Government, who shall be:
   (a) an expert in the field of management organisational structure or sociological movement or
   (b) an officer who is a member of a civil service of the Union or of an all India service or holds a civil post under the Union with appropriate experience.[63]

The Chairperson and every Member shall hold office for such period, not exceeding three years, as may be specified by the Cent Government. The Chairperson or a Member (other than the Member-Secretary who is a member of a civil service the Union or of an all India service or holds a civil post under the Union) may, by writing and addressed to the Central Government, resign from the office of Chairperson or, as the case may be, of the Member at any time.

The Central Government shall remove a person from the office of Chairperson or a Member after giving him a reasonable opportunity of being heard if that person:

- becomes an undischarged insolvent
- gets convicted and sentenced to imprisonment for an offence which in the opinion of the Central Government involves moral turpitude
- becomes of unsound mind and stands so declared by a competent Court
- refuses to act or becomes incapable of acting
- is, without obtaining leave of absence from the Commission, absent from three consecutive meetings of the Commission
- in the opinion of the Central Government has so abused the position of Chairperson or Member to render that person's continuance in office detrimental to the public interest.

A vacancy caused or otherwise shall be filled by fresh nomination. The salaries and allowances payable to, and the other terms and conditions of service of, the Chairperson and Members shall be such as may be prescribed.[64]

The Central Government shall provide the Commission with such officers and employees as may be necessary for the efficient performance of the function of the Commission under this Act. The salaries and allowances payable to, and the other terms and conditions of service of, the officer and other employees appointed for the purpose of the Commission shall be such as may be prescribed[65] and shall be paid out of the grants by the Central Government.

No act or proceeding of the Commissioner shall be questioned or shall be invalid on the ground merely of the existence of any vacancy or defect in the constitution of the Commission.[66]

The Commissioner may appoint such committees as may be necessary for dealing with such special issues as may be taken up by the Commission from time to time. The Commission shall have the power to co-opt as members of any such committee such number of persons, who are not Members of the Commission, as it may think fit and the persons so co-opted shall have the right to attend the meetings of the committee and take part in its proceedings but shall not have the right to vote. The persons so co-opted shall be entitled to receive such allowances for attending the meetings of the committee as may be prescribed.[67]

The Commission or a committee thereof shall meet as and when necessary and shall meet at such time and place as the Chairperson may think fit. The Commission shall regulate its own procedure and the procedure of the Committees thereof. All orders and decisions of the Commission shall be authenticated by the Member-Secretary or any other officer of the Commission duly authorised by the Member-Secretary in this behalf.[68]

The Chairperson, Members and staff of the Commission are to be public servants.[69] The Central Government shall consult the Commission on all major policy matters affecting women.[70]

**The Functions of the Commission**[71]

The functions of the Commission are to:

- Investigate and examine all matters relating to the safeguards provided for women under the Constitution and other laws.
- The Commission, while investigating any matter, has all the powers of a Civil Court trying a suit.
- present to the Central Government, annually and at such other times as the Commission may deem fit, reports upon the working of those safeguards.

- Make in such reports recommendations for the effective implementation of those safeguards for improving the conditions of women by the Union or any State.
- Review, from time to time, the existing provisions of the Constitution and other laws affecting women and recommend amendments thereto so as to suggest remedial legislative measures to meet any lacunae, inadequacies or shortcomings in such legislations
- Take up the cases of violation of the provisions of the Constitution and of other laws relating to women with the appropriate authorities.
- Look into complaints and take suo moto notice of matters relating to:
  - the deprivation of women's rights
  - the non-implementation of laws enacted to provide protection to women and also to achieve the objective of equality and development
  - the non-compliance of policy decisions, guidelines or instructions aimed at mitigating hardships and ensuring welfare and providing relief to women, and take up the issues arising out of such matters with appropriate authorities
- Call for special studies or investigations into specific problems or situations arising out of discrimination and atrocities against women and identify the constraints so as to recommend strategies for their removal.
- Undertake promotional and educational research so as to suggest ways of ensuring due representation of women in all-spheres and identify factors responsible for impeding their advancement, such as, lack of access to housing and basic services, inadequate support services and technologies for reducing drudgery and occupational health hazards and for increasing their productivity.
- Participate and advise on the planning process for the socio-economic development of women.
- Evaluate the progress of the development of women under the Union and any State.
- Inspect or cause to be inspected a gaol, remand home, women's institution or other place of custody where women

are kept as prisoners or otherwise, and take up with the concerned authorities for remedial action, if found necessary.

- Fund litigation involving issues affecting a large body of women.
- Make periodical reports to the Government on any matter pertaining to women.
- Deal with any other matter which may be referred to it by Central Government.

The Central Government shall cause all the reports of the Commission to be laid before each House of Parliament along with a memorandum explaining the action taken or proposed to be taken on the recommendations relating to the Union and the reasons for the non-acceptance, if any, of any of such recommendations.

Where any such report or any part thereof relates to any matter with which any State Government is concerned, the Commission shall forward a copy of such report or part to such State Government who shall cause it to be laid before the Legislature of the State along with a memorandum explaining the action taken or proposed to be taken on the recommendations relating to the State and the reasons for the non-acceptance, if any, of any of such recommendations.

The Commission shall, while investigating any matter, have all the powers of a Civil Court trying a suit and, in particular in respect of the following matters:

(a) summoning and enforcing the attendance of any person from any part of India and examining him on oath
(b) requiring the discovery and production of any document
(c) receiving evidence on affidavits
(d) requisitioning any public record or copy thereof from any Court or office
(e) issuing commissions for the examination of witnesses and documents and
(f) any other matter which may be prescribed.

**Finance**[72]

The Central Government shall, after due appropriation made by Parliament by law in this behalf, pay to the Commission by way of grants such sums of money as the Central Government may think fit for being utilised for the purposes of this Act. The Commission may spend such sums as it thinks fit for performing the functions under this Act, and such sums shall be treated as expenditure payable out of these grants.

**Accounts and audit**[73]

The Commission shall maintain proper accounts and other relevant records and prepare an annual statement of accounts in such form as may be prescribed by the Central Government in consultation with the Comptroller and Auditor-General of India.

The accounts of the Commission shall be audited by the Comptroller and Auditor-General at such intervals as may be specified by him and any expenditure incurred in connection with such audit shall be payable by the Commission to the Comptroller and Auditor-General.

The Comptroller and Auditor-General and any person appointed by him in connection with the audit of the accounts of the Commission under this Act shall have the same rights and privileges and the authority in connection with such audit as the Comptroller and Auditor-General generally has in connection with the audit of Government accounts and, in particular, shall have the right to demand the production of books, accounts, connected vouchers and other documents and papers and to inspect any of the offices of the Commission.

The accounts of the Commission, as certified by the Comptroller and Auditor-General or any other person appointed by him in this behalf, together with the audit report thereon shall be forwarded annually to the Central Government by the Commission.

**Annual report**

The Commission shall prepare in such form and at such time, for each financial year, as may be prescribed, its annual report, giving a full account of its activities during the previous financial year and forward a copy thereof to the Central Government. [74]

Annual report and audit report to be laid before Parliament. The Central Government shall cause the annual report together with a memorandum of action taken on the recommendations contained therein, in so far as they relate to the Central Government, and the reasons for the non-acceptance, if any, of any of such recommendations and the audit report to be laid as soon as may be after the reports are received, before each House of Parliament.[75]

**Rules**

The Central Government may, by notification in the Official Gazette, make rules for carrying out the provisions of this Act. Every rule made under this Act shall be laid, as soon as may be after it is made, before each House of Parliament, while it is in session, for a total period of thirty days which may be comprised in one session or in two or more successive sessions, and if, before the expiry of the session immediately following the session or successive sessions aforesaid, both Houses agree in making any modification in the rule or both Houses agree that the rule should not be made, the rule shall thereafter have effect only in such modified form or be of no effect, as the case may be; so, however, that any such modification or annulment shall be without prejudice to the validity of anything previously done under that rule.[76]

## THE PRENATAL DIAGNOSTIC TECHNIQUES ACT

The Act to provides for the regulation of the use of Prenatal Diagnostic Techniques for the purpose of detecting genetic or metabolic disorders or chromosomal abnormalities or certain congenital malformations or sex linked disorders and for the prevention of the misuse of such techniques for the purpose of Prenatal sex determination leading to female foeticide; and, for matters connected therewith or incidental thereto. It extends to the whole of India except the State of Jammu and Kashmir.

### Definitions[77]

'Genetic Counselling Centre' means an institute, hospital, nursing home or any place, by whatever name called, which provides for genetic counselling to patients.

'Genetic Clinic' means a clinic, institute, hospital, nursing home or any place, by whatever name called, which is used for conducting Prenatal Diagnostic Procedures.

'Genetic Laboratory' means a laboratory and includes a place where facilities are provided for conducting analysis or tests of samples received from Genetic Clinic for Prenatal diagnostic test.

'Gynaecologist' means a person who possesses a post-graduate qualification in gynaecology and obstetrics.

'Medical geneticist' means a person who possesses a degree or diploma or certificate in medical genetics in the field of Prenatal Diagnostic Techniques or has experience of not less than two years in such field after obtaining any one of the medical qualifications recognised under the Indian Medical Council Act, 1956 a post-graduate degree in biological sciences.

'Paediatrician' means a person who possesses a post-graduate qualification in paediatrics.

'Prenatal Diagnostic Procedures' means all gynaecological or obstetrical or medical procedures such as ultrasonography foetoscopy, taking or removing samples of amniotic fluid, chorionic villi, blood or any tissue of a pregnant woman for being sent to a Genetic Laboratory or Genetic Clinic for conducting Prenatal diagnostic test.

'Prenatal Diagnostic Techniques' includes all Prenatal Diagnostic Procedures and Prenatal diagnostic tests.

'Prenatal diagnostic test' means ultrasonography or any test or analysis of amniotic fluid, chorionic villi, blood or any tissue of a pregnant woman conducted to detect genetic or metabolic disorders or chromosomal abnormalities or congenital anomalies or haemoglobinopathies or sex-linked diseases.

'Registered medical practitioner' means a medical practitioner who possesses any recognised medical qualification as defined in the Indian Medical Council Act, 1956, and whose name has been entered in a State Medical Register.

'Regulations' means regulations framed by the Central Supervisory Board under this Act.

## Provisions

### *The regulation of genetic counselling centres, genetic laboratories and genetic clinics*[78]

(1) No Genetic Counselling Centre, Genetic Laboratory or Genetic Clinic unless registered under this Act, shall conduct or associate with or help in, conducting activities relating to Prenatal Diagnostic Techniques.

(2) No Genetic Counselling Centre, Genetic Laboratory or Genetic Clinic shall employ or cause to be employed any person who does not possess the prescribed qualifications.

(3) No medical geneticist, gynaecologist, paediatrician registered medical practitioner or any other person shall conduct or cause to be conducted or aid in conducting by himself or through any other person, any Prenatal Diagnostic Techniques at a place other than a place registered under this Act.

**Regulation of Prenatal Diagnostic Techniques[79]**

No place including a registered Genetic Counselling Centre or Genetic Laboratory or Genetic Clinic shall be used or caused to be used by any person for conducting Prenatal Diagnostic Techniques except for the following purposes and after satisfying any of the specified conditions.

No Prenatal Diagnostic Techniques shall be conducted except for the purposes of detection of any of the following abnormalities:

(1) chromosomal abnormalities

(2) genetic metabolic diseases

(3) haemoglobinopathies

(4) sex-linked genetic diseases

(5) congenital anomalies

(6) other abnormalities or diseases

No Prenatal Diagnostic Techniques shall be used or conducted unless the person qualified to do so is satisfied that any of the following conditions are fulfilled:

1. The age of the pregnant woman is above thirty-five years.
2. The pregnant woman has undergone of two or more spontaneous abortions or foetal loss.
3. The pregnant woman had been exposed to potentially teratogenic agents such as drugs, radiation, infection or chemicals.
4. The pregnant woman has a family history of mental retardation or physical deformities such as spasticity or any other genetic disease.
5. Any other condition as may be specified by the Central Supervisory Board.

No person, being a relative or the husband of the pregnant woman shall seek or encourage the conduct of any Prenatal Diagnostic Techniques on her except for the purposes specified earlier.

***Written consent of pregnant woman and prohibition of communicating the sex of foetus[80]***

No person shall conduct the Prenatal Diagnostic Procedures unless:

(1) he has explained all known side and after effects of such procedures to the pregnant woman concerned.

(2) he has obtained in the prescribed form her written consent to undergo such procedures in the language which she understands and

(3) a copy of her written consent is given to the pregnant woman.

No person conducting Prenatal Diagnostic Procedures shall communicate to the pregnant woman concerned or her relatives the sex of the foetus by words, signs or in any other manner.

*Determination of sex prohibited*[81]

No Genetic Counselling Centre or Genetic Laboratory or Genetic Clinic shall conduct or cause to be conducted in its Centre, Laboratory or Clinic, Prenatal Diagnostic Techniques including ultrasonography, for the purpose of determining the sex of a foetus.

No person shall conduct or cause to be conducted any Prenatal Diagnostic Techniques including ultrasonography for the purpose of determining the sex of a foetus.

**The Central Supervisory Board**[82]

The Central Government shall constitute a Board to be known as the Central Supervisory Board to exercise the powers and perform the functions conferred on the Board under this Act.

The Board shall have the following functions:

(1) to advise the Government on policy matters relating to use of Prenatal Diagnostic Techniques

(2) to review implementation of the Act and the rules made under it and recommend changes in the said Act and rules to the Central Government

(3) to create public awareness against the practice of prenatal determination of sex and female foeticide

(4) to lay down code of conduct to be observed by persons working at Genetic Counselling Centres, Genetic Laboratories and Genetic Clinics

(5) do any other functions as may be specified under the Act.[83]

***The Board shall consist of***

- the Minister in charge of the Ministry or Department of Family Welfare, who shall be the Chairman, ex officio

- the Secretary to the Government of India in charge of the Department of Family Welfare, who shall be the Vice-Chairman, ex officio
- two members to be appointed by the Central Government to represent the Ministries of Central Government in charge of woman and Child Development and of Law and Justice, ex officio
- the Director General of Health Services of the Central Government, ex officio
- ten members to be appointed by the Central Government, two each from amongst:
  - eminent medical geneticists
  - eminent gynaecologists and obstetricians
  - eminent paediatricians
  - eminent social scientists
  - representatives of women welfare organisations.
- three women Members of Parliament, of whom two shall be elected by the House of the People and one by the Council of States
- four members to be appointed by the Central Government by rotation to represent the States and the Union territories, two in the alphabetical order and two in the reverse alphabetical order provided that no appointment under this clause shall be made except on the recommendation of the State Government or, as the case may be, the Union territory
- an officer, not below the rank of a Joint Secretary or equivalent of the Central Government, in charge of Family Welfare, who shall be the Member-Secretary, ex officio.

The term of office of a member, other than an ex officio member, shall be in case of experts and Members of Parliament, one year.

If a casual vacancy occurs in the office of any other members, whether by reason of his death, resignation or inability to discharge his functions owing to illness or other incapacity, such vacancy shall be filled by the Central Government by making a fresh appointment and the member so appointed shall hold office for the remainder of the term of office of the person in whose place he is so appointed.

The Vice-Chairman shall perform such functions as may be assigned to him by the Chairman from time to time. The procedure to be followed by the members in the discharge of their functions shall be such as may be prescribed.[84]

A person shall be disqualified for being appointed as a member if he:

(1) has been convicted and sentenced to imprisonment for an offence which, in the opinion of the Central Government, involves moral turpitude

(2) is an undischarged insolvent

(3) is of unsound mind and stands so declared by a competent Court

(4) has been removed or dismissed from the service of the Government or a Corporation owned or controlled by the Government

(5) has in the opinion of the Central Government, such financial or other interest in the Board as is likely to affect prejudicially the discharge by him of his functions as a member

(6) has, in the opinion of the Central Government, been associated with the use or promotion of prenatal diagnostic technique for determination of sex.[85]

Subject to the other terms and conditions of service as may be prescribed, any person ceasing to be a member shall be eligible for reappointment as such member.[86]

The Board shall meet at such time and place, and shall observe such rules of procedure in regard to the transaction of business at its meetings (including the quorum at such meetings) as may be provided by regulations provided that the Board shall meet at least once in six months.

The Chairman and in his absence the Vice-Chairman shall preside at the meetings of the Board. If for any reason the Chairman or the Vice-Chairman is unable to attend any meeting of the Board, any other member chosen by the members present at the meeting shall preside at the meeting.

All questions which come up before any meeting of the Board shall be decided by a majority of the votes of the members present and voting, and in the event of an equality of votes, the Chairman or in his absence, the person presiding, shall have and exercise a second or casting vote.

Members other than ex officio members shall receive such allowances, if any, from the Board as may be prescribed.[87]

No act or proceeding of the Central Supervisory Board shall be invalid merely by reason of:

(a) any vacancy in or any defect in the constitution of the Board

(b) any defect in the appointment of a person acting as a member of the Board

(c) any irregularity in the procedure of the Board not affecting the merits of the case.

The Board may associate with itself, in such manner and for such purposes as may be determined by regulations, any person whose assistance or advice it may desire in carrying out any of the provisions of this Act. Such a person shall have a right to take part in the discussions relevant to that purpose, but shall not have a right to vote at a meeting of the Board and shall not be a member for any other purpose.[88]

For the purpose of enabling it efficiently to discharge its functions under this Act, the Board may, subject to such regulations as may be made in this behalf, appoint (whether on deputation or otherwise) such number of officers and other employees as it may consider necessary provided that the appointment of such category of officers, as may be specified in such regulations, shall be subject to the approval of the Central Government. Every officer or other employee appointed by the Board shall be subject to such conditions of service and shall be entitled to such remuneration as may be specified in the regulations.[89]

All orders and decisions of the Board shall be authenticated by the signature of the Chairman or any other member authorised by the Board in this behalf, and all other instruments issued by the Board shall be authenticated by the signature of the Member-Secretary or any other officer of the Board authorised in like manner in this behalf.[90]

**The Appropriate Authority and the Advisory Committee[91]**

The Central Government shall appoint, by notification in the Official Gazette, one or more Appropriate Authorities for each of the Union territories for the purposes of this Act.

The State Government shall appoint, by notification in the Official Gazette, one or more Appropriate Authorities for the whole or part of the State for the purposes of this Act having regard to the intensity of the problem of prenatal sex determination leading to female foeticide.

The officers appointed as Appropriate Authorities shall be:

(a) when appointed for the whole of the State or the Union territory, of or above the rank of the Joint Director of Health and Family Welfare and

(b) when appointed for any part of the State or the Union territory, of such other rank as the State Government or the Central Government, as the case may be, may deem fit.

The Appropriate Authority shall have the following functions:

(a) to grant, suspend or cancel registration of a Genetic Counselling Centre, Genetic Laboratory or Genetic Clinic;

(b) to enforce standards prescribed for the Genetic Counselling Centre, Genetic Laboratory and Genetic Clinic;

(c) to investigate complaints of breach of the provisions of this Act or the rules made thereunder and take immediate action; and

(d) to seek and consider the advice of the Advisory Committee on application for registration and on complaints for suspension or cancellation of registration.

The Central Government or the State Government, as the case may be, shall constitute an Advisory Committee for each Appropriate Authority to aid and advise the Appropriate Authority in the discharge of its functions, and shall appoint one of the members of the Advisory Committee to be its Chairman.

*The Advisory Committee shall consist of*

1. Three medical experts from amongst gynaecologists, obstetricians, paediatricians and medical geneticists.
2. One legal expert.
3. One officer to represent the department dealing with information and publicity of the State Government or the Union territory, as the case may be.
4. Three eminent social workers of whom not less than one shall be from amongst representatives of women's organisations.

No person who, in the opinion of the Central Government or the State Government, as the case may be, has been associated with the use or promotion of prenatal diagnostic technique for determination of sex shall be appointed as a member of the Advisory Committee.

The Advisory Committee may meet as and when it thinks fit or on the request of the Appropriate Authority for consideration of any application for registration or any complaint for suspension or cancellation of registration and to give advice thereon provided that the period intervening between any two meetings shall not exceed the prescribed period.

The terms and conditions subject to which a person may be appointed to the Advisory Committee and the procedure to be followed by such Committee in the discharge of its functions shall be such as may be prescribed.

**Registration of Genetic Counselling Centres, Genetic Laboratories or Genetic Clinics**[92]

No person shall open any Genetic Counselling Centre, Genetic Laboratory or Genetic Clinic after the commencement of this Act unless such Centre, Laboratory or Clinic is duly registered separately or jointly under this Act.

Every application for registration shall be made to the Appropriate Authority in such form and in such manner and shall be accompanied by such fees as may be prescribed.

Every Genetic Counselling Centre, Genetic Laboratory or Genetic Clinic engaged in counselling or conducting Prenatal Diagnostic Techniques shall cease to conduct any such counselling or technique on the expiry of six months from the date of commencement of this Act unless such Centre, Laboratory or Clinic has applied for registration and is so registered separately or jointly or till such application is disposed of, whichever is earlier.

No Genetic Counselling Centre, Genetic Laboratory or Genetic Clinic shall be registered under this Act unless the Appropriate Authority is satisfied that such Centre, Laboratory or Clinic is in a position to provide such facilities, maintain such equipment and standards as may be prescribed.

**Certificate of Registration**[93]

The Appropriate Authority shall, after holding an inquiry and after satisfying itself that the applicant has complied with all the requirements of this Act and the rules made thereunder and having regard to the advice of the Advisory Committee in this behalf, grant a certificate of registration in the prescribed form jointly or separately to the Genetic Counselling Centre, Genetic Laboratory or Genetic Clinic, as the case may be.

If, after the inquiry and after giving an opportunity of being heard to the applicant and having regard to the advice of the Advisory Committee, the Appropriate Authority is satisfied that the applicant has not complied with the requirements of this Act or the rules, it shall, for reasons to be recorded in writing, reject the application for registration.

Every certificate of registration shall be renewed in such manner and after such period and on payment of such fees as may be prescribed. The certificate of registration shall be displayed by the registered Genetic Counselling Centre, Genetic Laboratory or Genetic Clinic in a conspicuous place at its place of business.

**Cancellation or suspension of registration**[94]

The Appropriate Authority may suo moto or on complaint, issue a notice to the Genetic Counselling Centre, Genetic Laboratory or Genetic Clinic to show cause why its registration should not be suspended or cancelled for the reasons mentioned in the notice.

If, after giving a reasonable opportunity of being heard to the Genetic Counselling Centre, Genetic Laboratory or Genetic Clinic and having regard to the advice of the Advisory Committee, the Appropriate Authority is satisfied that there has been a breach of the provisions of this Act or the rules, it may, without prejudice to any criminal action that it may take against such Centre Laboratory or Clinic, suspend its registration for such period as it may think fit or cancel its registration, as the case may be. However, if the Appropriate Authority is of the opinion that it is necessary or expedient so to do in the public interest, it may, for reasons to be recorded in writing, suspend the registration of any Genetic Counselling Centre, Genetic Laboratory or Genetic Clinic without issuing any such notice referred to earlier.

**Appeals**[95]

The Genetic Counselling Centre, Genetic Laboratory or Genetic Clinic may, within thirty days from the date of receipt of the order of suspension or cancellation of registration passed by the Appropriate Authority, prefer an appeal against such order to:

- the Central Government, where the appeal is against the order of the Central Appropriate Authority and
- the State Government, where the appeal is against the order of the State Appropriate Authority, in the prescribed manner.

**Prohibition of advertisement relating to prenatal determination of sex and punishment for contravention**[96]

No person organisation, Genetic Counselling Centre, Genetic Laboratory or Genetic Clinic shall issue or cause to be issued any advertisement in any manner regarding facilities of prenatal determination of sex available at such Centre, Laboratory, Clinic or any other place.

No person or organisation shall publish or distribute or cause to be published or distributed any advertisement in any manner regarding facilities of prenatal determination of sex available at any Genetic Counselling Centre, Genetic Laboratory, Genetic Clinic or any other place.

Any person who contravenes these provisions shall be punishable with imprisonment for a term which may extend to three years and with fine which may extend to ten thousand rupees.

('Advertisement' includes any notice, circular, label wrapper or other document and also includes any visible representation made by means of any light, sound, smoke or gas.)

**Offences and penalties**

Every offence under this Act shall be cognizable, non-bailable and non-compoundable.[97]

Notwithstanding anything in the Indian Evidence Act, 1872, the Court shall presume unless the contrary is proved that the pregnant woman has been compelled by her husband or the relative to undergo prenatal diagnostic technique and such person shall be liable for abetment of offence.[98]

Any medical geneticist, gynaecologist, registered medical practitioner or any person who owns a Genetic Counselling Centre, a Genetic Laboratory or a Genetic Clinic or is employed in such a Centre, Laboratory or Clinic and renders his professional or technical services to or at such a Centre, Laboratory or Clinic, whether on an honorary basis or otherwise, and who contravenes any of the provisions of this Act or rules made thereunder shall be punishable with imprisonment for a term which may extend to three years and with fine which may extend to ten thousand rupees and on any subsequent conviction, with imprisonment which may extend to five years and with fine which may extend to fifty thousand rupees.

The name of the registered medical practitioner who has been so convicted by the Court shall be reported by the Appropriate Authority to the respective State Medical Council for taking necessary action including the removal of his name from the register or the Council for a period of two years for the first offence and permanently for the subsequent offence.

Any person who seeks the aid of a Genetic Counselling Centre, Genetic Laboratory or Genetic Clinic or of a medical geneticist, gynaecologist or registered medical practitioner for conducting

Prenatal Diagnostic Techniques on any pregnant woman (including such woman unless she was compelled to undergo such diagnostic techniques) for purposes other than those permitted shall, be punishable with imprisonment for a term which may extend to three years and with fine which may extend to ten thousand rupees and on any subsequent conviction with imprisonment which may extend to five years and with fine which may extend to fifty thousand rupees.[99]

Whoever contravenes any of the provisions of this Act or any rules made thereunder, for which no penalty has been elsewhere provided in this Act, shall be punishable with imprisonment for a term which may extend to three months or with fine, which may extend to one thousand rupees or with both and in the case of continuing contravention with an additional fine which may extend to five hundred rupees for every day during which such contravention continues after conviction for the first such contravention.[100]

No Court shall take cognizance of an offence under this Act except on a complaint made by:

(a) The Appropriate Authority concerned or any officer authorised in this behalf by the Central Government or State Government, as the case may be or the Appropriate Authority.

(b) A person who has given notice of not less than thirty days in the manner prescribed, to the Appropriate Authority, of the alleged offence and of his intention to make a complaint to the Court.

'Person' includes a social organisation. The Court may, on demand by such person, direct the Appropriate Authority to make available copies of the relevant records in its possession to such person.

No Court other than that of a Metropolitan Magistrate or a Judicial Magistrate of the first class shall try any offence punishable under this Act.[101]

Where any offence, punishable under this Act has been committed by a company, every person who, at the time the offence was committed was in charge of, and was responsible to, the company for the conduct of the business of the company, as well as the company, shall be deemed to be guilty of the offence and shall be liable to be proceeded against and punished accordingly provided that nothing contained in this subsection shall render any such person liable to any punishment, if he proves that the offence was committed without his knowledge or that he had exercised all due diligence to prevent the commission of such offence.

However, where any offence punishable under this Act has been committed by a company and it is proved that the offence has been committed with the consent or connivance of or is attributable to any neglect on the part of, any director, manager, secretary or other officer of the company, such director, manager, secretary or other officer shall also be deemed to be guilty of that offence and shall be liable to be proceeded against and punished accordingly.

(a) 'Company' means any body corporate and includes a firm or other association of individuals, and

(b) 'Director', in relation to a firm, means a partner in the firm.[102]

No suit, prosecution or other legal proceeding shall lie against the Central or the State Government or the Appropriate Authority or any officer authorised by the Central or State Government or by the Authority for anything which is in good faith done or intended to be done in pursuance of the provisions of this Act.[103]

**Records**

All records, charts, forms, reports, consent letters and all other documents required to be maintained under this Act and the rules shall be preserved for a period of two years or for such period as may be prescribed provided that, if any criminal or other proceedings are instituted against any Genetic Counselling Centre, Genetic Laboratory or Genetic Clinic, the records and all other documents of such Centre, Laboratory or Clinic shall be preserved till the final disposal of such proceedings.

All such records shall, at all reasonable times, be made available for inspection to the Appropriate Authority or to any other person authorised by the Appropriate Authority in this behalf. [104]

If the Appropriate Authority has reason to believe that an offence under this Act has been or is being committed at any Genetic Counselling Centre, Genetic Laboratory or Genetic Clinic, such Authority or any officer authorised thereof in this behalf may, subject to such rules as may be prescribed, enter and search at all reasonable times with such assistance, if any, as such authority or officer considers necessary, such Genetic Counselling Centre, Genetic Laboratory or Genetic Clinic and examine any record, register, document, book, pamphlet, advertisement or any other material object found therein and seize the same if such Authority or officer has reason to believe that it may furnish evidence of the commission of an offence punishable under this Act.

The provisions of the Code of Criminal Procedure, 1973 relating to searches and seizures shall, so far as may be, apply to every search or seizure made under this Act.[105]

**Rules and regulations**

The Central Government may make rules for carrying out the provisions of this Act.[106]

The Board may, with the previous sanction of the Central Government, by notification in the Official Gazette, make regulations not inconsistent with the provisions of this Act and the rules made thereunder to provide for:

(a) the time and place of the meetings of the Board and the procedure to be followed for the transaction of business at such meetings and the number of members which shall form the quorum

(b) the manner in which a person may be temporarily associated with the Board

(c) the method of appointment, the conditions of service and the scales of pay and allowances of the officer and other employees of the Board appointed

(d) generally for the efficient conduct of the affairs of the Board.[107]

Every rule and every regulation made under this Act shall be laid, as soon as may be after it is made, before each House of Parliament, while it is in session, for a total period of thirty days which may be comprised in one session or in two or more successive sessions, and if, before the expiry of the session immediately following the session or the successive sessions aforesaid, both Houses agree in making any modification in the rule or regulation or both Houses agree that the rule or regulation should not be made, the rule or regulation shall thereafter have effect only in such modified form or be of no effect, as the case may be; so, however, that any such modification or annulment shall be without prejudice to the validity of anything previously done under that rule or regulation.[108]

## THE PROTECTION OF WOMEN AGAINST DOMESTIC VIOLENCE ACT

This Act was passed in 2005. It provides for more effective protection of the rights of women guaranteed under the Constitution who are victims of violence of any kind occurring within the family and for matters connected therewith or incidental thereto. It extends to the whole of India except the State of Jammu and Kashmir.

**Definitions**[109]

'Aggrieved person' means any woman who is or has been, in a domestic relationship with the respondent and who alleges to have been subjected to any act of domestic violence by the respondent.

'Child' means any person below the age of eighteen years and includes any adopted, step or foster child.

'Domestic incident report' means a report made in the prescribed form on receipt of a complaint of domestic violence from an aggrieved person.

'Domestic relationship' means a relationship between two persons who live or have, at any point of time, lived together in a shared household, when they are related by consanguinity, marriage or through a relationship in the nature of marriage, adoption or are family members living together as a joint family.

'Magistrate' means the Judicial Magistrate of the first class or as the case may be, the Metropolitan Magistrate, exercising jurisdiction under the Code of Criminal Procedure, 1973 in the area where the aggrieved person resides temporarily or otherwise or the respondent resides or the domestic violence is alleged to have taken place.

'Monetary relief' means the compensation which the Magistrate may order the respondent to pay to the aggrieved person, at any stage during the hearing of an application seeking any relief under this Act, to meet the expenses incurred and the losses suffered by the aggrieved person as a result of the domestic violence.

'Respondent' means any adult male person who is or has been, in a domestic relationship with the aggrieved person and against whom the aggrieved person has sought any relief under this Act provided that an aggrieved wife or female living in a relationship in the nature of a marriage may also file a complaint against a relative of the husband or the male partner.

'Shared household' means a household where the person aggrieved lives or at any stage has lived in a domestic relationship either singly or along with the respondent and includes such a household whether owned or tenanted either jointly by the aggrieved person and the respondent or owned or tenanted by either of them in respect of which either the aggrieved person or the respondent or both jointly or singly have any right, title, interest or equity and includes such a household which may belong to the joint family of which the respondent is a member, irrespective of whether the respondent or the aggrieved person has any right, title or interest in the shared household.

'Shelter home' means any shelter home as may be notified by the State Government to be a shelter home for the purposes of this Act.

**Provisions**

*The Definition of Domestic Violence*[110]

Any act, omission or commission or conduct of the respondent shall constitute domestic violence if it:

- harms or injures or endangers the health, safety, life, limb or well-being, whether mental or physical, of the aggrieved person or tends to do so and includes causing physical abuse, sexual abuse, verbal and emotional abuse and economic abuse
- harasses, harms, injures or endangers the aggrieved person with a view to coerce her or any other person related to her to meet any unlawful demand for any dowry or other property or valuable security
- has the effect of threatening the aggrieved person or any person related to her by any conduct mentioned in clause (a) or clause (b)
- otherwise injures or causes harm, whether physical or mental, to the aggrieved person.

*Explanation I:* For the purposes of this Section:

(a) 'Physical Abuse' means any act or conduct which is of such a nature as to cause bodily pain, harm or danger to life, limb or health or impair the health or development of the aggrieved person and includes assault, criminal intimidation and criminal force.

(b) 'Sexual Abuse' includes any conduct of a sexual nature that abuses, humiliates, degrades or otherwise violates the dignity of woman.

(c) 'Verbal and Emotional Abuse' includes:

- insults, ridicule, humiliation, name calling and insults or ridicule specially with regard to not having a child or a male child

- repeated threats to cause physical pain to any person in whom the aggrieved person is interested.

(d) 'Economic Abuse' includes:

- deprivation of all or any economic or financial resources to which the aggrieved person is entitled under any law or custom whether payable under an order of a Court or otherwise or which the aggrieved person requires out of necessity including, but not limited to, household necessities for the aggrieved person and her children, if any, Stridhan, property, jointly or separately owned by the aggrieved person, payment of rental related to the shared household and maintenance
- disposal of household effects, any alienation of assets whether movable or immovable, valuables, shares, securities, bonds and the like or other property in which the aggrieved person has an interest or is entitled to use by virtue of the domestic relationship or which may be reasonably required by the aggrieved person or her children or her Stridhan or any other property jointly or separately held by the aggrieved person
- prohibition or restriction to continued access to resources or facilities which the aggrieved person is entitled to use or enjoy by virtue of the domestic relationship including access to the shared household.

*Explanation II:* For the purpose of determining whether any act, omission, commission or conduct of the respondent constitutes 'domestic violence' under this Section, the overall facts and circumstances of the case shall be taken into consideration.

**Information to Protection Officer and exclusion of liability of informant[111]**

Any person who has reason to believe that an act of domestic violence has been or is being or is likely to be committed, may give information about it to the concerned Protection Officer. No liability, civil or criminal, shall be incurred by any person for giving information in good faith.

**Duties of police officers, service providers and Magistrate[112]**

A police officer, Protection Officer, service provider or Magistrate who has received a complaint of domestic violence or is otherwise present at the place of an incident of domestic violence or when the incident of domestic violence is reported to him, shall inform the aggrieved person:

- of her right to make an application for obtaining a relief by way of a protection order, an order for monetary relief, a custody order, a residence order, a compensation order or more than one such order under this Act
- of the availability of services of service providers
- of the availability of services of the Protection Officers
- of her right to free legal services under the Legal Services Authorities Act, 1987
- of her right to file a complaint under Section 498 A of the Indian Penal Code wherever relevant provided that nothing in this Act shall be construed in any manner as to relieve a police officer from his duty to proceed in accordance with law upon receipt of information as to the commission of a cognizable offence.

**Duties of shelter homes**[113]

If an aggrieved person or on her behalf a Protection Officer or a service provider requests the person-in-charge of a shelter home to provide shelter to her, such person-in-charge of the shelter home shall provide shelter to the aggrieved person in the shelter home.

**Duties of medical facilities**[114]

If an aggrieved person or, on her behalf a Protection Officer or a service provider requests the person-in-charge of a medical facility to provide any medical aid to her, such person-in-charge of the medical facility shall provide medical aid to the aggrieved person in the medical facility.

**Protection Officers**

The State Government shall, by notification, appoint such number of Protection Officers in each district as it may consider necessary and shall also notify the area or areas within which a Protection Officer shall exercise the powers and perform the duties conferred on him by or under this Act. The Protection Officers shall, as far as possible, be women and shall possess such qualifications and experience as may be prescribed. The terms and conditions of service of the Protection Officer and the other officers subordinate to him shall be such as may be prescribed.[115]

It shall be the duty of the Protection Officer:

- to assist the Magistrate in the discharge of his functions under this Act
- to make a domestic incident report to the Magistrate, in such form and in such manner as may be prescribed, upon receipt of a complaint of domestic violence and forward copies thereof to the police officer in charge of the police station within the local limits of whose jurisdiction domestic violence is alleged to have been committed and to the service providers in that area
- to make an application in such form and in such manner as may be prescribed to the Magistrate, if the aggrieved person so desires, claiming relief for issuance of a protection order
- to ensure that the aggrieved person is provided legal aid under the Legal Services Authorities Act, 1987 (39 of 1987) and make available free of cost the prescribed form in which a complaint is to be made
- to maintain a list of all service providers providing legal aid or counselling, shelter homes and medical facilities in a local area within the jurisdiction of the Magistrate
- to make available a safe shelter home, if the aggrieved person so requires and forward a copy of his report of having lodged the aggrieved person in a shelter home to the police station and the Magistrate having jurisdiction in the area where the shelter home is situated
- to get the aggrieved person medically examined, if she has sustained bodily injuries and forward a copy of the medical report to the police station and the Magistrate having jurisdiction in the area where the domestic violence is alleged to have taken place
- to ensure that the order for monetary relief (under Section 20) is complied with and executed, in accordance with the procedure prescribed under the Code of Criminal Procedure, 1973
- to perform such other duties as may be prescribed.

The Protection Officer shall be under the control and supervision of the Magistrate, and shall perform the duties imposed on him by the Magistrate and the Government by or under, this Act.[116]

If any Protection Officer fails or refuses to discharge his duties as directed by the Magistrate in the protection order without any sufficient cause, he shall be punished with imprisonment of either description for a term which may extend to one year or with fine which may extend to twenty thousand rupees or with both.[117]

No prosecution or other legal proceeding shall lie against the Protection Officer unless a complaint is filed with the previous sanction of the State Government or an officer authorised by it in this behalf.[118]

No suit, prosecution or other legal proceeding shall lie against the Protection Officer for any damage caused or likely to be caused by anything which is in good faith done or intended to be done under this Act or any rule or order made thereunder.[119] The provisions of this Act shall be in addition to, and not in derogation of the provisions of any other law, for the time being in force.[120]

The Central Government may, by notification, make rules for carrying out the provisions of this Act. Every rule made under this Act shall be laid, as soon as may be after it is made, before each House of Parliament, while it is in session, for a total period of thirty days which may be comprised in one session or in two or more successive sessions, and if, before the expiry of the session immediately following the session or the successive sessions aforesaid, both Houses agree in making any modification in the rule or both Houses agree that the rule should not be made, the rule shall thereafter have effect only in such modified form or be of no effect, as the case may be; so, however, that any such modification or annulment shall be without prejudice to the validity of anything previously done under that rule.[121]

**Service providers**[122]

Subject to such rules as may be made in this behalf, any voluntary association registered under the Societies Registration Act, 1860 or a company registered under the Companies Act, 1956 or any other law for the time being in force with the objective of protecting the rights and interests of women by any lawful means including providing of legal aid, medical, financial or other assistance shall register itself with the State Government as a service provider for the purposes of this Act.

A registered service provider shall have the power to:

(a) record the domestic incident report in the prescribed form if the aggrieved person so desires and forward a copy thereof to the Magistrate and the Protection Officer having jurisdiction in the area where the domestic violence took place

(b) get the aggrieved person medically examined and forward a copy of the medical report to the Protection Officer and the police station within the local limits of which the domestic violence took place ensure that the aggrieved person is provided shelter in a shelter home, if she so requires and forward a report of the lodging of the aggrieved person in the shelter home to the police station within the local limits of which the domestic violence took place.

No suit, prosecution or other legal proceeding shall lie against any service provider or any member of the service provider who is or who is deemed to be, acting or purporting to act under this Act, for anything which is in good faith done or intended to be done in the exercise of powers or discharge of functions under this Act towards the prevention of the commission of domestic violence.

**Duties of Government[123]**

The Central Government and every State Government shall take all measures to ensure that:

- the provisions of this Act are given wide publicity through public media including the television, radio and the print media at regular intervals
- the Central Government and State Government officers including the police officers and the members of the judicial services are given periodic sensitization and awareness training on the issues addressed by this Act
- effective co-ordination between the services provided by concerned Ministries and Departments dealing with law, home affairs including law and order, health and human resources to address issues of domestic violence is established and periodical review of the same is conducted
- protocols for the various Ministries concerned with the delivery of services to women under this Act including the Courts are prepared and put in place.

**An Application to a Magistrate**

An aggrieved person or a Protection Officer or any other person on behalf of the aggrieved person may present an application to the Magistrate seeking one or more reliefs under this Act provided that before passing any order on such application, the Magistrate shall take into consideration any domestic incident report received by him from the Protection Officer or the service provider.

The relief sought may include a relief for issuance of an order for payment of compensation or damages without prejudice to the right of such person to institute a suit for compensation or damages for the injuries caused by the acts of domestic violence committed by the respondent provided that where a decree for any amount as compensation or damages has been passed by any Court in favour of the aggrieved person, the amount, if any, paid or payable in pursuance of the order made by the Magistrate under this Act shall be set off against the amount payable under such decree and the decree shall, notwithstanding anything contained in the Code of Civil Procedure or any other law for the time being in force, be executable for the balance amount, if any, left after such set off.

Every application shall be in such form and contain such particulars as may be prescribed or as nearly as possible thereto. The Magistrate shall fix the first date of hearing, which shall not ordinarily be beyond three days from the date of receipt of the application by the Court.

The Magistrate shall endeavour to dispose of every application within a period of sixty days from the date of its first hearing. [124]

A notice of the date of hearing fixed shall be given by the Magistrate to the Protection Officer, who shall get it served by such means as may be prescribed on the respondent, and on any other person, as directed by the Magistrate within a maximum period of two days or such further reasonable time as may be allowed by the Magistrate from the date of its receipt. A declaration of service of notice made by the Protection Officer in such form as may be prescribed shall be the proof that such notice was served upon the respondent and on any other person as directed by the Magistrate unless the contrary is proved.[125]

If the Magistrate considers that the circumstances of the case so warrant, and if either party to the proceedings so desires, he may conduct the proceedings under this Act in camera. [126]

**Counselling[127]**

The Magistrate may, at any stage of the proceedings under this Act, direct the respondent or the aggrieved person, either singly or jointly, to undergo counselling with any member of a service provider who possesses such qualifications and experience in counselling as may be prescribed. Where the Magistrate has issued any direction, he shall fix the next date of hearing of the case within a period not exceeding two months.

**Assistance of welfare expert[128]**

In any proceeding under this Act, the Magistrate may secure the services of such person, preferably a woman, whether related to the aggrieved person or not, including a person engaged in promoting family welfare as he thinks fit, for the purpose of assisting him in discharging his functions.

**Right to Reside in a Shared Household**[129]

Notwithstanding anything contained in any other law for the time being in force, every woman in a domestic relationship shall have the right to reside in the shared household, whether or not she has any right, title or beneficial interest in the same.

The aggrieved person shall not be evicted or excluded from the shared household or any part of it by the respondent save in accordance with the procedure established by law.

**Protection Orders**[130]

The Magistrate may, after giving the aggrieved person and the respondent an opportunity of being heard and on being prima facie satisfied that domestic violence has taken place or is likely to take place, pass a protection order in favour of the aggrieved person and prohibit the respondent from:

- committing any act of domestic violence
- aiding or abetting in the commission of acts of domestic violence
- entering the place of employment of the aggrieved person or, if the person aggrieved is a child, its school or any other place frequented by the aggrieved person
- attempting to communicate in any form, whatsoever, with the aggrieved person, including personal oral or written or electronic or telephonic contact alienating any assets, operating bank lockers or bank accounts used or held or enjoyed by both the parties, jointly by the aggrieved person and the respondent or singly by the respondent, including her Stridhan or any other property held either jointly by the parties or separately by them without the leave of the Magistrate
- causing violence to the dependants, other relatives or any person who give the aggrieved person assistance from domestic violence
- committing any other act specified in the protection order.

A protection order shall be in force till the aggrieved person applies for discharge. If the Magistrate, on receipt of an application from the aggrieved person or the respondent, is satisfied that there is a change in the circumstances requiring alteration, modification or revocation of any order made under this Act, he may, for reasons to be recorded in writing pass such order, as he may deem appropriate.[131]

**Residence Orders**[132]

The Magistrate may, on being satisfied that domestic violence has taken place, pass a residence order:

- restraining the respondent from dispossessing or in any other manner disturbing the possession of the aggrieved person from the shared household, whether or not the respondent has a legal or equitable interest in the shared household
- directing the respondent to remove himself from the shared household unless the respondent is a woman
- restraining the respondent or any of his relatives from entering any portion of the shared household in which the aggrieved person resides
- restraining the respondent from alienating or disposing off the shared household or encumbering the same
- restraining the respondent from renouncing his rights in the shared household except with the leave of the Magistrate
- directing the respondent to secure the same level of alternate accommodation for the aggrieved person as enjoyed by her in the shared household or to pay rent for the same, if the circumstances so require

While making an order, the Magistrate may impose on the respondent obligations relating to the discharge of rent and other payments, having regard to the financial needs and resources of the parties.

The Magistrate may impose any additional conditions or pass any other direction which he may deem reasonably necessary to protect or to provide for the safety of the aggrieved person or any child of such aggrieved person.

The Magistrate may require from the respondent to execute a bond, with or without sureties, for preventing the commission of domestic violence. Such an order shall be deemed to be an order under Chapter VIII of the Code of Criminal Procedure, 1973 and shall be dealt with accordingly.

While passing an order, the Court may also pass an order directing the officer in charge of the nearest police station to give protection to the aggrieved person or to assist her or the person making an application on her behalf in the implementation of the order.

The Magistrate may direct the officer in-charge of the police station in whose jurisdiction the Magistrate has been approached to assist in the implementation of the protection order.

The Magistrate may direct the respondent to return to the possession of the aggrieved person her Stridhan or any other property or valuable security to which she is entitled to.

**Monetary Relief**[133]

While disposing of an application, the Magistrate may direct the respondent to pay monetary relief to meet the expenses incurred and losses suffered by the aggrieved person and any child of the aggrieved person as a result of the domestic violence and such relief may include, but not limited to:

1. the loss of earnings
2. the medical expenses
3. the loss caused due to the destruction, damage or removal of any property from the control of the aggrieved person and
4. the maintenance for the aggrieved person as well as her children, if any, including an order under or in addition to an order of maintenance under Section 125 of the Code of Criminal Procedure, 1973 or any other law for the time being in force.

The monetary relief granted under this Section shall be adequate, fair and reasonable and consistent with the standard of living to which the aggrieved person is accustomed.

The Magistrate shall have the power to order an appropriate lump sum payment or monthly payments of maintenance, as the nature and circumstances of the case may require. He shall send a copy of the order for monetary relief made to the parties to the application and to the in charge of the police station within the local limits of whose jurisdiction the respondent resides.

The respondent shall pay the monetary relief granted to the aggrieved person within the period specified in the order.

Upon the failure on the part of the respondent to make payment in terms of the order, the Magistrate may direct the employer or a debtor of the respondent, to directly pay to the aggrieved person or to deposit with the Court a portion of the wages or salaries or debt due to or accrued to the credit of the respondent, which amount may be adjusted towards the monetary relief payable by the respondent.

### Custody Orders[134]

Notwithstanding anything contained in any other law for the time being in force, the Magistrate may, at any stage of hearing of the application for protection order or for any other relief under this Act grant temporary custody of any child or children to the aggrieved person or the person making an application on her behalf and specify, if necessary, the arrangements for visit of such child or children by the respondent provided that if the Magistrate is of the opinion that any visit of the respondent may be harmful to the interests of the child or children, the Magistrate shall refuse to allow such visit.

### Compensation Orders[135]

In addition to other reliefs as may be granted under this Act, the Magistrate may on an application being made by the aggrieved person, pass an order directing the respondent to pay compensation and damages for the injuries, including mental torture and emotional distress, caused by the acts of domestic violence committed by that respondent.

### Interim Orders, etc.[136]

In any proceeding before him under this Act, the Magistrate may pass such interim order as he deems just and proper.

If the Magistrate is satisfied that an application prima facie discloses that the respondent is committing or has committed an act of domestic violence or that there is a likelihood that the respondent may commit an act of domestic violence, he may grant an ex parte order on the basis of the affidavit in such form, as may be prescribed, of the aggrieved person against the respondent. [137]

The Magistrate shall, in all cases where he has passed any order under this Act order that a copy of such order, shall be given free of cost, to the parties to the application, the police officer in-charge of the police station in the jurisdiction of which the Magistrate has been approached, and any service provider located within the local limits of the jurisdiction of the Court and if any service provider has registered a domestic incident report, to that service provider. [138]

### Relief

Relief may also be sought in any legal proceeding, before a Civil Court, family Court or a Criminal Court, affecting the aggrieved person and the respondent whether such proceeding was initiated before or after the commencement of this Act.

Any such relief may be sought for in addition to and along with any other relief that the aggrieved person may seek in such suit or legal proceeding before a civil or Criminal Court.

In case any relief has been obtained by the aggrieved person in any proceedings other than a proceeding under this Act, she shall be bound to inform the Magistrate of the grant of such relief.[139]

### Jurisdiction[140]

The Court of Judicial Magistrate of the first class or the Metropolitan Magistrate, as the case may be, within the local limits of which:

- the person aggrieved permanently or temporarily resides or carries on business or is employed
- the respondent resides or carries on business or is employed
- the cause of action has arisen, shall be the competent Court to grant a protection order and other orders under this Act and to try offences under this Act.

Any order made under this Act shall be enforceable throughout India.

### Procedure

Save as otherwise provided in this Act, all proceedings shall be governed by the provisions of the Code of Criminal Procedure, 1973 although the Court from laying down its own procedure for disposal of an application or with regard to interim and ex parte orders.[141]

An appeal shall lie to the Court of Session within thirty days from the date on which the order made by the Magistrate is served on the aggrieved person or the respondent, as the case may be, whichever is later.[142]

The Protection Officers and members of service providers, while acting or purporting to act in pursuance of any of the provisions of this Act or any rules or orders made thereunder shall be deemed to be public servants within the meaning of Section 21 of the Indian Penal Code.[143]

A breach of protection order or of an interim protection order, by the respondent shall be an offence under this Act and shall be-punishable with imprisonment of either description for a term which may extend to one year or with fine which may extend to twenty thousand rupees or with both.[144]

Such an offence shall be cognizable and non-bailable. Upon the sole testimony of the aggrieved person, the Court may conclude that such an offence has been committed by the accused.[145]

The offence shall as far as practicable be tried by the Magistrate who had passed the order, the breach of which has been alleged to have been caused by the accused.[146]

While framing charges, the Magistrate may also frame charges under Section 498 A of the Indian Penal Code or any other provision of that Code or the Dowry Prohibition Act, 1961, as the case may be, if the facts disclose the commission of an offence under those provisions.[147]

## NOTES

1. Section 22; The Commission of Sati (Prevention) Act, 1987
2. Section 20; The Commission of Sati (Prevention) Act, 1987
3. Section 2; The Commission of Sati (Prevention) Act, 1987
4. Section 3; The Commission of Sati (Prevention) Act, 1987
5. Section 4; The Commission of Sati (Prevention) Act, 1987
6. Section 16; The Commission of Sati (Prevention) Act, 1987
7. Section 5; The Commission of Sati (Prevention) Act, 1987
8. Section 18; The Commission of Sati (Prevention) Act, 1987
9. Section 17; The Commission of Sati (Prevention) Act, 1987
10. Section 15; The Commission of Sati (Prevention) Act, 1987
11. Section 19; The Commission of Sati (Prevention) Act, 1987
12. Section 6; The Commission of Sati (Prevention) Act, 1987
13. Section 7; The Commission of Sati (Prevention) Act, 1987
14. Section 8; The Commission of Sati (Prevention) Act, 1987
15. Section 15; The Commission of Sati (Prevention) Act, 1987
16. Section 10; The Commission of Sati (Prevention) Act, 1987
17. Section 11; The Commission of Sati (Prevention) Act, 1987
18. Section 12; The Commission of Sati (Prevention) Act, 1987
19. Section 13; The Commission of Sati (Prevention) Act, 1987
20. Section 14; The Commission of Sati (Prevention) Act, 1987
21. Section 21; The Commission of Sati (Prevention) Act, 1987

22. Rule 3; The Commission of Sati (Prevention) Rules, 1988
23. Rule 4; The Commission of Sati (Prevention) Rules, 1988
24. Rule 5; The Commission of Sati (Prevention) Rules, 1988
25. Rule 6; The Commission of Sati (Prevention) Rules, 1988
26. Rule 7; The Commission of Sati (Prevention) Rules, 1988
27. Section 2; The Immoral Traffic (Prevention) Act, 1956
28. Section 3; The Immoral Traffic (Prevention) Act, 1956
29. Section 4; The Immoral Traffic (Prevention) Act, 1956
30. Section 5; The Immoral Traffic (Prevention) Act, 1956
31. Section 6; The Immoral Traffic (Prevention) Act, 1956
32. Section 7; The Immoral Traffic (Prevention) Act, 1956
33. Section 8; The Immoral Traffic (Prevention) Act, 1956
34. Section 9; The Immoral Traffic (Prevention) Act, 1956
35. Section 13; The Immoral Traffic (Prevention) Act, 1956
36. Section 14; The Immoral Traffic (Prevention) Act, 1956
37. Section 15; The Immoral Traffic (Prevention) Act, 1956
38. Section 16; The Immoral Traffic (Prevention) Act, 1956
39. Section 17; The Immoral Traffic (Prevention) Act, 1956
40. Section 17 A; The Immoral Traffic (Prevention) Act, 1956
41. Section 18; The Immoral Traffic (Prevention) Act, 1956
42. Section 19; The Immoral Traffic (Prevention) Act, 1956
43. Section 20; The Immoral Traffic (Prevention) Act, 1956
44. Section 21; The Immoral Traffic (Prevention) Act, 1956
45. Section 21; The Immoral Traffic (Prevention) Act, 1956
46. Section 21 A; The Immoral Traffic (Prevention) Act, 1956
47. Section 22 A; The Immoral Traffic (Prevention) Act, 1956
48. Section 22 AA; The Immoral Traffic (Prevention) Act, 1956
49. Section 22 B; The Immoral Traffic (Prevention) Act, 1956
50. Section 23; The Immoral Traffic (Prevention) Act, 1956
51. Section 24; The Immoral Traffic (Prevention) Act, 1956
52. Section 25; The Immoral Traffic (Prevention) Act, 1956
53. Section 2; The Indecent Representation of Women (Prohibition) Act, 1986

54. Section 3; The Indecent Representation of Women (Prohibition) Act, 1986
55. Section 4; The Indecent Representation of Women (Prohibition) Act, 1986
56. Section 5; The Indecent Representation of Women (Prohibition) Act, 1986
57. Section 6; The Indecent Representation of Women (Prohibition) Act, 1986
58. Section 7; The Indecent Representation of Women (Prohibition) Act, 1986
59. Section 8; The Indecent Representation of Women (Prohibition) Act, 1986
60. Section 9; The Indecent Representation of Women (Prohibition) Act, 1986
61. Section 10; The Indecent Representation of Women (Prohibition) Act, 1986
62. Section 2; The National Commission for Women Act, 1990
63. Section 3; The National Commission for Women Act, 1990
64. Section 4; The National Commission for Women Act, 1990
65. Section 5; The National Commission for Women Act, 1990
66. Section 7; The National Commission for Women Act, 1990
67. Section 8; The National Commission for Women Act, 1990
68. Section 9; The National Commission for Women Act, 1990
69. Section 15; The National Commission for Women Act, 1990
70. Section 16; The National Commission for Women Act, 1990
71. Section 10; The National Commission for Women Act, 1990
72. Section 11; The National Commission for Women Act, 1990
73. Section 12; The National Commission for Women Act, 1990
74. Section 13; The National Commission for Women Act, 1990
75. Section 14; The National Commission for Women Act, 1990
76. Section 17; The National Commission for Women Act, 1990
77. Section 2; The Prenatal Diagnostic Techniques Act, 1994
78. Section 3; The Prenatal Diagnostic Techniques Act, 1994
79. Section 4; The Prenatal Diagnostic Techniques Act, 1994
80. Section 5; The Prenatal Diagnostic Techniques Act, 1994

81. Section 6; The Prenatal Diagnostic Techniques Act, 1994
82. Section 7; The Prenatal Diagnostic Techniques Act, 1994
83. Section 16; The Prenatal Diagnostic Techniques Act, 1994
84. Section 8; The Prenatal Diagnostic Techniques Act, 1994
85. Section 14; The Prenatal Diagnostic Techniques Act, 1994
86. Section 15; The Prenatal Diagnostic Techniques Act, 1994
87. Section 9; The Prenatal Diagnostic Techniques Act, 1994
88. Section 11; The Prenatal Diagnostic Techniques Act, 1994
89. Section 12; The Prenatal Diagnostic Techniques Act, 1994
90. Section 13; The Prenatal Diagnostic Techniques Act, 1994
91. Section 17; The Prenatal Diagnostic Techniques Act, 1994
92. Section 18; The Prenatal Diagnostic Techniques Act, 1994
93. Section 19; The Prenatal Diagnostic Techniques Act, 1994
94. Section 20; The Prenatal Diagnostic Techniques Act, 1994
95. Section 21; The Prenatal Diagnostic Techniques Act, 1994
96. Section 22; The Prenatal Diagnostic Techniques Act, 1994
97. Section 27; The Prenatal Diagnostic Techniques Act, 1994
98. Section 24; The Prenatal Diagnostic Techniques Act, 1994
99. Section 23; The Prenatal Diagnostic Techniques Act, 1994
100. Section 25; The Prenatal Diagnostic Techniques Act, 1994
101. Section 28; The Prenatal Diagnostic Techniques Act, 1994
102. Section 26; The Prenatal Diagnostic Techniques Act, 1994
103. Section 31; The Prenatal Diagnostic Techniques Act, 1994
104. Section 29; The Prenatal Diagnostic Techniques Act, 1994
105. Section 30; The Prenatal Diagnostic Techniques Act, 1994
106. Section 32; The Prenatal Diagnostic Techniques Act, 1994
107. Section 33; The Prenatal Diagnostic Techniques Act, 1994
108. Section 34; The Prenatal Diagnostic Techniques Act, 1994
109. Section 2; The Protection of Women Against Domestic Violence Act, 2005
110. Section 3; The Protection of Women Against Domestic Violence Act, 2005
111. Section 4; The Protection of Women Against Domestic Violence Act, 2005

112. Section 5; The Protection of Women Against Domestic Violence Act, 2005
113. Section 6; The Protection of Women Against Domestic Violence Act, 2005
114. Section 7; The Protection of Women Against Domestic Violence Act, 2005
115. Section 8; The Protection of Women Against Domestic Violence Act, 2005
116. Section 9; The Protection of Women Against Domestic Violence Act, 2005
117. Section 33; The Protection of Women Against Domestic Violence Act, 2005
118. Section 34; The Protection of Women Against Domestic Violence Act, 2005
119. Section 35; The Protection of Women Against Domestic Violence Act, 2005
120. Section 36; The Protection of Women Against Domestic Violence Act, 2005
121. Section 37; The Protection of Women Against Domestic Violence Act, 2005
122. Section 10; The Protection of Women Against Domestic Violence Act, 2005
123. Section 11; The Protection of Women Against Domestic Violence Act, 2005
124. Section 12; The Protection of Women Against Domestic Violence Act, 2005
125. Section 13; The Protection of Women Against Domestic Violence Act, 2005
126. Section 16; The Protection of Women Against Domestic Violence Act, 2005
127. Section 14; The Protection of Women Against Domestic Violence Act, 2005
128. Section 15; The Protection of Women Against Domestic Violence Act, 2005
129. Section 17; The Protection of Women Against Domestic Violence Act, 2005
130. Section 18; The Protection of Women Against Domestic Violence Act, 2005

131. Section 25; The Protection of Women Against Domestic Violence Act, 2005
132. Section 19; The Protection of Women Against Domestic Violence Act, 2005
133. Section 20; The Protection of Women Against Domestic Violence Act, 2005
134. Section 21; The Protection of Women Against Domestic Violence Act, 2005
135. Section 22; The Protection of Women Against Domestic Violence Act, 2005
136. Section 23; The Protection of Women Against Domestic Violence Act, 2005
137. Section 23; The Protection of Women Against Domestic Violence Act, 2005
138. Section 24; The Protection of Women Against Domestic Violence Act, 2005
139. Section 26; The Protection of Women Against Domestic Violence Act, 2005
140. Section 27; The Protection of Women Against Domestic Violence Act, 2005
141. Section 28; The Protection of Women Against Domestic Violence Act, 2005
142. Section 29; The Protection of Women Against Domestic Violence Act, 2005
143. Section 30; The Protection of Women Against Domestic Violence Act, 2005
144. Section 31; The Protection of Women Against Domestic Violence Act, 2005
145. Section 32; The Protection of Women Against Domestic Violence Act, 2005
146. Section 31; The Protection of Women Against Domestic Violence Act, 2005
147. Section 31; The Protection of Women Against Domestic Violence Act, 2005

# REFERENCES

## SELECTED BIBLIOGRAPHY

Bakshi, P. M. (2003 ), The Constitutional Law of India; Universal Law Publishing Co. Pvt. Ltd.

Bone, Sheila and Rutherford, Leslie (ed.); Osborne's Concise Law Dictionary; Universal Law Publishing Co. Pvt. Ltd.

Jaisingh, Indira (ed.) (2005), Men's Laws, Women's Lives; Women Unlimited.

Kannabiran, Kalpana (ed.) (2005), The violence of normal times; Women Unlimited.

Malarek, Victor (2003), The Natashas; Arcade Publishing.

Pandey, J. N. (2005), Constitutional Law of India; Central Law Agency.

Ratanlal and Dhirajlal; The Law of Evidence; Wadhwa; 21st Edition.

Ratanlal and Dhirajlal; The Indian Penal Code; Wadhwa; 30th Edition.

# INDEX


**A**

Abortion xi, 15, 16

Adultery 34, 130, 219

Agamemnon 36

Agni 130

Alexandrowicz 134

Ambedkar 131

Amnesty International 25, 135

Anatole France 120

Ancient Monuments
  Archeological Sites Act, 67

Arthashastra 6

Arthur Canon Doyle
  The Speckled Band, xii

Assault 73, 74, 172

**B**

Bahamani Kingdom 9

Bangladesh 17, 105

Battered Women's Syndrome
  117

Beijing Conference the 123

Beijing Plantform of Action 135,
  138

Beijing Statement the 82

Bigamy 245

Blank Noise Project 76

Bombay Court Fee Act 138

Bonded Labour 125

Brahmin 7, 9, 12, 36

British, the 28, 75, 118

Burgundian Tribe, the 118

**C**

Cassandra 36

Caste 6, 32

Child Marriage 147

Child Marriage Restraint Act,
  143, 146, 147, 149, 150

Children 54, 93, 126, 145

Christine de Pisan 36

Churchill 62

Clytemnestra 36

Code of Criminal Procedure, the 49, 148, 155, 177, 181, 182, 191, 192, 201, 205, 244, 249, 250, 252

Commission of Sati (Prevention) Act, 18, 57, 58

Community Intervention 131

Companies Act, 245

Consent 94, 95, 105, 215

Constitution 11, 12, 41, 77, 78, 82, 102, 118-121, 126, 127, 129, 131, 135, 137, 149, 150, 155, 222, 223, 239

Contempt of Court 122

Contract Act 72

Convention on the Elimination of All Forms of Discrimination against Women 83, 103, 124, 135

Corrective Institutions 200, 201

Counselling 247

Criminal Force 212

Criminal Intimidation 219

Cruelty 40, 209, 219

Custom 15

**D**

Dalit xii

Daphne Programme, the 39

Declaration on the Elimination of Violence against Women 21, 25, 135, 138, 158

Declaration of Rights of Child 126

Declaration of Human Rights Act, 126, 127

Delhi Sultanate 9

Devdasis 126

Directive Principles of State Policy 129. 131

Discrimination vi

Diwani Adalats 118

DNA Test 125

Domestic Violence v, 14, 34, 37, 53, 55, 85, 241

Donald Rumsfeld 1

Double Jeopardy 95

Dowry 13, 44, 45, 210, 241

Dowry Deaths 44, 46, 52, 20, 9, 210

Dowry Prohibition Act 14, 43, 44-46, 210, 211, 253

Draupadi 1

Dying Defloration, 48, 50, 51

**E**

Ec Treaty 37

Edouard Manet 69

Education 18, 139

Electra 36

Equality 120, 121

Erin Pizzey 39

Euripides 36

Eurobarometer Survey

European Community 37

Eve Teasing 76

Evidence Act 30, 40, 41, 46, 47, 49, 61, 91, 93, 95, 207, 237

Exploitation 125

**F**

Female philosophers
Gargi, Maitreyee 5

Feminist 36

Foeticide 28

Francis Power Cobbe 37

Friar Cherubino 35

Fundamental Rights 118, 120, 127

Frenetic Counseling Centres 29, 30

**G**

George Bush 102

George Mikes 2

Geraldine Brooks

Gotra 7

Grievous Hurt 213, 219

Gurney Champion 120

**H**

Hannah Claire Foster 161

Helen Duncan 62

High Court 11, 90, 91, 96, 119, 127, 182, 191, 200

Hindu Adoptions and Maintenance Act 13

Hindu Marriage Act 6, 7, 11, 13, 32

Hindu Minority and Guardianship Act 120

HIV/AIDS 54, 103

Holland 5

Homer 36

Homosexuality 75

Honour Killings 31, 33

Human Rights Court 78, 157

Hussain, M. F. 70

Hysterectomy 137

**I**

Immoral Traffic Prevention Act 13, 100-103

Indecent Representation of Women Act 13, 65-67

Indian Culture 2, 3

Indian Mutiny 120

Indian Penal Code 42, 41, 46, 47, 65, 72, 73, 75, 91, 93, 97, 174, 175, 177, 191, 195, 208-210

Indian Women 40

Indira Jaisingh 119

Infanticide 16

Information Technology Act, 65, 68, 226

International Covenant on Civil and Political Rights, the 136, 143, 155

International Covenant on Economic, Social and Cultural Rights, the 82, 144, 155

International Law 135
Iphigenia 36

J
Jauhar 60
Jawaharlal Nehru 15
Jehangir 10
Jeremy Blachman 14
John Stuart Mill 37
Johns Hopkins University 25
Juliet 60
Jus Cogens 135

K
K.R. Narayanan 1, 13
Kalidas 8
Kamasutra 1
Kauravas 1
Kautiliya 6
Khajuraho 1
Khasis 5
Kidnapping 104, 212, 213
Kofi Annan 54
Kshatriya 7

L
Labour Laws vi
Law Commission 1, 75, 96
*Le Dejuner sur l'Herbe* 69
Legal Aid
Liberty 124
Literacy 140, 144
Lombard Tribe the 118
Legal Services Authorities Act 243

M
Magna Carta 120
Charter of Liberties of Henry II 120
Mahatma Gandhi 13, 146
Malimath Committee 42
Maninder Pal Singh Kohli 161
Manusmriti 3,5
Marital Rape
Marriage ix, 3, 7, 8, 44, 45, 46, 118, 144-147
Marriage, Types of 7, 8
Martin Luther King, Jr. xiii
Mary Wollstonecraft 37
Matriarchy
Matrimonial Proceedings and Property Act 11
Medical Termination of Pregnancy Act 13, 15, 29
Mentally-disabled Women 117, 155
Migration 105
Mimansa Principles 10
Miscarriage 210. 211
Modesty 64
Mughal 9

Mughal Empire 9
Muslim Rulers, 3, 9
NNGOS, 38, 77, 81, 100, 153

**N**

Nair Community 9
Narada Smriti 6
National Commission for Human Rights 155
National Commission for Women 13. 96. 146. 151. 152
National Commission for Women Act 151. 154. 120. 222-225
National Crime Records Bureau 26. 40
National Human Rights Commission 158, 161, 162
Native Marriage Act, 12, 146
Nayar 9
Neha Kubadia 27
Noor Jehan 10
Nyay Panchayat, 129

**P**

Panchayat 129
Pardhi Tribe 130
Paternity Test 125
Patriarchy 8
Personal Laws 118, 119
Phoolan Devi
  Bandit Queen 70
Police 38, 42, 75, 161, 162, 173, 178, 179, 215, 242
Polygamy 9
Polyandry, 9
Pornography 71, 72
Poverty 14
Prenatal Diagnostic Techniques Act 13, 16, 20, 226
Prevention of Domestic Violence Bill, 2002 14
Prevention of Witch Practices Act 62
Privacy 73
Probation of Offenders Act 190, 195, 197
Prostitutes 100, 101, 105, 155, 156
Prostitution 5, 100-105, 147, 156-190, 202, 203, 212-214
*Protection of Human Rights Act* 78, 82, 161
Protection of Women Against Domestic Violence Act 52, 53, 239
Protective Homes 198, 199
Provocation 212
Prushashukta Hymn 5
Psychopaths 143
PTSD 54
Purdah 9

**Q**

Queen Victoria
  Victorian 1

**R**

Radhika Coomaraswamy 135
Raja of Porbandar 28

Rajput 57
Ramayana. 130
Rape 3, 25, 24, 95, 96, 98, 142, 209, 214-217
Reformatory School Act, 203
Refugees 105
Régis Debray 1
Representation of People Act, 59, 77, 124, 179
Res Gestae 98
Right to Die 125
Right to Life
Rishi 4, 7
Roman Empire, the 3, 118
Ryairi Dougal 95

S

Salt Satyafraha, 13
Sapinda 7
Sati 10, 12, 56-61, 135, 175, 179-184
Sati Act 175, 179
Savitri
    Satyavan 151
Scriptures 28
Self Defence
Sex Ratio 31
Sexual Harassment 25, 72, 75-81, 146, 214-219
Sexual Desire 135
Sexual History 95, 96
Sexual Intercourse 88, 89
Sex Slavery 164
Sex Slaves, 102
Sex Workers 100, 101
Shakuntala 8
Shalishi 161
Shashi Tharoor 243
Shelters 6
Shudras 130
Slavder of Women Act, 95
Sita 130
Smriti 7
Societies Regn. Act, 245
Sonal Mansingh 4
Soonamai Desai 17
Special Courts 176, 177, 180, 181, 183, 184
State Human Rights Commission, 158
Suicide
Sukra
Supreme Court 67, 70, 73, 79, 82, 84-86, 90, 94, 96, 99, 103, 117, 120, 122-129, 135, 136, 145, 147, 162
Swami Vivekananda 4, 5

T

Tata Institute of Social Sciences 41
Teen Abuse Survey of Great Britain 54
Tess of the d'Urbervilles 94

The American Society for the Preventior of Cruelty of Animals xiii

The Society for the Prevention of Cruelty to Children xiii

Tiru-Valluvar 8, 151

Torture 135

Trafficking 100-103, 125, 212

Travancore Christian Succession Act 119

Trial by Ordeal 130

Troy 36

Two-finger Test 196

**U**

UN 44, 54, 135

UN Charter 124

Uniform Civil Code 119

Universal Declaration of Human Rights, the 121, 126, 127, 135, 143

**V**

Vaishya 7

Valentine's Day 2, 3

Vedas 4, 5, 8

Vedic Period 3, 5, 6

Victor Malarek 103, 104, 141, 142

Village Panchayat, 129, 133

Vidhava Vivah Movement, 146

Vijayanagar Kingdom 9

Virginity Test 125

Visigoth Tribe, the 118

**W**

Warren Hastings' Judicial Plan 118

Western Influences 2

Widow Remarriage Act 912

Widows 9

Witchcraft Act 61

World Conf. on Human Right, 135

**Y**

Yajnavalkya Smriti 6